THE CLAY SANSKRIT LIBRARY
FOUNDED BY JOHN & JENNIFER CLAY

WWW.CLAYSANSKRITLIBRARY.COM
WWW.NYUPRESS.ORG

First Edition 2005

The Clay Sanskrit Library is co-published by
New York University Press
and the JJC Foundation.

Further information about this volume
and the rest of the Clay Sanskrit Library
is available on the following Websites:
www.claysanskritlibrary.com
www.nyupress.org.

ISBN 0-8147-1661-X

Artwork by Robert Beer.
Typeset in Adobe Garamond at 10.25 : 12.3+pt.
Printed in Great Britain by St Edmundsbury Press Ltd,
Bury St Edmunds, Suffolk, on acid-free paper.
Bound by Hunter & Foulis Ltd, Edinburgh, Scotland.

RĀKṢASA'S RING
BY VIŚĀKHADATTA

EDITED AND TRANSLATED BY
MICHAEL COULSON

NEW YORK UNIVERSITY PRESS
JJC FOUNDATION
2005

Library of Congress Cataloging-in-Publication Data
Viśākhadatta
[Mudrārākṣasa. English & Sanskrit]
Rakshasa's ring / by Vishakhadatta ;
edited and translated by Michael Coulson.– 1st ed.
p. cm. – (The Clay Sanskrit library)
In English and Sanskrit; translated from Sanskrit.
Includes bibliographical references and index.
ISBN-13: 978-0-8147-1661-8 (cloth : alk. paper)
ISBN-10: 0-8147-1661-X (cloth : alk. paper)
1. India–History–Maurya dynasty, ca. 322 B.C.-ca. 185 B.C.–Drama.
I. Coulson, Michael. II. Title. III. Series.
PK3798.V82E5 2005
891'.22–dc22 2005011451

CONTENTS

CSL CONVENTIONS

SANSKRIT ALPHABETICAL ORDER

Vowels:	*a ā i ī u ū ṛ ṝ ḷ ḹ e ai o au ṃ ḥ*
Gutturals:	*k kh g gh ṅ*
Palatals:	*c ch j jh ñ*
Retroflex:	*ṭ ṭh ḍ ḍh ṇ*
Labials:	*p ph b bh m*
Semivowels:	*y r l v*
Spirants:	*ś ṣ s h*

GUIDE TO SANSKRIT PRONUNCIATION

a	b*u*t
ā, â	r*a*ther
i	s*i*t
ī, î	f*ee*
u	p*u*t
ū, û	b*oo*
ṛ	vocalic *r*, American p*ur*dy or English p*re*tty
ṝ	lengthened *ṛ*
ḷ	vocalic *l*, ab*le*
e, ê, ē	m*a*de, esp. in Welsh pronunciation
ai	b*i*te
o, ô, ō	r*o*pe, esp. Welsh pronunciation; Italian s*o*lo
au	s*ou*nd
ṃ	*anusvāra* nasalizes the preceding vowel
ḥ	*visarga*, a voiceless aspiration (resembling English *h*), or like Scottish lo*ch*, or an aspiration with a faint echoing of the preceding vowel so that *taiḥ* is pronounced *taih*[i]

k	lu*ck*
kh	blo*ckh*ead
g	*g*o
gh	bi*gh*ead
ṅ	a*n*ger
c	*ch*ill
ch	mat*chh*ead
j	*j*og
jh	aspirated *j*, he*dgeh*og
ñ	ca*ny*on
ṭ	retroflex *t*, *t*ry (with the tip of tongue turned up to touch the hard palate)
ṭh	same as the preceding but aspirated
ḍ	retroflex *d* (with the tip of tongue turned up to touch the hard palate)
ḍh	same as the preceding but aspirated
ṇ	retroflex *n* (with the tip of tongue turned up to touch the hard palate)
t	French *t*out
th	ten*t h*ook

d	*d*inner
dh	guil*dh*all
n	*n*ow
p	*p*ill
ph	u*ph*eaval
b	*b*efore
bh	a*bh*orrent
m	*m*ind
y	*y*es
r	trilled, resembling the Italian pronunciation of *r*
l	*l*inger
v	*w*ord
ś	*sh*ore
ṣ	retroflex *sh* (with the tip of the tongue turned up to touch the hard palate)
s	hi*ss*
h	*h*ood

CSL PUNCTUATION OF ENGLISH

The acute accent on Sanskrit words when they occur outside of the Sanskrit text itself, marks stress, e.g. Ramáyana. It is not part of traditional Sanskrit orthography, transliteration or transcription, but we supply it here to guide readers in the pronunciation of these unfamiliar words. Since no Sanskrit word is accented on the last syllable it is not necessary to accent disyllables, e.g. Rama.

The second CSL innovation designed to assist the reader in the pronunciation of lengthy unfamiliar words is to insert an unobtrusive middle dot between semantic word breaks in compound names (provided the word break does not fall on a vowel resulting from the fusion of two vowels), e.g. Maha·bhárata, but Ramáyana (not Rama·áyana). Our dot echoes the punctuating middle dot (·) found in the oldest surviving forms of written Sanskrit, the Ashokan inscriptions of the third century BCE.

The deep layering of Sanskrit narrative has also dictated that we use quotation marks only to announce the beginning and end of every direct speech, and not at the beginning of every paragraph.

CSL PUNCTUATION OF SANSKRIT

The Sanskrit text is also punctuated, in accordance with the punctuation of the English translation. In mid-verse, the punctuation will not alter the *sandhi* or the scansion. Proper names are capitalized. Most Sanskrit metres have four "feet" *(pāda):* where possible we print the common *śloka* metre on two lines. In the Sanskrit text, we use French

Guillemets (e.g. *«kva saṃcicīrṣuḥ?»*) instead of English quotation marks (e.g. "Where are you off to?") to avoid confusion with the apostrophes used for vowel elision in *sandhi*.

Sanskrit presents the learner with a challenge: *sandhi* ("euphonic combination"). *Sandhi* means that when two words are joined in connected speech or writing (which in Sanskrit reflects speech), the last letter (or even letters) of the first word often changes; compare the way we pronounce "the" in "the beginning" and "the end."

In Sanskrit the first letter of the second word may also change; and if both the last letter of the first word and the first letter of the second are vowels, they may fuse. This has a parallel in English: a nasal consonant is inserted between two vowels that would otherwise coalesce: "a pear" and "an apple." Sanskrit vowel fusion may produce ambiguity. The chart at the back of each book gives the full *sandhi* system.

Fortunately it is not necessary to know these changes in order to start reading Sanskrit. For that, what is important is to know the form of the second word without *sandhi* (pre-*sandhi*), so that it can be recognized or looked up in a dictionary. Therefore we are printing Sanskrit with a system of punctuation that will indicate, unambiguously, the original form of the second word, i.e., the form without *sandhi*. Such *sandhi* mostly concerns the fusion of two vowels.

In Sanskrit, vowels may be short or long and are written differently accordingly. We follow the general convention that a vowel with no mark above it is short. Other books mark a long vowel either with a bar called a macron (*ā*) or with a circumflex (*â*). Our system uses the macron, except that for initial vowels in *sandhi* we use a circumflex to indicate that originally the vowel was short, or the shorter of two possibilities (*e* rather than *ai*, *o* rather than *au*).

When we print initial *â*,	before *sandhi* that vowel was *a*
î or *ê*,	*i*
û or *ô*,	*u*
âi,	*e*
âu,	*o*
ā,	*ā* (i.e., the same)
ī,	*ī* (i.e., the same)
ū,	*ū* (i.e., the same)

ē,	*ī*
ō,	*ū*
āi,	*ai*
āu,	*au*
', before *sandhi* there was a vowel *a*	

FURTHER HELP WITH VOWEL SANDHI

When a final short vowel (*a*, *i* or *u*) has merged into a following vowel, we print ' at the end of the word, and when a final long vowel (*ā*, *ī* or *ū*) has merged into a following vowel we print " at the end of the word. The vast majority of these cases will concern a final *a* or *ā*.

Examples:

What before *sandhi* was	is represented as
atra asti	*atr' âsti*
atra āste	*atr' āste*
kanyā asti	*kany" âsti*
kanyā āste	*kany" āste*
atra iti	*atr' êti*
kanyā iti	*kany" êti*
kanyā īpsitā	*kany" ēpsitā*

Finally, three other points concerning the initial letter of the second word:

(1) A word that before *sandhi* begins with *ṛ* (vowel), after *sandhi* begins with *r* followed by a consonant: *yatha" rtu* represents pre-*sandhi* *yathā ṛtu*.

(2) When before *sandhi* the previous word ends in *t* and the following word begins with *ś*, after *sandhi* the last letter of the previous word is *c* and the following word begins with *ch*: *syāc chāstravit* represents pre-*sandhi* *syāt śāstravit*.

(3) Where a word begins with *h* and the previous word ends with a double consonant, this is our simplified spelling to show the pre-*sandhi* form: *tad hasati* is commonly written as *tad dhasati*, but we write *tadd hasati* so that the original initial letter is obvious.

COMPOUNDS

We also punctuate the division of compounds (*samāsa*), simply by inserting a thin vertical line between words. There are words where the decision whether to regard them as compounds is arbitrary. Our principle has been to try to guide readers to the correct dictionary entries.

EXAMPLE

Where the Deva·nágari script reads:

कुम्भस्थली रक्षतु वो विकीर्णसिन्दूररेणुर्द्विरदाननस्य ।
प्रशान्तये विघ्नतमश्छटानां निष्ठ्यूतबालातपपल्लवेव ॥

Others would print:

kumbhasthalī rakṣatu vo vikīrṇasindūrareṇur dviradānanasya /
praśāntaye vighnatamaśchaṭānāṃ niṣṭhyūtabālātapapallaveva //

We print:

Kumbha|sthalī rakṣatu vo vikīrṇa|sindūra|reṇur dvirad'|ānanasya
praśāntaye vighna|tamaś|chaṭānāṃ niṣṭhyūta|bāl'|ātapa|pallav" êva.

And in English:

"May Ganésha's domed forehead protect you! Streaked with vermilion dust, it seems to be emitting the spreading rays of the rising sun to pacify the teeming darkness of obstructions."

"Nava·sáhasanka and the Serpent Princess" I.3 by Padma·gupta

DRAMA

Classical Sanskrit literature is in fact itself bilingual, notably in drama. There women and characters of low rank speak one of several Prakrit dialects, an "unrefined" *(prākṛta)* vernacular as opposed to the "refined" *(saṃskṛta)* language. Editors commonly provide such speeches with a Sanskrit paraphrase, their "shadow" *(chāyā)*. We mark Prakrit speeches with ⌜opening and closing⌟ corner brackets, and supply the Sanskrit *chāyā* in endnotes. Some stage directions are original to the author but we follow the custom that sometimes editors supplement these; we print them in italics (and within brackets, in mid-text).

WORDPLAY

Classical Sanskrit literature can abound in puns *(śleṣa)*. Such paronomasia, or wordplay, is raised to a high art; rarely is it a *cliché*. Multiple meanings merge *(śliṣyanti)* into a single word or phrase. Most common are pairs of meanings, but as many as ten separate meanings are attested. To mark the parallel senses in the English, as well as the punning original in the Sanskrit, we use a *slanted* font (different from *italic*) and a triple colon *(⁝)* to separate the alternatives. E.g.

> Yuktaṃ Kādambarīṃ śrutvā kavayo maunam āśritāḥ
> *Bāṇa/dhvanāv* an|adhyāyo bhavat' îti smṛtir yataḥ.
>
> It is right that poets should fall silent upon hearing the Kádambari, for the sacred law rules that recitation must be suspended when *the sound of an arrow ⁝ the poetry of Bana* is heard.
>
> Soméshvara·deva's "Moonlight of Glory" I.15

INTRODUCTION

Vishákha·datta

Although Vishákha·datta furnishes the names of his father and grandfather, we know little else about him. Estimates of the date of "Rákshasa's Ring" *(Mudrā/ Rākṣasa)* have varied widely. Professor A. L. Basham suggests the sixth century CE, which would put the work neatly halfway between Kali·dasa's "Shakúntala" and Bhava·bhuti's "Málati and Mádhava."[1] However, if the reference to Chandra·gupta in the final, benedictory stanza of the play is authentic, there are good arguments for identifying this monarch as Chandra·gupta II, who reigned about 376–415 CE. The intention can hardly be to refer to the emperor Chandra·gupta Maurya, of seven hundred years before, who appears in the play, since these final stanzas are not attached to the dramatic situation but are addressed directly to the audience. But variant readings that appear to center on the name Avánti·varman also occur, and the question cannot be taken as settled. "Rákshasa's Ring" is Vishákha·datta's only surviving play, although there exist fragments of another work probably to be ascribed to him.

The titles of Vishákha·datta's father and grandfather do indicate one point of interest: that he came from a princely family, certain to have been involved in political administration at least at a local level. It seems very possible, in fact, that Vishákha·datta came to literature from the world of affairs. Stylistically he stands a little apart from other dramatists. A proper literary education is clearly in no way lacking, and in formal terms he operates within the normal conventions of Sanskrit literature, but one does not feel that he cultivates these conventions very enthusiastically for their own sake. It would be as much a travesty to suggest that one can detect in his writing a clipped, quasi-military diction as it would be to think of Kali·dasa as an untutored child of nature simply because he shows himself less steeped than Bhava·bhuti in philosophical erudition. But it is fair to say that Vishákha·datta's prose passages in particular often have a certain stiffness compared with the supple idiom of both Kali·dasa and Bhava·bhuti. And in relative rather than absolute terms his style inclines toward the principle of "more matter and less art."

There have been other cases of contributions to Sanskrit literature by men of action—for instance, the three plays ascribed to the celebrated monarch Harsha·várdhana. The ascription is plausible, and the plays are talented and worthy pieces. But unlike "Rákshasa's Ring" they adhere closely to conventional literary ideals. Harsha no doubt wished to show that he could write as well as he could rule: yet in the last resort one suspects that he would have been more interesting to know as a man than as a dramatist. We do not know whether Vishákha·datta, on the other hand, if he was some kind of politician, was as such either original or successful; but as a playwright he is both.

The historical setting of the play is, as mentioned above, at least seven hundred years earlier than Vishákha·datta's own time, and belongs to the period immediately following Alexander the Great's Indian expedition of 327–325 BCE. Alexander effectively penetrated no further than the area of modern Pakistan. To the east lay the empire of the Nandas, with its capital of Pátali·putra, the modern Patna. Greek sources tell us that a young Indian called Sandracottus tried unsuccessfully to persuade Alexander to attack this empire. Sandracottus is the Chandra·gupta of our play, and after Alexander's withdrawal he managed the task for himself and seized the throne, thereby founding the great empire of the Mauryas—his grandson Ashóka is the best known and most remarkable of all the kings of ancient India. It is very likely that Chandra·gupta Maurya was indeed aided by a minister called Kautílya or Chanákya, but we need not suppose that he was as dependent on his guidance as the present play makes out.

"Rákshasa's Ring"

"Rákshasa's Ring" is unique in Sanskrit literature. If, as I will further suggest below, a Sanskrit play may be looked on as a fairy tale subjected to a process of literary sophistication, then this play is such a fairy tale subjected to a further process of political sophistication. It cannot be seen, that is to say, as a realistic political drama—even in the ancient Indian context, where cloak-and-dagger enterprise and Machiavellian intrigue probably made a more significant contribution than they would today to the course of important political events. The work is unashamedly a piece of colorful storytelling, but deeply imbued at the same time with a sense of man as a political animal—a celebration, in fact, of the human goal of *artha*, or worldly advancement.

Indian tradition distinguished three Ends of Man: *dharma*, duty to God and one's fellow creatures; *artha*, worldly (and, more particularly, political) advancement; and *kāma*, sensual (especially sexual) pleasure. (A fourth goal, transcending these three, was often added: that of *mokṣa*, or release from worldly bondage.) The theme of *dharma* is never absent from Sanskrit literature. But the theme of *artha* is more prominent in this play than is that of *kāma* in "Shakúntala" or even in "Málati and Mádhava." And just as Bhava·bhuti shows himself conversant with the Indian ars amatoria, and indeed at one point actually quotes directly from the "Kama Sutra," so Vishákha·datta shows himself equally conversant with the theory of statecraft (*artha/śāstra* or *nīti/śāstra*) and in Act III makes a direct reference to its teachings.

Nothing shows the political sophistication of the play more plainly than the nature of the conflict between the two main characters. The hero is Rákshasa, the exiled Chief Minister of the deposed dynasty of the Nandas, a man in equal measure intelligent, experienced, courageous and loyal. But his political opponent, far from being the villain of the piece, is a sort of superhero—the inhumanly competent ascetic Kautílya, the man who originally engineered the Nandas' destruction. And the theme of the play is Kautílya's struggle not to destroy Rákshasa but to win him over to his own side to be his successor as Chandra·gupta's Chief Minister, so that he himself can retire from all involvement in practical politics. Rákshasa is outmaneuvered because of the poor quality and treachery of his associates, the undisciplined warmth of his human feelings, and ultimately his unswerving loyalty—the very quality, above all, which Kautílya values him for.

The fact that Rákshasa is outsmarted by Kautílya at every turn would make him a poor sort of hero if the two characters were on the same dramatic level.

But Kautílya is presented as no ordinary human being, in fact scarcely as a real person at all. He has no human weaknesses—for the anger that inspired his implacable enmity toward the Nanda Emperor is no more seen as a weakness than is that of the sage Durvásas in "Shakúntala." Rather, he is the idealized embodiment of *artha/śāstra*, statecraft, itself. Indeed, the "Artha Shastra," the textbook on statecraft which has come down to us under that name, is traditionally attributed to his authorship (though the attribution is certainly false), and the audience would have been keenly aware of this fact, which underlines his mythical and semi-divine character. His differing status from Rákshasa is emphasized also by the difference in their relationship to the young Emperor. Kautílya is Chandra·gupta's guru, the man who chose to put him on the throne: the question of his being a loyal or disloyal servant of the Emperor cannot arise, since the obligation is all on the other side.

Rákshasa, on the other hand, once he has been maneuvered into accepting Chandra·gupta as the true heir of the Nandas' power (and it is hinted that the young man is in fact an illegitimate son of the late Emperor), transfers to the new monarch the absolute commitment that he had given to the old. It becomes a central part of his own particular *dharma* to put his political talents unreservedly at the disposal of his new master.

Kautílya, the austere and self-disciplined sage, lacks all worldly ties, and his motivations are not those of ordinary men. But in Rákshasa, utterly loyal servant and devoted friend and husband as well as experienced statesman, the conflicting claims of *dharma*, *artha* and *kāma* meet and take their proper place within a single human being.

One of the delights of "Rákshasa's Ring" is its intricate and perfectly interlocking plot. To help the reader a little in keeping the characters distinct, I have taken one minor liberty with nomenclature. While the playwright alternates the names Kautílya and Chanákya, I have eliminated the latter completely, since two other major characters have names beginning with "Chan°."

No reader should let himself be put off by Kautílya's long explanatory monologue at the beginning of Act I (which to my mind is something of a flaw in the dramatic construction, since few members of any audience could be expected to keep all of it clear in their heads): those who plunge straight on into the lively ensuing dialogue will find that the main lines of the plot unfold quite naturally as the play progresses.

Sanskrit Drama

In Sanskrit drama, not all of the dialogue is in Sanskrit. While men of high social status speak Sanskrit, the uneducated—men of inferior status, young children and almost all women—speak in varieties of Prakrit, the language that evolved from Sanskrit (rather as Italian evolved from Latin). Originally, this must have been at least in part a reflection of social realities. But as time passed the Prakrit dialects used in the drama became no more than a rigid literary convention, and likely to be less comprehensible to people of ordinary education than Sanskrit itself. The medieval commentator Hari·hara, in undertaking to explain the Prakrit used in

"Málati and Mádhava," describes it as "a source of terror to the dimwits of today" *(vitrāsa/kāri kudhiyām adhunātanā-nām).*

All classical Sanskrit literature, in fact, was written for a highly educated, highly sophisticated audience. It was recognized that drama had a greater breadth of appeal than other literary genres because it incorporated the elements of spectacle, music and dance. But on the literary side the dramatist made no compromise with popular taste. Dramatic verse is fully as complex as that of any other genre, and if the audience numbered some who could make little of it, they are clearly not the ones at whom the poet was directing his work.

Drama in Action

There were no vast amphitheatres with mass audiences, as in the Greek tradition. The typical performance would have been held either under private patronage (in a palace, for example) or as a contribution to a religious festival, and given in a hall of comparatively modest size, though preferably one specially constructed for the performance of plays. The style of performance was intimate and suited to a small audience, with attention paid to subtleties of gesture and expression.

We know in outline the conditions of stage presentation, though many questions remain unanswered. No curtain separated the stage from the audience. There was no scenery, and props were very little used: the ancient handbook on the theatre, the "Natya Shastra" *(Nāṭya/śāstra)*, cursorily dismisses any suggestion that realism is desirable, for example when someone is represented as riding in a chariot or sailing in a boat, by observing that no one expects an actor to die when the character he is playing does so. However, importance is attached to costume and adornment, and in general the focus of attention is on the actor rather than on his physical environment.

A curtain did separate the back of the stage from the actors' changing room *(nepathya)*. Normally, when an actor came onstage part of this curtain was drawn aside for him by attendants. Occasionally a sudden and dramatic entry was marked by the actor's pushing through the curtain for himself. The stage was divided (in the minds, that is, of spectators and actors) into zones, so that an actor could indicate a change of locality, such as a visit to a friend's house, by moving from one part of the stage to another: this is the significance of the frequent stage direction "he walks about." By means of this convention, different groups of actors could occupy the stage simultaneously without supposedly being visible to one another. The action can switch in turn from one group to another in a way that might well be aided on the modern stage by the use of a spotlight.

A character often speaks "to himself," i.e., voices his thoughts for the benefit of the audience without any of the other characters hearing. The frequency with which this device is employed in the course of ordinary dialogue goes well beyond the normal use of soliloquy and asides in the Western theatre, and gives Sanskrit drama a flexibility in representing the private thoughts and attitudes of its characters which rivals a modern "multiple viewpoint" novel.

Someone may also speak privately to a companion, while remaining unheard by others who are present. In addition, characters in one zone may speak without being heard by those in another zone, but this convention is not indicated by any special instruction in the text.

The stage directions form an integral part of the original text of the plays, and I have been careful to preserve them exactly as written.[2] Again, they are entirely actor-oriented and never include a direct indication of setting. In other words, the written text consists of two sets of instructions to the actors: what to say ("Who is that coming this way?") and how to behave ("he peers anxiously"). This fact emphasizes the integral part played by mime in Sanskrit drama. The actor communicated not merely by words but by the controlled use of his body and facial expressions. It was the elaboration of this art which made it possible to dispense with material props: actions such as riding in a chariot, flying through the air, watering flowers, and being pestered by a bee were all conveyed clearly by the actor's skill alone. The language of these stage directions is terse and conventional, and the modern reader is left to fill out the picture from his own imagination.

One stage direction may sound rather puzzling, the not infrequent "enter seated." The meaning of this in dramatic terms is not in doubt: it corresponds to the "is discovered seated" on a stage with a front curtain or a spotlighting system. But how this particular direction was realized in practice is less clear—perhaps simply by entering and then assuming a seated posture.

MUSICAL THEATRE

It is evident that music contributed significantly to the performance. The "Natya Shastra" compares a play without music to an unpainted building, and in another passage says that song, instrumental music and acting should be blended into one, like the circle of a whirling firebrand. Among the more important instruments were the *vīṇā*, or lute, the flute, drums and cymbals; while, on the vocal side, female singers were more highly admired than male. Before the play began, the musicians, including the singers, would take up their positions at the back of the stage and embark on a series of elaborate preliminaries that served the dual purpose of "tuning up" and of setting the mood for the coming performance. And throughout the play music was used to reinforce the action—thus a drunkard's staggering gait would be underlined on the drum.

Particularly intriguing are the descriptions of the Prakrit mood-songs, called *dhruvā*, which it seems frequently accompanied the entrances and exits of the characters, and could be used at other points also to attune the expectations of the audience (one useful variety, the "fill-in" *(antarā dhruvā)*, was available to cover up any hitch in an actor's performance). Typically the language of such a song would take the form of a symbolic description of nature: thus a song about a mighty elephant crashing through the jungle would mark the appearance of the hero roaming desperately in search of his beloved.

Responsibility for the composition and performance of these songs seems to have rested essentially with the musicians rather than with the playwright and actors, and it is difficult to say how prominently they would have figured in a performance of a classical drama. In one recension of Ka·li·dasa's play "The Hero and the Nymph" *(Vikram'/Ôrvaśī)* which has come down to us, the fourth act incorporates material of this kind; but it is generally agreed that, in the form in which we have it, this version is late, and we cannot be sure how accurately it reflects the ordinary tradition of stage performance even of this particular piece, let alone of classical drama in general. Clearly, tact would have been needed to avoid a clash between such material and the subtle heightenings of mood conveyed by the dramatist's own poetry—just as, in the modern cinema, banal and over-obvious background music can ruin the artistic impact of a film.

Prose and Verse

Many of the features that give Sanskrit drama its distinctive nature will be apparent from the translation in this volume. One of the most fundamental is the blending of prose and verse. The word "poetry" has no direct equivalent in Sanskrit: because a vast quantity of scientific writing is in metrical form, verse has no special association with belles lettres. The nearest term, *kāvya*, embraces every variety of creative literature. Within it, the three major forms of extended creative writing are: narrative poems, entirely metrical; prose romances, entirely non-metrical; and dramas. The prose of the romances ("novels" would be a rather misleading term for this, the least important of the three genres) is often highly ornate. By contrast, the prose of the dramas, which forms a counterpart of the verse, is generally clear and simple.

The distinction between prose and verse in the play is again something I have been careful to keep. In general I have aimed at a fairly close translation, and the preservation rather than the naturalization of culturally unfamiliar images and ideas, except perhaps where these are wholly incidental to what is being said and might therefore be distracting. By keeping the four-line structure of Sanskrit stanzas, I have hoped to suggest something of the variety of long and short meters used in the original. It will be obvious enough that my translation is often extremely low-key, and is not intended to be an addition to the corpus of English poetry. But I would resist the suggestion that I might just as well have used prose.

Free-verse translation can serve a useful function in suggesting a metrical original, and this is particularly important where the work translated alternates between verse and prose. Undoubtedly it can be claimed that the formal beauty of Sanskrit verse can adequately be represented only by a highly melodious and formally patterned, perhaps therefore rhymed, English equivalent. But this calls both for considerable poetic talent and for an appreciably greater degree of freedom in adapting the original, and in practice the results seldom seem to justify the liberties taken. Even when it is reasonably successful, the final effect of a rhymed English translation is usually to suggest a minor English poet rather than a great Indian one, and one wonders easily whether it is right to turn someone like Kali·dasa into raw material for the exercise of frustrated poetic ambitions.

Sanskrit Style

Translators from all languages have a difficult and thankless task: in the end there are no degrees of success, only degrees of failure. But translators of Sanskrit *kāvya* have more to complain about than most. To translate a Sanskrit stanza so that it merely bores rather than bewilders the reader can be an achievement in itself. The chief reason is a syntactical one, and lies in the way in which the classical poets exploited the structural possibilities of the language. In classical Sanskrit subordinate phrases and clauses are largely replaced by compound-noun formations. Not infrequently, a stanza of verse is wholly organized around a small nucleus of subject-verb-object. Here is a piece of English verse that has something of the pace and cadence of a Sanskrit stanza:

For the clear voice suddenly singing, high up in the
convent wall,
The scent of elder bushes, the sporting prints in the hall,
The croquet matches in summer, the handshake,
the cough, the kiss,
There is always a wicked secret, a private reason for this.

W. H. Auden

And here is a literal English rendering of the grammatical structure such a verse might have in Sanskrit (one should perhaps caution the linguistically unsophisticated against importing into Sanskrit the English notion that long compounds have a comic flavor to them):

*Convent-wall-height-sudden-clearsinging-voice-
signalled,
Elderbush-scent-hinted, hall-hung-sportingprints-
lurking,
Summer-held-croquetmatch-implicit, handshake-cough-
kiss betrayed,
Everywhere are found wicked private-reason-based
secrets.*

This is a straightforward example. Factors such as the existence of a type of compound called *bahu/vrīhi* (i.e., "[a land where there is] much rice;" cf., e.g., Bluebeard, home-cooked, etc.) and the highly inflected nature of Sanskrit would make similar renderings of other stanzas quite incomprehensible. The function that a compound plays in a sentence depends on its grammatical ending, and many stanzas are tightly organized mosaics that defy literal translation. The baffled translator resorts to breaking up and rearranging this carefully constructed artifact, and two features of the original, order of ideas and syntactical unity, tend to be regarded as particularly expendable. No one would really find it necessary to resort to such rearrangement in the above example, but the following is a parody of the kind of thing that can happen:

Everywhere one finds wicked secrets based on private reasons: they are signalled by the sudden clear-singing voice in the heights of a convent wall; the scent of elder bushes hints at them, and they lurk among the sporting prints hung in the hall; croquet matches in summer imply them; handshakes, coughs and kisses betray them.

Faced with standard "literal" versions of this kind, which are prosaic for a far more fundamental reason than the lack of rhyme and meter, it is difficult for the Western reader to guess at Sanskrit originals as tuneful and evocative as the verse by AUDEN.

I stress the tunefulness of Sanskrit verse, since it is relevant to the complementary roles of verse and prose in the theatrical idiom. The distinction is almost one of "recitative and aria." The perpetual alternation between the directness of the prose and the lyricism of the verse is fundamental to the dramatic rhythm. Except occasionally for motives of stylistic variety, verse is not used as a way of carrying the story forward. Its function is rather one of crystallization, of commenting on the situation and developing its implications. Even when characters talk to each other directly in verse, the verse tends to be preceded by a short remark in prose, a headline, as it were, for the following story ("I am disappointed in you," "your eyes are so beautiful," "who is that figure standing beside you?"). Deictic references ("look at this," "here is the person who") are often kept out of the stanza even if they are grammatically part of it—one of the reasons that stanzas from Sanskrit plays can often appear in anthologies without their dramatic origin being apparent.

The suggestion that Sanskrit drama is generally "undramatic," while it no doubt has an element of truth, is in my view rather exaggerated, and perhaps stems from an over-preoccupation with the verse and a certain failure to recognize the important complementary role played by the prose. (One critical edition of "Shakúntala" actually quotes variant readings only for the verses!)

Heroic Drama

"Rákshasa's Ring" is classified as *nāṭaka*, or heroic drama. The plot of the heroic drama, the most highly regarded dramatic form, in taken from tradition. "Rákshasa's Ring" is not, however, entirely typical in the source of its plot. It is based not on legend at all but on historical fact, though to its audience the exploits of Chandra·gupta were probably more remote than those of the "Ramáyana," for example.

But, whether they derive from tradition or the writer's imagination, the characters in these dramas are types rather than individuals. The method of the Indian poet was not to elevate particular people to universal status but to take universal types and then infuse them with individual human life. The atmosphere of Sanskrit drama is of the fairy story taken to an ultimate pitch of sophistication. It is often said that the nearest parallel in Western tradition to plays such as "Shakúntala" is Shakespearean comedy. There is the same blend of gentleness, grace and fantasy with a calm maturity and wisdom. Tragedy in the Greek sense does not occur, and unhappy endings of any kind are as foreign to the conventions of Sanskrit drama as they are, for instance, to the novels of Jane Austen. Even a play such as Bhava·bhuti's "Later Story of Rama" *(Uttara|Rāma|carita)*, in which the Sorrowful *rasa* (for which see below) predominates, modulates into serenity and reconciliation at the end.

Cultural Context

A Western reader, of course, cannot hope to come to a Sanskrit play in the same state of preparedness as its original audience. There is not merely the question of cultural references (some of which at least can be explained in footnotes) and of the general context of life shared by the poet and his public. There is also the question of the literary tradition itself. A work of art, as well as being a reflection of the culture that produces it, is more specifically a comment on the works of art that have preceded it. This is particularly true where, as in India, the tradition has been a long, articulate and self-conscious one. When the poet embroiders on what has gone before, his work may seem strained and far-fetched to the outsider unfamiliar with what has gone before—a consideration that applies particularly to the use of figures of speech in Sanskrit poetry, which were elaborated and refined over a long period.

It is where cultural differences and literary tradition reinforce each other that the Western reader is likely to feel least at home. The Indian varieties of the lotus and the water lily, for example, have a degree of symbolic value more than comparable with that of the rose in Western poetry. To select one aspect, the lotus, opening out at dawn and folding its petals again toward evening, is regarded as having a particular affinity with the sun, while the night-blossoming water lily is regarded as being under the tutelage of the moon: these relationships, as part of the natural order of things, may be taken for granted or seen as mysterious and paradoxical (as in "Málati and Mádhava"—"the searing sun makes the lotus bloom"), but either way they serve as a paradigm of many other such affinities in the world about us. Again, the comparison between the human eye and the deep color of the dark-blue variety of water lily was so familiar that two people gazing long and deep into each other's eyes could be described as "linked by a garland of dark water lilies" (also relevant to this image is the fact that the process of seeing was conceived in terms of an outgoing radiation from the eye).

When in Act IX of "Málati and Mádhava" Mádhava is overcome with grief at the signs of the approach of the monsoon, this is because the season of the rains, being unsuitable for traveling, is a time symbolizing domestic tranquility and the reunion of loved ones, when separation is especially bitter (a period comparable, in this respect, with Christmastide).

As in the West, the season of spring is believed to inflame amorous feeling: but when lovers grow tormented by the intensity of their passion and their doubts as to its being reciprocated, they attain a state of such hypersensitivity that even the cool rays of the moon can burn them like fire. However, the pallor and emaciation brought on by love-fever are felt to heighten their physical attractiveness.

The idea of female beauty is one of extreme shapeliness. The waist must be slim and the breasts youthfully firm, but if these conditions are met, every pound of flesh on breasts and hips augments a woman's attractions. For this reason we are often told that her breasts are too heavy for her slender waist to bear, or that when she walks the exertion of moving her bulky hips causes her to break out in a fine sweat. (Conveniently, the wasting effect of lovesickness usually seems to manifest itself less strikingly on the breasts and hips than on other parts of the body—most particularly the arms, on which bracelets in consequence grow loose.)

The mention of sweating has pleasant associations, for in other amorous contexts it may give a lover a clue to his sweetheart's emotional state. Sweating, like other involuntary physical reactions such as tears or trembling, is valued by poets as a means whereby ideals of self-discipline suffer an honorable defeat at the hands of invincible nature. One such involuntary reaction features far more prominently in Indian than in Western literature—horripilation ("gooseflesh"), frequently seen as a sign of sexual excitement.

While the depiction of these involuntary physical reactions is common to all Sanskrit literature, the need for them to be realized in concrete visual terms on the stage gives them prominence of a particular sort in the drama; and, formalized into eight involuntary states, they provide one element in an ancient and important tradition of dramatic analysis, the theory of *rasa*.

The Theory of *Rasa*

Critics divided the effect that a drama, or a passage in a drama, might have on its audience into eight possible different flavors (flavor is the literal meaning of the term *rasa*)—Romantic, Comic, Sorrowful, Violent, Heroic, Terrifying, Repulsive and Marvelous. Later critics, who extended the theory to non-dramatic literature, added the Peaceful *rasa*. But how does the audience's experience ("tasting") of such a *rasa* relate to what is going on onstage? To describe this, the elements of determinants, states and consequents were distinguished.

In the Terrifying *rasa*, determinants might include a deserted house at night, the sudden hooting of an owl, the apparition of a ghostly figure. States might include apprehensiveness, shock and fear. Consequents might include bulging eyes, trembling, a cry of alarm, an agitated attempt to get away. The states (other than the involuntary states, which became a special sub-class within the general category of consequents) are divided between thirty-three transitory or subsidiary states and eight or nine permanent or predominant states. These latter are each tied to a particular *rasa*, and they are, in order, Love, Mirth, Grief, Fury, Resoluteness, Fear, Revulsion, Wonder and Peace.

The expectations of an Indian audience were schooled to a significant extent by this way of looking at a play. A dramatist was judged largely by the effectiveness with which he evoked the *rasa* he was aiming at, and every detail of play and performance was expected to contribute directly or indirectly to the evocation of *rasa*. The description of setting, and especially of natural phenomena, and the selection of imagery in simile and metaphor were consciously guided by a search for harmony and the heightening of a particular mood. To take just one example, at the beginning of Act VI of "Rákshasa's Ring" (stanza 11 ff.), the Transitory state of Despair, established by Rákshasa's direct expression of his hurt and frustration, is reinforced by the natural images of blight and decay that surround him. The audience would take such reinforcement for granted, and be alert to notice not whether it was done but only how well.

In this system of dramatic analysis, clearly the states are, in broad terms, the states of mind represented as belonging to the characters of the drama, and communicated to the audience both by the determinants, i.e., the dramatic situation, and by the consequents, i.e., above all the actor's performance. But the question of the relationship between raw and corresponding permanent state was one that fascinated Indian thinkers.

If in ordinary life we seek to avoid grief, why should tasting the Sorrowful *rasa* be a pleasant and even ennobling experience?—one comparable, in fact, with the exalted state of consciousness of the mystic. But if, on the other hand, the *rasa* is the permanent state not personally undergone but merely observed, why should someone who is moved by the sight of two lovers on the stage be quite likely to respond with such feelings as embarrassment, jealousy or indifference on seeing two lovers together in real life? In fact, since the emotion in a play is merely fictitious, why should one not a fortiori go through life tasting *rasa* at every true instance of strong emotion that one comes across?

The answer, in its finally accepted form, was that the Sorrowful *rasa* is grief experienced as it never is or can be in ordinary life, as directly and vividly as if it were one's own response to real circumstances (not at all as if it were the observed grief of some other person), yet with such complete detachment that one feels no anxiety, no wish to assert oneself in any way. It is the grief neither of oneself in a particular situation nor of any other person distinct from oneself: in other words, it is grief generalized. The function of literature is to generalize emotion so that it can be tasted in this way. We can respond only insofar as the emotion evoked already lies within our experience. The tasting of *rasa* is nothing more nor less than the re-experience *(anuvyavasāya)* of our own emotions. That is why it is pleasant. Consciousness resents the intrusion of anything distinct from itself which wrests it from its state of repose. But the emotion awoken by art is a calm, unthreatening, recreative ordering of what is already within us.

This is the formulation arrived at by the great critic and philosopher Abhináva·gupta, writing in the eleventh century CE, some five hundred years later than Vishákha·datta's "Rákshasa's Ring." I mention his account both because it represents a drawing out within the Indian tradition of the implications of the original theory and because it is an analysis by a man of intelligence and sensibility of his own response to just such works as those here translated. The determinants will often seem strange to the Western reader, and the ancient actors are not here to help evoke the consequents. But I hope that, even through the thick veil of translation into an alien tongue, something of the essential *rasa* of these plays does still survive.

The Sanskrit Text

In the *Mudrā/Rākṣasa*, the usual problem of markedly different recensions does not arise. In general, I have followed Hillebrandt's edition while taking some readings from his apparatus rather than from his text.

BIBLIOGRAPHY

W. H. AUDEN Song VIII in *From Twelve Songs*, 1933–1938.

Mudrārākṣasa by Viśākhadatta; edited from manuscripts. . . by Alfred HILLEBRANDT. Breslau : M. & H. Marcus, 1912. Indische Forschungen;4 Heft.

Nāṭyaśāstra of Bharatamuni with the Commentary Abhinavabhāratī by Abhinavaguptācārya. Ed. M. RAMAKRISHNA KAVI, revised [. . .] by K.S. RAMASVAMI SHASTRI, 2nd ed. Baroda 1956, (Gaekwad Oriental Series 36).

NOTES

1 Michael COULSON will make further references to these other two plays because his translations of them were originally published together with the present work in a single volume. [Ed.]

2 But with one minor exception: the original never identifies the source of a 'voice offstage'—so that specific attribution, such as "king's voice offstage," merely represents my own inference from the context.

DRAMATIS PERSONÆ

Characters not appearing on stage are mentioned in brackets.

THE RULING FACTION

Rājā:	The EMPEROR of India, Chandra·gupta Maurya, familiarly called 'Vríshala'
Cāṇakyaḥ:	KAUTÍLYA, his preceptor and acting Chief Minister
Śiṣyaḥ:	Shárnga·rava, a PUPIL, living in KAUTÍLYA's household
Pratīhārī:	Shonóttara, FEMALE GUARD of the EMPEROR
Kañcukī:	Vaihínari, CHAMBERLAIN to the Emperor

KAUTÍLYA'S AGENTS

Caraḥ:	Nípunaka, a SPY, disguised as a votary of the God of Death
Siddhārthakaḥ:	SIDDHÁRTHAKA, pretending friendship to SHÁKATA·DASA and to RÁKSHASA
Kṣapaṇakaḥ:	JIVA·SIDDHI, a Jain monk, in reality a brahmin called Indu·sharman
Bhāgurāyaṇaḥ:	BHAGURÁYANA, pretending friendship to MÁLAYA·KETU
Puruṣaḥ:	MAN, supposed friend of a friend of CHÁNDANA·DASA
Samiddhārthakaḥ:	SAMIDDHÁRTHAKA, Siddhárthaka's friend

(Three brahmin brothers, the eldest called Vishva·vasu, disguised as traders)

(Bhadra·bhata, Púrusha·datta, Hingu·rata, Bala·gupta, Raja·sena, Rohitáksha, Vijaya·varman, allies of CHANDRA·GUPTA now supposedly disloyal)

THE OPPOSING FACTION

Malayaketuḥ:	Prince MÁLAYA·KETU, son of Chandra·gupta's murdered ally King Párvataka
Rākṣasaḥ:	RÁKSHASA, Chief Minister of the deposed Nanda dynasty, now adviser to MÁLAYA·KETU

Candanadāsaḥ:	CHÁNDANA·DASA, a rich jeweller, RÁKSHASA's friend
Śakaṭadāsaḥ:	SHÁKATA·DASA, a letter-writer, RÁKSHASA's friend
Virādhaguptaḥ/ Āhituṇḍikaḥ:	VIRÁDHA·GUPTA, RÁKSHASA's friend, now his agent and disguised as a SNAKE CHARMER
Dvitīyaḥ [Vaitālaikaḥ]:	SECOND BARD at Chandra·gupta's court, Stana·kálasha, RÁKSHASA's agent
Karabhakaḥ:	KÁRABHAKA, RÁKSHASA's agent
Puruṣaḥ:	MANSERVANT of RÁKSHASA, Priyam·vádaka
Kañcukī:	Jájali, CHAMBERLAIN to MÁLAYA·KETU
Pratīhārī:	Víjaya, FEMALE GUARD of Malaya·ketu
Puruṣaḥ:	Bhásvaraka, MANSERVANT, of BHAGURÁYANA

(Five princes, Chitra·varman, Simha·nada, Pushkaráksha, Sindhushéna, Megha·nada, allies of MÁLAYA·KETU)

Also FIRST Bard,
Rákshasa's DOORKEEPER,
a MANSERVANT of Málaya·ketu,
a MANSERVANT of Chandra·gupta,
WIFE and SON of Chándana·dasa

BENEDICTION

«Dhanyā k" êyam sthitā te śirasi?» «śaśi|kalā.»
«kiṃ nu nām' âitad asyāḥ?»
«nām' âiv' âsyās tad etat paricitam api te
vismṛtaṃ kasya hetoḥ?»
«nārīṃ pṛcchāmi n' êndum.» «kathayatu Vijayā,
na pramāṇaṃ yad' îndur.»
devyā nihnotum icchor iti Sura|saritaṃ
śāṭhyam avyād Vibhor vaḥ.

api ca,

pādasy' āvir|bhavantīm avanatim avane
rakṣataḥ svaira|pātaiḥ
saṃkocen' âiva doṣṇāṃ muhur abhinayataḥ
sarva|lok'|âtigānām
dṛṣṭiṃ lakṣyeṣu n' ôgrāṃ jvalana|kaṇa|mucaṃ
bibhrato dāha|bhīter
ity ādhār'|ânurodhāt Tripura|Vijayinaḥ
pātu vo duḥkha|nṛttam.

"Who is that lucky one on your head?"
"Moon crescent."
"Of course, but you knew it well—
how could you have forgotten?"
"My question concerns a woman, not your moon."
"Ask Víjaya, then, if the moon's no help."
Shiva's skill, thus guarding Ganga from his wife,
be your protection.

&

As with cautious steps he avoids the earth's certain
collapse
And mimes with arms always bent that could
outreach the universe,
Letting his blazing eye rest nowhere for fear of fire,
May the dance protect you, cramped by its stage,
of the Triple City's Victor.

PROLOGUE

nāndy|ante tataḥ praviśati SŪTRA|DHĀRAḤ.

SŪTRADHĀRAḤ: alam ativistareṇa. ājñāpito 'smi pariṣadā yath" âdya sāmanta|Vaṭeśvaradatta|pautrasya mahā|rāja| Bhāskaradatta|sūnoḥ kaver Viśākhadattasya kṛtir Mudrā| Rākṣasaṃ nāma nāṭakaṃ nāṭayitavyam iti. yat satyaṃ kāvya|viśeṣa|vedinyāṃ pariṣadi prayuñjānasya mam' âpi sumahān paritoṣaḥ prādur|bhavati. kutaḥ?

cīyate bāliśasy' âpi
  sat|kṣetra|patitā kṛṣiḥ
na śāleḥ stamba|karitā
  vaptur guṇam apekṣate.

tad yāvad idānīṃ gṛhaṃ gatvā gṛha|janena saha saṃgītakam anutiṣṭhāmi. *(parikramy' âvalokya ca)* ime no gṛhāḥ. yāvat praviśāmi. *(praviśy' âvalokya ca)* aye tat kim idam? asmad|gṛheṣu mah"|ôtsava iv' âdya sva|sva|karmaṇy adhikataram abhiyuktaḥ parijanaḥ. tathā hi:

1.5 vahati jalam iyaṃ pinaṣṭi gandhān
  iyam iyam udgrathate srajo vicitrāḥ
musalam idam iyaṃ ca pāta|kāle
  muhur anuyāti kalena huṃ|kṛtena.

bhavatu. kuṭumbinīm āhūya pṛcchāmi. *(nepathy'|âbhimukham avalokya)*

guṇavaty upāya|nilaye
  sthiti|heto sādhike tri|vargasya
mad|bhavana|nīti|vidye
  kāry'|ācārye drutam upaihi.

After the Benediction, enter the DIRECTOR.

DIRECTOR: Enough, enough! The audience directs me to present the play called "Rákshasa's Ring," a work of the writer Vishákha·datta, son of Maha·raja Bháskara·datta, and grandson of Lord Vatéshvara·datta. And indeed it gives me the greatest pleasure to perform before so discriminating a public. For,

Even a fool can farm
When he lights on fertile ground.
Rich crops have no need
Of merit in the sower.

So first I'll go home and rehearse my company. *(walking about and looking)* Here is our house. I'll enter. *(entering and looking)* Hallo, what's going on? Is it some celebration, with all the maidservants so busy? Look—

Here's one fetching water, here's one grinding 1.5
perfume,
Here's one weaving colorful garlands.
And here's one at the pestle
Humming softly as she works.

I must call my wife and ask her. *(looking offstage)*

Talented wife, treasure-house of contrivance,
Source of security, my path to Pleasure, Virtue and
Success,
Science of Polity incarnate in my household,
Teacher and counselor—come here at once.

pravíśya NAṬĪ: ⌜ajja, iaṃ mhi. āṇā|ṇioeṇa maṃ ajjo aṇugeṇhadu.⌟

SŪTRADHĀRAḤ: ārye, tiṣṭhatu tāvad ājñā|niyogaḥ. kathaya kim adya bhavatyā bhagavatāṃ brāhmaṇānām upanimantraṇena kuṭumbakam anugṛhītam abhimatā vā bhavanam atithayaḥ saṃprāptā yata eṣa pāka|viśeṣ'|ārambhaḥ?

1.10 NAṬĪ: ⌜ajja, āmantidā mae bhaavanto bamhaṇā.⌟

SŪTRADHĀRAḤ: kasmin nimitte?

NAṬĪ: ⌜ajja, uvarajjadi kila bhaavaṃ cando tti.⌟

SŪTRADHĀRAḤ: ārye, ka evam āha?

NAṬĪ: ⌜evaṃ khu ṇaara|ṇivāsī jaṇo mantedi.⌟

1.15 SŪTRADHĀRAḤ: ārye, kṛta|śramo 'smi catuḥṣaṣṭy|aṅge jyotiḥ|śāstre. tat pravartyatāṃ brāhmaṇān uddiśya pākaḥ. candr'|ôparāgaṃ prati tu ken' âpi vipralabdh" âsi. paśya—

Krūra|grahaḥ sa|Ketuś
  Candraṃ saṃpūrṇa|maṇḍalam idānīm
abhibhavitum icchati balāt—

ity ardh'|ôkte, nepathye:

āḥ ka eṣa mayi sthite?

Enter an ACTRESS*:*

Here I am, sir. Favor me with your commands.

DIRECTOR: Never mind my commands for the moment, dear wife. Tell me, have you favored our house by inviting holy brahmins here, or have honored guests perhaps turned up, to justify all this cooking?

ACTRESS: I have invited holy brahmins, sir. 1.10

DIRECTOR: For what purpose?

ACTRESS: Because there's going to be an eclipse of the moon.

DIRECTOR: Who says so?

ACTRESS: That's what people have been saying in the city.

DIRECTOR: My dear wife, I have laboured much upon the 1.15
sixty-four branches of the science of astronomy. By all means go on with your cooking for the brahmins. But, as for an eclipse of the moon, someone has been misleading you. Let me explain—

> Now the fierce Demon joins with Ketu,
> Seeking by force to overpower
> Chandra the full-orbed moon—

Interrupting him, a VOICE *offstage:*

Who! Who dares, while I am here!

SŪTRADHĀRAḤ:

1.20 —rakṣaty enaṃ tu Budha|yogaḥ.

NAṬĪ: ⌜ajja, ko uṇa eso dharaṇi|goaro bhavia candaṃ gahovarāādo rakkhiduṃ icchadi?⌟

SŪTRADHĀRAḤ: ārye, yat satyaṃ may" âpi n' ôpalakṣitaḥ. bhavatu bhūyo 'bhiyuktaḥ svara|vyaktim upalapsye.

Krūra|grahaḥ sa|Ketuś
  Candraṃ saṃpūrṇa|maṇḍalam idānīm
abhibhavitum icchati balāt—

nepathye:

āḥ, kathaya, kathaya, ka eṣa mayi sthite Candraguptam abhibhavitum icchati balāt?

1.25 SŪTRADHĀRAḤ: *(ākarṇya)* ārye, jñātam. Kauṭilyaḥ.

naṭī bhayaṃ nāṭayati.

Kauṭilyaḥ kuṭila|matiḥ sa eṣa yena
  krodh'|âgnau prasabham adāhi Nanda|vaṃśaḥ
«candrasya grahaṇam» iti śruteḥ sa|nāmno
  Maury'|êndor dviṣad|abhiyoga ity avaiti.

tad ita āvāṃ gacchāvaḥ.

iti niṣkrāntau.

DIRECTOR:

—But the wise planet Mercury safeguards him. 1.20

ACTRESS: Sir, who was that human being wanting to save the moon from an eclipse?

DIRECTOR: I couldn't tell, either. This time I'll listen carefully for his voice—

Now the fierce Demon joins with Ketu,
Seeking by force to overpower
Chandra the full-orbed moon—

A VOICE *offstage:*

Who! Who is it, who is it? Who while I am here dares try to overthrow Chandra·gupta?

DIRECTOR: *(listening)* Now I know! It is Kautílya— 1.25

The actress shows fear.

It is Kautílya of wily counsel,
Who consumed the House of Nanda in the fire of his anger.
Hearing mention of the moon's eclipse, he imagines
Some threat to the Maurya emperor who has the same name as the moon.

Let us be off.

They withdraw.

ACT I
KAUTÍLYA LAYS HIS PLANS

1.30 *tataḥ praviśati muktāṃ śikhāṃ parāmṛśan sa|kopaś* CĀṆAKYAḤ.

CĀṆAKYAḤ: kathaya, kathaya, ka eṣa mayi sthite Candraguptam abhibhavitum icchati balāt?

Nanda|kula|kāla|bhujagīṃ
  kop'|ânala|bahala|nīla|dhūma|latām
ady' âpi badhyamānāṃ
  vadhyaḥ ko n' êcchati śikhāṃ me.

api ca,

ullaṅghayan mama samujjvalataḥ pratāpaṃ
  kopasya Nanda|kula|kānana|dhūmaketoḥ
sadyaḥ parātma|parimāṇa|viveka|mūḍhaḥ
  kaḥ śālabhena vidhinā labhatāṃ vināśam?

1.35 Śārṅgarava, Śārṅgarava.

praviśya ŚIṢYAḤ: upādhyāya, ājñāpaya.

CĀṆAKYAḤ: vatsa, upaveṣṭum icchāmi.

ŚIṢYAḤ: upādhyāya, nanv iyaṃ saṃnihita|vetr'|āsan" âiva dvāra|prakoṣṭha|śālā. tad asyām upaveṣṭum arhaty upādhyāyaḥ.

CĀṆAKYAḤ: vatsa, kāry'|âbhiyoga ev' âsmān ākulayati na punar upādhyāya|sahabhūḥ śiṣya|jane duḥśīlatā. *(nāṭyen' ôpaviśy' ātma|gatam)* kathaṃ prakāśatāṃ gato 'yam arthaḥ paureṣu yathā kila Nanda|kula|vināśa|janita|roṣo Rākṣasaḥ pitṛ|vadh'|āmarṣitena sakala|Nanda|rājya|paripaṇa|protsāhitena Parvataka|putreṇa Malayaketunā saha saṃdhāya tad upagṛhītena ca mahatā Mleccha|rāja|balena parivṛto Vṛṣalam abhiyoktum udyata iti. *(vicintya)*

Enter, angrily fingering his loosened braid of hair, KAUTÍLYA.* 1.30

KAUTÍLYA: Who is it, who is it? Who while I am here dares try to overthrow Chandra·gupta?

> Who is that doomed fool who even now
> Wants to see this lock of hair unbound,
> This dark serpent that bit the House of Nanda,
> This thick black plume of smoke from the fire of
> my wrath?

&

> Who blunders like a moth into my blazing anger
> Which burned the Nanda forest,
> So little able to measure his strength and mine
> That he invites his own destruction?

Shárnga·rava, Shárnga·rava! 1.35

Enter his PUPIL: Command me, preceptor.

KAUTÍLYA: A seat, boy.

PUPIL: Why, sir, there is a bamboo seat already here in the entrance hall. Please be seated, sir.

KAUTÍLYA: I have many affairs on my mind, dear boy—don't think I'm just a teacher picking fault with his pupil. *(to himself, sitting down)* So the news is out, is it, that Rákshasa* has made a pact with Párvataka's son Málaya·ketu, and, with the large forces of the barbarian princes whom Málaya·ketu has won to his side, is getting ready to attack the Emperor—Rákshasa in revenge for the destruction of the House of Nanda, Málaya·ketu indignant at his father Párvataka's murder and inflamed by the prospect of winning the whole Nanda empire. *(reflecting)* But

atha|vā yena mayā sarva|loka|prakāśaṃ Nanda|vaṃśa|va-dhaṃ pratijñāya nistīrṇā dustarā pratijñā|sarit so 'ham idānīṃ prakāśī|bhavantam apy enam arthaṃ samarthaḥ praśamayitum. kuta etat?

1.40 śyāmī|kṛty' ānan'|êndūn ripu|yuvati|diśāṃ
saṃtataiḥ śoka|dhūmaiḥ
kāmaṃ mantri|drumebhyo naya|pavana|hṛtaṃ
moha|bhasma prakīrya
dagdhvā saṃbhrānta|paura|dvija|gaṇa|rahitān
Nanda|vaṃśa|prarohān
dāhy'|âbhāvān na khedāj jvalana iva vane
śāmyati krodha|vahniḥ.

api ca,

śocanto 'vanatair nar'|âdhipa|bhayād
dhik|śabda|garbhair mukhair
mām agr'|āsanato 'vakṛṣṭam avaśaṃ
ye dṛṣṭavantaḥ purā
te paśyantu tath" âiva saṃprati janā
Nandaṃ mayā s'|ânvayaṃ
siṃhen' êva gaj'|êndram adri|śikharāt
siṃh'|āsanāt pātitam.

so 'ham idānīm avasita|pratijñā|bhāro 'pi Vṛṣal'|âpekṣayā śastraṃ dhārayāmi.

what of it? No matter how strong the public alarm is, I can quiet it—I am Kautílya, who vowed before the whole world to slay the Nanda race, and then fulfilled that impossible vow:

Clouding the moon-lovely faces of my enemy's 1.40
wives with the smoke of grief,
Spattering his counselors with ashes of confusion
borne on the wind of strategy,
Burning the tender shoots of his House, while his
subjects scattered like startled birds,
My forest fire of wrath has paused for lack of fuel,
not from exhaustion.

&

Those who once in helpless grief saw me dragged
from my high place,
Their gaze averted, protests dying on their lips for
fear of the King,
Let them now see how Nanda with all his brood
Lies felled from the throne, like an elephant felled
from the mountaintop by a lion.

Now, with the burden of my vow discharged, it is only regard for Vríshala that keeps me in office. For I

samutkhātā Nandā
nava hṛdaya|rogā iva bhuvaḥ
kṛtā Maurye lakṣmīḥ
sarasi nalin" îva sthira|padā
dvayoḥ sāraṃ tulyaṃ
dvitayam abhiyuktena manasā
phalaṃ kopa|prītyor
dviṣati ca vibhaktaṃ suhṛdi ca.

1.45 atha|vā: agṛhīte Rākṣase kim utkhātaṃ Nanda|vaṃśasya kiṃ vā sthairyam utpāditaṃ Candragupta|lakṣmyāḥ. *(vicintya)* aho Rākṣasasya Nanda|vaṃśe niratiśayo bhakti|guṇaḥ. sa khalu kasmiṃś cid api jīvati Nand'|ânvay'|âvayave Vṛṣalasya sācivyaṃ grāhayituṃ na śakyate. tad abhiyogaṃ prati nirudyogair asmābhir avasthātum ayuktam ity anay" âiva buddhyā tapo|vana|gato 'pi ghātitas tapasvī Sarvārthasiddhiḥ. yāvad asau Malayaketum aṅgī|kṛty' âsmad|ucchedāya vipulataraṃ prayatnam upadarśayaty eva. *(pratyakṣavad ākāśe lakṣyaṃ baddhvā)* sādhu, amātya|Rākṣasa, sādhu. sādhu, mantri|Bṛhaspate, sādhu. kutaḥ?

aiśvaryād an|apetam īśvaram ayaṃ
loko 'rthataḥ sevate
taṃ gacchanty anu ye vipattiṣu punas
te tat pratiṣṭh"|āśayā
bhartur ye pralaye 'pi pūrva|sukṛt'|â-
saṅgena niḥsaṅgayā
bhaktyā kārya|dhuraṃ vahanti kṛtinas
te durlabhās tvādṛśāḥ.

Have uprooted the Nine Nandas like a canker from
the soil,
And planted sovereignty in the Maurya as surely
as a lotus in a pool.
On friend and foe with full deliberation
I have justly apportioned the fruits of my
displeasure or regard.

But no. Until I have Rákshasa, the House of Nanda is undisturbed and Chandra·gupta's sovereignty has no firm roots. *(reflectively)* Oh how unswerving is Rákshasa's loyalty to the Nandas! While even a single member of the Nanda family remained alive, it would have been impossible to get him to serve under Vríshala. But once blocked on that front, he'll be manageable. That was why I had the wretched Sarvártha·siddhi killed, though he retired to a hermitage. Meanwhile, Rákshasa has won Málaya·ketu to his side, and shows himself more determined than ever to destroy me. *(addressing himself to the air)* Bravo, Minister Rákshasa! Bravo, divine pattern of a counselor! 1.45

While he has power, people serve their lord for
gain,
And those who follow him into adversity are
hoping for his restoration.
Hard it is to find men with loyalty such as yours,
Selflessly shouldering the burden of duty even
when their master is dead.

ata ev' âsmākaṃ tvat|saṃgrahe yatnaḥ katham asau Vṛṣalasya sācivya|grahaṇena s'|ânugrahaḥ syād iti. kutaḥ?

aprājñena ca kātareṇa ca guṇaḥ
  syād bhakti|yuktena kaḥ?
prajñā|vikrama|śālino 'pi hi bhavet
  kiṃ bhakti|hīnāt phalam?
prajñā|vikrama|bhaktayaḥ samuditā
  yeṣāṃ guṇā bhūtaye
te bhṛtyā nṛpateḥ kalatram itare
  saṃpatsu c' āpatsu ca.

tan may" âpy asmin vastuni na śayānena sthīyate. yathā|śakti kriyate tad|grahaṇaṃ prati yatnaḥ. katham iti?

1.50 atra tāvad «‹Vṛṣala|Parvatakayor anyatara|vināśen' âpi Cāṇakyasy' âpakṛtaṃ bhavat' îti› viṣa|kanyayā Rākṣasen' âsmākam atyant'|ôpakāri mitraṃ ghātitas tapasvī Parvataka iti» saṃcārito jagati jan'|âpavādaḥ. loka|pratyay'|ârtham asy' âiv' ârthasy' âbhivyaktaye «pitā te Cāṇakyena ghātita iti» rahasi trāsayitvā Bhāgurāyaṇen' âpavāhitaḥ Parvataka|putro Malayaketuḥ. śakyaḥ khalv eṣa Rākṣasa|mati|parigṛhīto 'pi vyuttiṣṭhamānaḥ prajñayā nivārayituṃ, na punar asya nigrahāt Parvataka|vadh'|ôtpannam ayaśaḥ prakāśī|bhavat pramārṣṭum iti.

That is why I strive to win you to our side, to persuade you to favor us by accepting office under Vríshala.

What merit has a timid, stupid man, however loyal?
What use is a brave and clever man if he lacks loyalty?
Those who unite brains, courage and devotion are the servants
That profit a king. In good times or in bad the rest are concubines.

And so I am unresting in my struggle to win him over. This is what I have done:

First, I have used the mystery of King Párvataka's murder. I 1.50
have made sure that among the people a rumor unfavorable to Rákshasa circulates, that it was he who employed the poison-girl to kill our great ally, in the belief that the murder of Párvataka would harm me as much as the murder of Vríshala himself. To convince everyone that this was obviously true, my agent Bhaguráyana spoke privately to the murdered man's son, Prince Málaya·ketu, and first alarmed him with the opposite tale—that it was I, Kautílya, who had had his father killed—then helped him to escape. For if Málaya·ketu leads a rebellion against me, even one backed by Rákshasa, I can deal with him; but for me to have arrested him here would have wiped out all the mounting unpopularity that King Párvataka's murder has been earning Rákshasa.

prayuktāś ca sva|pakṣa|para|pakṣayor anurakt'|âparakta|jana|jijñāsayā bahu|vidha|deśa|veṣa|bhāṣ"|ācāra|saṃcāra|vedino nānā|vyañjanāḥ praṇidhayaḥ. anviṣyante ca Kusumapura|nivāsināṃ Nand'|âmātya|suhṛdāṃ nipuṇaṃ pracāra|gatayaḥ.

tat|tat|kāraṇam utpādya kṛta|kṛtyatām āpāditāś Candragupta|sah'|ôtthāyino Bhadrabhaṭa|prabhṛtayaḥ pradhāna|puruṣāḥ.

śatru|prayuktānāṃ ca tīkṣṇa|rasa|dāyināṃ pratividhānaṃ praty apramādinaḥ parīkṣita|bhaktayaḥ kṣiti|pati|pratyāsannā niyuktās tatr' āpta|puruṣāḥ.

asti c' âsmākaṃ sah'|âdhyāyi mitraṃ Induśarmā nāma brāhmaṇaḥ. sa c' Âuśanasyāṃ daṇḍa|nītau catuḥṣaṣṭy|aṅge jyotiḥ|śāstre ca paraṃ prāvīṇyam upagataḥ. sa ca mayā Kṣapaṇaka|liṅga|dhārī Nanda|vaṃśa|vadha|pratijñ"|ânantaram eva Kusumapuram upanīya sarva|Nand'|âmātyaiḥ saha sakhyaṃ grāhito viśeṣataś ca tasmin Rākṣasaḥ samutpanna|viśrambhaḥ. ten' êdānīṃ mahat|prayojanam anuṣṭheyaṃ bhaviṣyati.

1.55 tad evam asmatto na kiṃ cit parihāsyate. Vṛṣala eva kevalaṃ pradhāna|prakṛtiṣv asmāsv āropita|rājya|tantra|bhāraḥ satatam udāste. atha|vā yat svayam abhiyoga|duḥkhair asādhāraṇair apākṛtaṃ tad eva rājyaṃ sukhayati. kutaḥ?

svayam āhṛtya bhuñjānā
  balino 'pi sva|bhāvataḥ
nar'|êndrāś ca mṛg'|êndrāś ca
  prāyaḥ sīdanti duḥkhitāḥ.

Second, I have used spies disguised in various ways and commanding a variety of manners, costumes and dialects to help me learn who is loyal and who is mutinous both among ourselves and among the enemy. They are using their talents to investigate people living here in Pátali·putra who were friends of Rákshasa.

Then, there are Bhadra·bhata and certain others who fought on Chandra·gupta's side: various pretexts have been manufactured to give the enemy the impression that they can be easily seduced from their allegiance to us.

Fourth, I have ensured that the King is constantly attended by men of proven reliability, alert against any poisoners the enemy may employ.

And last, there is my friend and colleague of student days, the brahmin Indu·sharman. He is a man learned both in political science and in all branches of astrology. When I first swore to destroy the race of Nanda, I introduced him into this city disguised as a Jain monk and had him cultivate the friendship of all the Nanda ministers. In particular he enjoys Rákshasa's full confidence. He plays an important part in my plans.

So I have left nothing to chance. Vríshala himself sits at ease, 1.55
entrusting all cares of state to me, his Chief Minister. But then kingship cannot bring pleasure unless it is free of the special vexations that accompany it:

If they must forage for themselves,
Then, however strong they are,
Lords of men and lords of the herd alike
Grow vexed and weary.

tataḥ praviśati saha Yama|paṭena CARAḤ.

CARAḤ:

⌜paṇamaha Jamassa calaṇe
kiṃ kajjaṃ devaehi aṇṇehiṃ?
eso kkhu aṇṇa|bhattāṇa
haraï jīvaṃ dhaḍaphadantam.⌟

1.60 ⌜avi a,⌟ ⌜purisassa jīviavvaṃ
visamāo hoi bhatti|gahiāo
mārei savva|loaṃ
jo teṇa Jameṇa jīvāmo.⌟

⌜jāva edaṃ gehaṃ pavisia Jama|vaḍaṃ daṃsaaṃto gīdāïṃ gāāmi.⌟ *(iti parikrāmati)*

ŚIṢYAḤ: *(avalokya)* bhadra, bhadra, na praveṣṭavyam.

CARAḤ: ⌜haṃho bamhaṇā, kassa edaṃ gehaṃ?⌟

ŚIṢYAḤ: asmākam upādhyāyasya sugṛhīta|nāmna ācārya|Cāṇakyasya.

1.65 CARAḤ: *(vihasya)* ⌜haṃho bamhaṇā, attaṇo kerakassa jjeva dhamma|bhāduassa gharaṃ bhodi. tā dehi me pavesaṃ jāva tuha uvajjhāassa dhammaṃ uvadisāmi.⌟

ŚIṢYAḤ: *(sa|kopam)* aye mūrkha, kiṃ bhavān asmākam upādhyāyād dharmavittaraḥ?

CARAḤ: ⌜haṃho bamhaṇā, mā kuppa. nakkhu savvo savvaṃ jāṇadi. kiṃpi tuha uvajjhāo jānadi kiṃpi amhārisā vi jāṇanti.⌟

Enter a SPY *with a canvas depicting the God of Death.*

SPY:

> Bow at the feet of Death—
> What use of other gods?
> O you who worship other gods,
> It is he who will snatch your throbbing life.
>
> From this harsh god, appeased by prayer, 1.60
> Man's life is won.
> From him who slaughters all,
> From the God of Death we have our being.

I'll enter this house, show my death-canvas and sing my songs. *(He walks about.)*

PUPIL: *(seeing him)* Good fellow, you can't come in here.

SPY: Hallo, my fine brahmin, whose house is this?

PUPIL: It is the house of my teacher, the revered preceptor Kautílya.

SPY: *(with a laugh)* Why, then, it is the house of my very 1.65
own religious brother. S o let me in, and I'll instruct your preceptor in the true faith.

PUPIL: *(angrily)* Dolt! Do you know more of such things than he does?

SPY: Don't be annoyed, young brahmin. After all, no one can know everything. Your preceptor has his knowledge, and people like me have our own.

ŚIṢYAḤ: mūrkha, sarvajñatām upādhyāyasya corayitum icchasi?

CARAḤ: ⌜haṃho bamhaṇā, jaï tuha uvajjhāo savvaṃ jāṇadi tā jāṇadu dāva kāṇaṃ cando aṇahippedo tti.⌟

1.70 ŚIṢYAḤ: kim anena jñātena bhavati?

CARAḤ: ⌜haṃho bamhaṇā, tuha uvajjhāo jjeva jāṇissadi jaṃ ediṇā jāṇideṇa bhodi. tumaṃ uṇa ettiaṃ jeva jāṇāsi kamalāṇaṃ cando aṇahippedo tti.⌟

⌜kamalāṇa maṇa|harāṇa vi
rūvāhiṃto visaṃvaaï sīlaṃ
saṃpuṇṇa|maṇḍalammi vi
jāïṃ cande viruddhāïṃ.⌟

CĀṆAKYAḤ: *(ākarṇy' ātma|gatam)* aye, «Candraguptād aparaktān puruṣān jānām' îty» upakṣiptam anena.

ŚIṢYAḤ: mūrkha, kim idam asaṃbaddham abhidhīyate?

1.75 CARAḤ: ⌜haṃho bamhaṇā, susaṃbaddhaṃ jeva edaṃ bhave jaï—⌟

ŚIṢYAḤ: yadi kiṃ syāt?

CARAḤ: jaï suṇāduṃ jāṇantaṃ jaṇaṃ lahe.

CĀṆAKYAḤ: bhadra, praviśa. lapsyase śrotāraṃ jñātāraṃ ca.

CARAḤ: ⌜esa pavisāmi.⌟ *(praviśya)* ⌜jaadu jaadu ajjo!⌟

PUPIL: Blockhead! You question my preceptor's omniscience?

SPY: If your preceptor is omniscient, sir, he should know whom the moon displeases.

PUPIL: What use could there be in knowing that? 1.70

SPY: Your preceptor, sir, will know the point of knowing it. As for you, you need only know this much—the moon displeases the lotuses:

> The lotuses, fair though they be,
> Belie their looks by their behavior,
> For they are the enemy
> Of the full-orbed splendor of the moon.

KAUTÍLYA: *(listening, to himself)* Ha! He means that he knows of men disloyal to Chandra·gupta.

PUPIL: What nonsense is this, you idiot?

SPY: Why, sir, it would all make sense enough— 1.75

PUPIL: If what?

SPY: If I could find someone who understood to listen to me.

KAUTÍLYA: Come in, good fellow. You'll find someone to listen, and to understand.

SPY: I enter! *(entering)* Victory to you, sir.

I.80 CĀṆAKYAḤ: *(viloky' ātma|gatam)* katham, ayaṃ prakṛti|citta|parijñāne niyukto Nipuṇakaḥ. *(prakāśam)* bhadra, svāgatam. upaviśyatām.

CARAḤ: ⌜jaṃ ajjo āṇavedi.⌟ *(iti bhūmāv upaviṣṭaḥ)*

CĀṆAKYAḤ: bhadra, varṇay' êdānīṃ sva|niyoga|vṛttāntam. api Vṛṣalam anuraktāḥ prakṛtayaḥ?

CARAḤ: ⌜adha iṃ? ajjeṇa kkhu tesuṃ tesuṃ virāa|kāraṇesuṃ parihariantesuṃ sugihīda|ṇāma|dheaṃ devaṃ Candaüttaṃ diḍhadaraṃ aṇurattāo païdīo. kiṃ uṇa dāṇi atthi ettha ṇaare amacca|Rakkhaseṇa saha paḍhamaṃ samuppaṇṇa|seṇeha|bahumāṇā tiṇṇi purisā je devassa Candasiriṇo siriṃ ṇa sahanti.⌟

CĀṆAKYAḤ: *(sa|krodham)* nanu vaktavyaṃ «sva|jīvitaṃ na sahanta iti.» bhadra, api jñāyante nāmataḥ?

I.85 CARAḤ: ⌜ajja, a|suṇida|ṇāma|dheā ajjassa khadhaṃ ṇivedīanti?⌟

CĀṆAKYAḤ: tena hi śrotum icchāmi.

CARAḤ: ⌜suṇādu ajjo. paḍhamaṃ dāva ajjassa riu|pakkhe baddha|pakkha|vādo Khavaṇao.⌟

CĀṆAKYAḤ: *(sa|harṣam ātma|gatam)* asmad|ripu|pakṣe baddha|pakṣa|pātaḥ Kṣapaṇakaḥ. *(prakāśam)* kiṃ nāma|dheyo hi saḥ?

CARAḤ: ⌜Jīvasiddhī ṇāma jeṇa sā amacca|Rakkhasa|ppaüttā visa|kaṇṇaā deve Pavvadīsare samāvesidā.⌟

I.90 CĀṆAKYAḤ: *(sva|gatam)* sa tāvaj Jīvasiddhir asmat|praṇidhiḥ. *(prakāśam)* bhadra, ath' âparaḥ kaḥ.

KAUTÍLYA: *(to himself, looking at him)* Ah, this is Nípuna- 1.80
ka, whom I employed to sound out feeling among the citizens. *(aloud)* You are welcome, my good fellow. Be seated.

SPY: As you command, sir. *(He seats himself on the floor.)*

KAUTÍLYA: Now, what progress? Are the citizens loyal to Vríshala?

SPY: More loyal than ever, sir, as you remove various possible reasons for discontent. But there are at present in this city three men who, out of the love and esteem they have always borne Rákshasa, cannot endure the glorious reign of His Majesty the Emperor.

KAUTÍLYA: *(in anger)* Cannot endure to live, you mean! Do you know their names?

SPY: Would I approach you, sir, if I did not? 1.85

KAUTÍLYA: Then I am waiting to hear them.

SPY: Yes, sir. First there is a Jain monk working for the enemy.

KAUTÍLYA: *(to himself, in pleased tones)* A Jain monk working for the enemy?* *(aloud)* What is his name?

SPY: He is called Jiva·siddhi, and he ensured that King Párvataka was killed by the poison-girl engaged by Rákshasa.

KAUTÍLYA: *(to himself)* That one, at any rate, is my own 1.90
agent. *(aloud)* Who else, my good fellow?

CARAḤ: ⌜ajja, avaro vi amacca|Rakkhasassa pia|vaasso kāattho Saaḍadāso ṇāma.⌟

CĀṆAKYAḤ: *(vihasy' ātma/gatam)* kāyastha iti laghvī mātrā. tath" âpi na yuktaṃ prākṛtam api puruṣam avajñātum. tasmin mayā suhṛc|chadmanā Siddhārthako niyuktaḥ. *(prakāśam)* bhadra, tṛtīyam api śrotum icchāmi.

CARAḤ: ⌜tadio vi amacca|Rakkhasassa dudiaṃ via hiaaṃ Pupphaüra|ṇivāsī maṇi|āra|seṭṭhī Candaṇadāso ṇāma jassa gehe kalattaṃ ṇāsī|kadua amacca|Rakkhaso ṇaarādo avakkanto.⌟

CĀṆAKYAḤ: *(ātma/gatam)* nūnaṃ suhṛttamaḥ. na hy an|ātma|sadṛśeṣu Rākṣasaḥ kalatraṃ nyāsī|kariṣyati. *(prakāśam)* bhadra, «Candanadāsasya gṛhe Rākṣasena kalatraṃ nyāsī|kṛtam» iti katham avagamyate bhavatā.

1.95 CARAḤ: ⌜iaṃ aṅguli|muddā ajjaṃ pi avagamaïssadi.⌟ *(iti mudrām arpayati.)*

CĀṆAKYAḤ: *(gṛhītvā vācayati nāma Rākṣasasya. sa/harṣaṃ sva/gatam)* nanu vaktavyaṃ «Rākṣasa ev' âsmad|aṅguli|praṇayī saṃvṛtta iti.» *(prakāśam)* bhadra, aṅguli|mudr"|âdhigamaṃ vistarataḥ śrotum icchāmi.

CARAḤ: ⌜suṇādu ajjo. atthi dāva ahaṃ ajjeṇa pora|jaṇa|carid'|aṇṇesaṇe ṇiutto. tado para|ghara|ppavese parassa asaṅkaṇīeṇa imiṇā Jama|vaḍeṇa hiṇḍamāṇo ajja maṇi|āra|seṭṭhi|Candaṇadāsassa gehaṃ paviṭṭho mhi tahiṃ ca Jama|vaḍaṃ pasāria paütto mhi gāïduṃ.⌟

SPY: There is another good friend of Minister Rákshasa, a letter-writer called Shákata·dasa.

KAUTÍLYA: *(to himself, smiling)* A letter-writer is a person of small consequence. But it would be wrong to disregard even the meanest opponent, and I have already ordered my agent Siddhárthaka to cultivate his acquaintance. *(aloud)* And the third?

SPY: The third, too, is an intimate friend, one very dear to Minister Rákshasa's heart, the master jeweler and banker Chándana·dasa. It was in his house that Minister Rákshasa placed his wife when he left the city.

KAUTÍLYA: *(to himself)* A close friend indeed! Rákshasa would never entrust the safety of his wife to a mere acquaintance. *(aloud)* Tell me, my dear fellow, how do you know that Rákshasa has left his wife in Chándana·dasa's house?

SPY: This signet ring should enlighten you, sir. *(He hands him a ring.)* 1.95

KAUTÍLYA: *(taking it and reading out the name Rákshasa to himself in delight)* Why, I have Rákshasa himself entwined around my finger! *(aloud)* Tell me in detail how you came by this ring.

SPY: Listen, sir. Being employed by you to inquire into the activities of the citizens, I was wandering the city with this death-canvas, by means of which I may enter strange houses without exciting suspicion, and I went into the house of the master jeweler Chándana·dasa, where I spread my canvas and began to chant my songs.

CĀṆAKYAḤ: tatas tataḥ.

CARAḤ: ⌜tado ekkādo avavaraādo pañca|varisa|desīo pia|daṃsaṇīa|sarīr'|ākidī kumārao bāla|jaṇa|sulaha|kodūhal'|upphullamāṇa|ṇaaṇa|jualo ṇikkamiduṃ paütto. tado «hā ṇiggado hā ṇiggado tti» saṅkā|pariggaha|ṇihuda|garuo tassa jjeva avavaraassa ante itthī|jaṇassa utthido mahanto kolāhalo. tado īsi|duvāra|desa|dāvida|muhīe ekkāe itthiāe so kumārao ṇikkamanto jjeva ṇibbhacchia avalambido komalāe bāhuladāe. tissāe kumāra|saṃgahaṇa|saṃbhama|calid'|aṅguliādo karādo puris'|aṅguli|pariṇāha|ppamāṇa|ghaḍidā vialidā iaṃ aṅguli|muddiā dehalī|vaṭṭe ṇivaḍidā. ucchalidā tāe aṇavabuddha jjeva mama calaṇa|pāsaṃ samāgacchia paṇāma|ṇihudā kula|vahu via ṇiccalā saṃvuttā. mae vi amacca|Rakkhasassa ṇām'|aṅkida tti ajjassa pāa|mūlaṃ pāvidā. tā eso imāe muddiāe āgamo tti.⌟

I.100 CĀṆAKYAḤ: bhadra, śrutaṃ. apasara. acirād asya pariśramasya phalam anurūpam adhigamiṣyasi.

CARAḤ: ⌜jaṃ ajjo āṇavedi.⌟ *(iti niṣkrāntaḥ.)*

CĀṆAKYAḤ: Śārṅgarava, Śārṅgarava!

ŚIṢYAḤ: *(praviśya)* upādhyāya, ājñāpaya.

CĀṆAKYAḤ: masī|bhājanaṃ pattraṃ c' ôpanaya.

I.105 ŚIṢYAḤ: yad ājñāpayaty upādhyāyaḥ. *(iti niṣkramya punaḥ praviśya)* upādhyāya, idaṃ masī|bhājanaṃ pattraṃ ca.

CĀṆAKYAḤ: *(gṛhītvā sva|gatam)* kim atra likhāmi? anena lekhanena Rākṣaso jetavyaḥ.

KAUTÍLYA: What happened?

SPY: From an inner apartment an attractive child about four or five years old, his two eyes widening in the easy curiosity of childhood, began to show himself. In the apartment I could hear sounds of confusion, alarmed women urgently whispering, "Oh, he's got out, he's got out!"; then a woman, just showing her face around the door, scolded the child and caught hold of him with a slender arm, while he was still emerging. As she moved her hand hastily to check him, that signet ring, which is made to fit a man's finger, slipped off and fell onto the threshold. It bounced off and rolled toward me, quite unnoticed by her, and lay motionless at my feet, like a well-bred woman silently saluting me. Seeing that it was engraved with Minister Rákshasa's name, I brought it to Your Honor. And that is the story of how I came by it.

KAUTÍLYA: I have noted it, my dear man. Go, and you will I.100
soon be well rewarded for your efforts.

SPY: As you command, sir. *(He goes out.)*

KAUTÍLYA: Shárnga·rava! Shárnga·rava!

PUPIL: *(entering)* Command me, sir.

KAUTÍLYA: Bring me an ink-pot and paper.

PUPIL: Yes, sir. *(withdrawing and re-entering)* Here you are, I.105
sir.

KAUTÍLYA: *(accepting them, to himself)* How shall I phrase this letter? It must bring victory over Rákshasa.

praviśya PRATĪHĀRĪ: ⌜jaadu jaadu ajjo.⌟

CĀṆAKYAḤ: *(sa|harṣam ātma|gatam)* gṛhīto 'yaṃ jaya|śabdaḥ. *(prakāśam)* Śoṇottare, kim āgamana|prayojanam?

PRATĪHĀRĪ: ⌜ajja, kamala|maül'|āāraṃ añjaliṃ sīse ṇivesia devo Candasirī ajjaṃ viṇṇavedi. «icchāmi ahaṃ ajjeṇa abbhaṇuṇṇādo devassa Pavvadīsarassa pāraloiaṃ kāduṃ teṇa a dhārida|puvvāïṃ bhūsaṇāïṃ bhaavantāṇaṃ bamhaṇāṇaṃ paḍivādemi tti.»⌟

I.110 CĀṆAKYAḤ: *(sa|harṣam ātma|gatam)* sādhu, Vṛṣala, sādhu. mam' âiva hṛdayena saha saṃmantrya saṃdiṣṭavān asi. *(prakāśam)* Śoṇottare ucyatām asmad|vacanād Vṛṣalaḥ: «sādhu, vatsa, sādhu. abhijñaḥ khalv asi loka|vyavahārāṇām. tad anuṣṭhīyatām ātmano 'bhiprāyaḥ. kiṃ tu Parvateśvara|dhṛta|pūrvāṇi bhūṣaṇāni guṇavanti guṇavadbhya eva brāhmaṇebhyaḥ pratipādanīyāni. tad eṣa svayaṃ parīkṣita|guṇān brāhmaṇān preṣayām' îti.»

PRATĪHĀRĪ: ⌜jaṃ ajjo āṇavedi.⌟ *(iti niṣkrāntā.)*

CĀṆAKYAḤ: Śārṅgarava Śārṅgarava!

ŚIṢYAḤ: ājñāpaya.

CĀṆAKYAḤ: ucyantām asmad|vacanād Viśvāvasu|prabhṛtayas trayo bhrātaraḥ. «Vṛṣalāt pratigrahaṃ pratigṛhy' âhaṃ bhavadbhir draṣṭavya iti.»

I.115 ŚIṢYAḤ: yad ājñāpayaty upādhyāyaḥ. *(iti niṣkrāntaḥ.)*

Enter the FEMALE GUARD: Victory be yours, Your Honor.

KAUTÍLYA: *(delightedly, to himself)* I accept the omen of victory! *(aloud)* Shonóttara, what brings you here?

FEMALE GUARD: Sir, His Glorious Majesty the Emperor Chandra·gupta salutes you with his hands folded to his forehead, and begs to say: "I wish with Your Honor's permission to perform the obsequies of His Majesty King Párvataka, and would therefore bestow the decorations he wore upon revered brahmins."

KAUTÍLYA: *(delightedly, to himself)* Well done, Vríshala! You have consulted with my own heart in expressing such a wish. *(aloud)* Shonóttara, answer Vríshala in my name as follows: "Bravo, dear child, bravo! You show that you know what is proper. Do what you propose. And as to the decorations worn by Párvataka, they are of the finest quality and should be bestowed upon brahmins worthy of them. I will send you therefore brahmins whose worth I can vouch for."

FEMALE GUARD: As you command, sir. *(She goes out.)*

KAUTÍLYA: Shárnga·rava, Shárnga·rava!

PUPIL: Sir?

KAUTÍLYA: I have a message for Vishva·vasu and his two brothers: they are to go to Vríshala to accept a gift, and then to come to me.

PUPIL: Yes, sir. *(He goes out.)*

CĀṆAKYAḤ: uttaro 'yaṃ lekh'|ârthaḥ pūrvaḥ katamo 'stu. *(vicintya)* āṃ jñātam. upalabdhavān asmi praṇidhibhyo yathā «tasya mleccha|rāja|balasya madhyāt pradhānatamāḥ pañca rājānaḥ parayā suhṛttayā Rākṣasam anuvartanta iti.» tad yathā—

Kaulūtaś Citravarmā Malaya|nara|patiḥ
Siṃhanādo nṛsiṃhaḥ
Kāśmīraḥ Puṣkarākṣaḥ
kṣata|ripu|mahimā Saindhavaḥ Sindhuṣeṇaḥ
Meghākṣaḥ pañcamo 'sau pṛthu|turaga|balaḥ
Pārasīk'|âdhirājo:
nāmāny eṣāṃ likhāmi dhruvam aham adhunā
Citraguptaḥ pramārṣṭu.

atha|vā na likhāmi. sarvam an|abhivyaktam eva tāvad āstām. Śārṅgarava, Śārṅgarava.

ŚIṢYAḤ: *(praviśya)* upādhyāya, ājñāpaya.

1.120 CĀṆAKYAḤ: vatsa, śrotriya|likhitāny akṣarāṇi prayatna|likhitāny api niyatam a|sphuṭāni bhavanti. tad ucyatām asmad|vacanāt Siddhārthakaḥ. «ebhir ev' âkṣaraiḥ Śakaṭadāsena ‹ken' âpi kasy' âpi vācyam› ity adatta|bāhya|nāmānaṃ lekhaṃ lekhayitvā māṃ upatiṣṭhasva. na c' ākhyeyam asmai Cāṇakyo lekhayat' îti.»

ŚIṢYAḤ: yad ājñāpayaty upādhyāyaḥ. *(iti niṣkrāntaḥ.)*

CĀṆAKYAḤ: *(sva|gatam)* hanta jito Malayaketuḥ!

KAUTÍLYA: I have the second half of the letter, but how shall it begin? *(after reflection)* Ah, yes! My agents inform me that prominent among the barbarian forces are five princes especially friendly with Rákshasa—

Chitra·varman of Kulúta, stout Simha·nada of Málaya,
Pushkaráksha of Kashmir, mighty Sindhu·shena of Sindh,
And, fifth, Megháksha, commander of horsemen, ruler of the Persians.
I'll write their names now, and leave them to be canceled by the Clerk of Death.

No, on second thought, I won't spell things out. Shárnga·rava, Shárnga·rava!

PUPIL: *(entering)* Yes, sir?

KAUTÍLYA: My boy, a scholar's handwriting is always illegible however hard he tries. So give Siddhárthaka this message: "Have the letter-writer Shákata·dasa copy out this letter. Explain that it has no address on it because it is intended to be read aloud. When you have done this, bring it to me here. And do not mention to him that it is Kautílya who wants it copied." 1.120

PUPIL: Yes, sir. *(He goes out.)*

KAUTÍLYA: *(to himself)* This means victory over Málaya·ketu!

praviśya lekha|hastaḥ.

SIDDHĀRTHAKAḤ: ⌜jaadu jaadu ajjo. ajja, aaṃ so Saaḍadāseṇa ālihido leho.⌟

I.125 CĀṆAKYAḤ: *(gṛhītvā)* aho darśanīyāny akṣarāṇi. *(ity anuvācya)* bhadra, anayā mudrayā mudray' âinam.

SIDDHĀRTHAKAḤ: ⌜jaṃ ajjo āṇavedi.⌟

CĀṆAKYAḤ: Śārṅgarava, Śārṅgarava!

ŚIṢYAḤ: *(praviśya)* upādhyāya, ājñāpaya.

CĀṆAKYAḤ: vatsa, ucyatām asmad|vacanād daṇḍa|pāśiko yathā Vṛṣalaḥ samājñāpayati: «ya eṣa Kṣapaṇako Jīvasiddhī Rākṣasa|prayukto viṣa|kanyayā Parvateśvaraṃ ghātitavān sa enam eva doṣaṃ prakhyāpya sa|nikāraṃ nagarān nirvāsyatām iti.»

I.130 ŚIṢYAḤ: yad ājñāpayaty upādhyāyaḥ. *(iti parikrāmati.)*

CĀṆAKYAḤ: tiṣṭha. «yo 'yam aparaḥ kāyasthaḥ Śakaṭadāso nāma Rākṣasa|prayukto nityam asmac|charīram abhidrogdhum iha prayatate sa enam eva doṣaṃ prakhyāpya śūlam āropyatāṃ gṛha|janaś c' âsya bandha|nāgāraṃ praveśyatām iti.»

ŚIṢYAḤ: yad ājñāpayaty upādhyāyaḥ. *(iti niṣkrāntaḥ.)*

SIDDHĀRTHAKAḤ: ⌜ajja, muddido leho. āṇavedu ajjo kiṃ avaraṃ aṇuciṭṭhīadu tti.⌟

CĀṆAKYAḤ: bhadra, kasmiṃś cid āpta|jan'|ânuṣṭheye karmaṇi tvāṃ vyāpārayitum icchāmi.

Enter SIDDHÁRTHAKA *with the letter.*

SIDDHÁRTHAKA: Victory be yours, sir. Here is the letter, copied by Shákata·dasa.

KAUTÍLYA: *(taking it)* Ah, a most attractive hand! *(after reading it through)* Siddhárthaka, seal it with this signet ring. I.125

SIDDHÁRTHAKA: Yes, sir.

KAUTÍLYA: Shárnga·rava, Shárnga·rava!

PUPIL: Yes, sir?

KAUTÍLYA: Boy, tell the Chief of Police in my name that the following is the Emperor's command: "The Jain monk Jiva·siddhi, who, being in the employ of Rákshasa, made use of a poison-girl to murder King Párvataka, shall after proclamation of the aforesaid offense be banished in disgrace from the city."

PUPIL: Yes, sir. *(He walks off.)* I.130

KAUTÍLYA: Wait, there is more. "And the letter-writer Shákata·dasa, who, being likewise in the employ of Rákshasa, is forever seeking to do violence to my person, shall after proclamation of the aforesaid offense be impaled, and his household imprisoned."

PUPIL: Yes, sir. *(He goes out.)*

SIDDHÁRTHAKA: I have sealed the letter: what now, sir?

KAUTÍLYA: My dear man, I have an extremely confidential task that I want to employ you on.

I.135 SIDDHĀRTHAKAḤ: *(sa|harṣam)* ⌜ajja, aṇuggihido mhi. tā āṇavedu ajjo jaṃ imiṇā dāsa|jaṇena ajjassa aṇuciṭṭhidavvaṃ.⌟

CĀṆAKYAḤ: prathamam tāvad vadhya|sthānaṃ gatvā ghātakāḥ sa|roṣaṃ dakṣin'|âkṣi|saṃkoca|saṃjñāṃ grāhayitavyāḥ. tatas teṣu gṛhīta|saṃjñeṣu bhay'|âpadeśād itas tataḥ pradruteṣu Śakaṭadāso vadhya|sthānād apanīya Rākṣasaṃ prāpayitavyas. tasmāc ca suhṛt|prāṇa|parirakṣaṇa|parituṣṭāt pāritoṣikaṃ gṛhītvā Rākṣasa eva kiṃ cit kāl'|ântaraṃ sevitavyaḥ. tataḥ pratyāsanneṣu pareṣu tvayā prayojanam idam anuṣṭheyam—*(karṇe)* evam eva! *(cintāṃ nāṭayitv" ātma|gatam)* api nāma durātmā Rākṣaso gṛhyate?

SIDDHĀRTHAKAḤ: ⌜ajja, gahido!⌟

CĀṆAKYAḤ: *(sa|harṣam ātma|gatam)* hanta gṛhīto durātmā Rākṣasaḥ! *(prakāśam)* atha ko 'yaṃ gṛhītaḥ?

SIDDHĀRTHAKAḤ: ⌜gahido mae ajjassa saṃdeso. tā gamissaṃ ahaṃ kajja|siddhīe.⌟

I.140 CĀṆAKYAḤ: *(s'|âṅguli|mudraṃ lekham arpayitvā)* bhadra Siddhārthaka, gamyatām. astu te kārya|siddhiḥ.

SIDDHĀRTHAKAḤ: ⌜jaṃ ajjo āṇavedi.⌟ *(iti praṇamya niṣkrāntaḥ.)*

praviśya ŚIṢYAḤ: upādhyāya, kāla|pāśiko daṇḍa|pāśikaś ca upādhyāyaṃ vijñāpayataḥ. idam anuṣṭhīyate devasya Candraguptasya śāsanam iti.

SIDDHÁRTHAKA: *(delightedly)* You do me too much honor, sir. What may this humble servant do for you? 1.135

KAUTÍLYA: First, go to the Execution Ground and angrily wink your right eye as a signal to the executioners. When they get the signal they will pretend to panic and run about, and you must rescue Shákata·dasa and convey him to Rákshasa. Rákshasa will be delighted with you for saving his friend's life: accept whatever gift of gratitude he makes you, and serve him devotedly thereafter. But when the enemy is close to this city I want you to do as follows—*(he whispers in his ear)* Like that! *(to himself, in preoccupied tones)* Have I the obstinate Rákshasa within my grasp?

SIDDHÁRTHAKA: Yes, fully grasped, sir!

KAUTÍLYA: *(to himself, in delight)* Ha! Rákshasa is fully grasped! *(aloud)* Fully grasped? How do you mean?

SIDDHÁRTHAKA: My instructions, sir. I know what to do. And so I'll be off to accomplish my mission.

KAUTÍLYA: *(handing him the sealed letter)* Go, my dear Siddhárthaka. And all success be yours in your task. 1.140

SIDDHÁRTHAKA: Yes, sir. *(He salutes and goes out.)*

Enter a PUPIL: Sir, the Chiefs of Police and Prison beg to inform Your Honor that His Majesty's commands are being fulfilled.

CĀṆAKYAḤ: vatsa, śobhanam. maṇi|kāra|śreṣṭhinaṃ Candanadāsam idānīṃ draṣṭum icchāmi.

ŚIṢYAḤ: yath" ājñāpayaty upādhyāyaḥ.

I.145 *iti niṣkramya* CANDANADĀSENA *saha punaḥ praviśya.*

ŚIṢYAḤ: ita itaḥ, śreṣṭhin.

CANDANADĀSAḤ: *(ātma|gatam)*

⌜Cāṇakkammi a|karuṇe
  sahasā saddāvidassa vaṭṭedi
ṇiddosassa vi saṅkā
  kiṃ uṇa saṃjāda|dosassa.⌟

⌜tā bhaṇidā mae Dhaṇaseṇa|ppamuhā tiṇṇi ghara|aṇa|sevaā. jadhā: kad" âï Cāṇakka|hadao gehaṃ pi me viciṇāvedi. tā avavāhedha bhaṭṭiṇo amacca|Rakkhasassa ghara|aṇaṃ. mama dāṇi jaṃ bhodu taṃ bhodu tti.⌟

I.150 ŚIṢYAḤ: ita itaḥ śreṣṭhin.

CANDANADĀSAḤ: ⌜ajja, aaṃ āacchāmi.⌟ *(ubhau parikrāmataḥ.)*

ŚIṢYAḤ: *(upasṛtya)* upādhyāya, ayaṃ śreṣṭhī Candanadāsaḥ.

CANDANADĀSAḤ: ⌜jaadu jaadu ajjo.⌟

CĀṆAKYAḤ: *(nāṭyen' âvalokya)* bhoḥ śreṣṭhin, svāgatam! idam āsanam—āsyatām.

KAUTÍLYA: Excellent, my boy. Now I should like to see the master jeweler Chándana·dasa.

PUPIL: Yes, sir.

He goes out and returns with CHÁNDANA·DASA. I.145

PUPIL: This way, Master Chándana·dasa.

CHÁNDANA·DASA: *(to himself)*

> When the ruthless Kautílya
> Sends an urgent summons,
> Even the innocent are worried,
> Let alone the guilty.

That is why I have told them at home that the accursed Kautílya may be going to have our house searched, and that they must smuggle my lord Rákshasa's family away—though, for myself, what must be must be.

PUPIL: This way, Master Chándana·dasa. I.150

CHÁNDANA·DASA: I am coming, good sir. *(They both walk about.)*

PUPIL: *(approaching Kautílya)* Here is the master jeweler Chándana·dasa, sir.

CHÁNDANA·DASA: Victory, sir, victory!

KAUTÍLYA: *(seeing him)* My dear Master Chándana·dasa! Welcome! Here is a seat for you—do sit down.

1.155 CANDANADĀSAḤ: ⌜kiṃ ṇa jāṇadi ajjo jadhā aṇucido uvaāro pari|aṇa|hiaassa parihavādo vi mahantaṃ dukkhaṃ uppādedi? tā idha jjeva ahaṃ ucidāe bhūmīe uvavisāmi.⌟

CĀṆAKYAḤ: bhoḥ śreṣṭhin, mā m" âivam. ucitam ev' âitad asmad|vidhaiḥ saha bhavataḥ samāsanam. tad upaviśyatām āsana eva.

CANDANADĀSAḤ: *(sva|gatam)* ⌜uvalakkhidaṃ aṇeṇa kiṃ pi.⌟ *(prakāśam)* ⌜jaṃ ajjo āṇavedi.⌟ *(ity upaviṣṭaḥ.)*

CĀṆAKYAḤ: bhoḥ śreṣṭhin, api pracīyante saṃvyavahārāṇāṃ lābhāḥ?

CANDANADĀSAḤ: ⌜ajja, adha iṃ. ajjassa pasāeṇa akhaṇḍidā jeva vaṇijjā.⌟

1.160 CĀṆAKYAḤ: api Candragupta|doṣā atikrānta|pārthiva|guṇān smārayanti prakṛtīḥ?

CANDANADĀSAḤ: *(karṇau pidhāya)* ⌜santaṃ pāvaṃ!⌟

⌜udideṇa sāraa|ṇisā
  vimalā via puṇṇimā|mig'|aṅkeṇa
deveṇa Candasiriṇā
  adhiaṃ ṇandanti païdīo.⌟

CĀṆAKYAḤ: bhoḥ śreṣṭhin, yady evaṃ prītābhyaḥ prakṛtibhyaḥ pratipriyam icchanti rājānaḥ.

CANDANADĀSAḤ: ⌜āṇavedu ajjo: kiṃ kettiaṃ vā imādo jaṇādo attha|jādaṃ icchīadi tti.⌟

CHÁNDANA·DASA: As Your Honor surely knows, inappropriate courtesies cause an inferior more discomfort than do insults. So let me just sit here on the ground as is fitting. 1.155

KAUTÍLYA: Oh, my dear Master Chándana·dasa, not a bit of it, not a bit of it! It is perfectly fitting for you to sit together with one such as my poor self. Sit, therefore, on the seat.

CHÁNDANA·DASA: *(to himself)* He's found out something. *(aloud)* As you say, sir. *(He sits down.)*

KAUTÍLYA: Tell me, Master Chándana·dasa, is business flourishing?

CHÁNDANA·DASA: Most certainly, sir. By Your Honor's favor, business is as good as ever.

KAUTÍLYA: Perhaps Chandra·gupta's shortcomings make 1.160
people remember the merits of bygone rulers?

CHÁNDANA·DASA: *(stopping his ears)* Perish the thought!

> Like a full moon risen
> On a clear autumn evening
> His Serene Majesty Chandra·gupta
> Gladdens the hearts of his people.

KAUTÍLYA: If so, Master Chándana·dasa, a king likes some return from his satisfied subjects.

CHÁNDANA·DASA: Command me, sir: what and how much do you want?

I.165 CĀṆAKYAḤ: bhoḥ śreṣṭhin, Candragupta|rājyam idaṃ na Nanda|rājyaṃ; yato Nandasy' âiv' ârtha|rucer artha|sambandhaḥ prītim utpādayati, Candraguptasya tu bhavatām a|parikleśa eva.

CANDANADĀSAḤ: *(sa|harṣam)* ⌜ajja, aṇuggihido mhi.⌟

CĀṆAKYAḤ: bhoḥ śreṣṭhin, «sa c' â|parikleśaḥ katham āvir|bhavat' îti» nanu praṣṭavyā vayam eva bhavatā.

CANDANADĀSAḤ: ⌜āṇavedu ajjo.⌟

CĀṆAKYAḤ: saṃkṣepato rājany a|viruddhābhir vṛttibhiḥ.

I.170 CANDANADĀSAḤ: ⌜ajja, ko eso a|dhaṇṇo jo raṇṇā saha viruddho tti ajjeṇa avagacchīadi?⌟

CĀṆAKYAḤ: bhavān eva tāvat prathamaḥ.

CANDANADĀSAḤ: *(karṇau pidhāya)* ⌜santaṃ pāvaṃ! kīdiso tiṇāṇaṃ aggiṇā saha viroho?⌟

CĀṆAKYAḤ: īdṛśo virodho yat tvaṃ rājā|pathya|kāriṇo Rākṣasasya gṛha|janaṃ gṛhe rakṣasi.

CANDANADĀSAḤ: ⌜ajja, aliaṃ edaṃ keṇ'|âvi aṇ|ajjeṇa ajjassa ṇivedidaṃ.⌟

I.175 CĀṆAKYAḤ: bhoḥ śreṣṭhin, alam āśaṅkayā. bhītāḥ pūrva|rāja|puruṣāḥ paurāṇām an|icchatām api gṛheṣu gṛha|janaṃ nikṣipya deś'|ântaraṃ prayānti yatas tat|pracchādana|mātraṃ doṣam utpādayati.

KAUTÍLYA: Master Chándana·dasa! This is the reign of Cha- 1.165
ndra·gupta, not the reign of the Nandas! What pleased Nanda, with his itch for money, was the piling up of wealth; what pleases Chandra·gupta is your peace of mind.

CHÁNDANA·DASA: I am favored, sir.

KAUTÍLYA: Master Chándana·dasa, I was waiting to hear you say, "And how may one show one's peace of mind?"

CHÁNDANA·DASA: Command me, sir.

KAUTÍLYA: In a word, by not acting against the Emperor.

CHÁNDANA·DASA: Your Honor, what unlucky man do you 1.170
suppose to be acting against the Emperor?

KAUTÍLYA: You, for a start.

CHÁNDANA·DASA: *(stopping his ears)* Perish the thought! How can straws act against fire?

KAUTÍLYA: They can, as you have, harbor in their house the family of Rákshasa, a man who is acting treasonably.

CHÁNDANA·DASA: Your Honor, this is some calumny that some villain or other has reported to you.

KAUTÍLYA: Do not be alarmed, my dear Master Chándana· 1.175
dasa. When frightened officials of a former king leave their families in the houses of citizens (all unwilling though those citizens may be) before making off somewhere else, there is no crime except in subsequent concealment of the family.

CANDANADĀSAḤ: ⌜evaṃ ṇ' edam. tassiṃ samae āsi amha|ghare amacca|Rakkhasassa ghara|aṇo.⌟

CĀṆAKYAḤ: prathamam an|ṛtam idānīm «āsīd iti» paraspara|virodhinī vacana|śṛṅkhalā.

CANDANADĀSAḤ: ⌜ajja, etth' antare atthi me vāā|chalam.⌟

CĀṆAKYAḤ: bhoḥ śreṣṭhin, Candragupte rājany a|parigrahaś «chalānāṃ.» tat samarpaya Rākṣasasya gṛha|janam. a|cchalaṃ bhavatu bhavataḥ.

I.180 CANDANADĀSAḤ: ⌜ajja, ṇaṃ viṇṇavemi tassiṃ samae āsi amha|ghare amacca|Rakkhasassa ghara|aṇo tti.⌟

CĀṆAKYAḤ: ath' êdānīṃ kva?

CANDANADĀSAḤ: ⌜ṇa āṇāmi kahiṃ gado tti.⌟

CĀṆAKYAḤ: *(smitaṃ kṛtvā)* kathaṃ na jñāyate nāma? bhoḥ śreṣṭhin, śirasi bhayaṃ dūre tat|pratīkāraḥ. anyac ca Nandam iva Viṣṇuguptaḥ—*(ity ardh'|ôkte lajjāṃ nāṭayati)* nanu Nandam iva Candraguptam amātya|Rākṣasaḥ samucchetsyat' îti m" âivaṃ maṃsthāḥ. paśya—

CHÁNDANA·DASA: Yes, you are right. Minister Rákshasa's family was left in my house at that time.

KAUTÍLYA: First a calumny, now "it was left there"! Your words have a certain lack of internal consistency.

CHÁNDANA·DASA: I did speak misleadingly, sir.

KAUTÍLYA: While Chandra·gupta is on the throne, Master Chándana·dasa, no "misleading" will be tolerated. So hand over Minister Rákshasa's family, and let all misleading cease.

CHÁNDANA·DASA: Please, sir, what I mean to say is that 1.180
Minister Rákshasa's family was in my house, then.

KAUTÍLYA: And is now where?

CHÁNDANA·DASA: I don't know.

KAUTÍLYA: *(smiling grimly)* Oh, you don't know? Master jeweler, the danger, as we say, is about you, and the healing herbs far away on the mountaintop. And let me tell you this: you need be under no illusion that just as Nanda was overthrown by Vishnu·gupta*—*(breaking off and showing modesty)* I mean of course by Chandra·gupta, so Chandra·gupta in turn might be overthrown by Rákshasa. Consider—

vikrāntair naya|śālibhiḥ su|sacivaiḥ
śrīr Vakranās'|ādibhiḥ
Nande jīvati yā nṛpe na gamitā
sthairyaṃ calantī muhuḥ
tām ekatvam upāgatāṃ dyutim iva
prahlādayantīṃ jagat
kaś candrād iva Candragupta|nṛpateḥ
kartuṃ vyavasyet pṛthak?

1.185 api ca,

āsvādita|dvi|rada|śoṇita|śoṇa|śobhām
sandhy'|âruṇām iva kalāṃ śaśa|lāñchanasya
jṛmbhā|vidārita|mukhasya mukhāt sphurantīm
ko hartum icchati hareḥ paribhūya daṃṣṭrām?

CANDANADĀSAḤ: *(sva|gatam)* ⌜phaleṇa saṃpādidaṃ sohadi de vikatthidaṃ.⌟

nepathye tata utsāraṇā kriyate.

CĀṆAKYAḤ: Śārṅgarava, Śārṅgarava, jñāyatāṃ kim etat.

1.190 ŚIṢYAḤ: yad ājñāpayaty upādhyāyaḥ. *(iti niṣkramya punaḥ praviśya)* upādhyāya, eṣa rājñaś Candraguptasy' ājñayā rāj'|âpathya|kārī Kṣapaṇako Jīvasiddhiḥ sa|nikāraṃ nagarān nirvāsyate.

CĀṆAKYAḤ: ahaha Kṣapaṇakaḥ! atha|vā anubhavatu rāj'|âpathya|kāritvasya phalam. bhoḥ śreṣṭhiṃś Candanadāsa, evam apathya|kāriṣu tīkṣṇa|daṇḍo rājā. tat kriyatāṃ pathyaṃ suhṛd|vacaḥ. samarpyatāṃ Rākṣasasya gṛha|janaḥ. anubhūyatāṃ ciraṃ vicitra|phalo rāja|prasādaḥ.

All those brave and brilliant counselors, like
  Vakra·nasa,
Could not make the light of sovereignty rest
  tranquilly on Nanda.
Now that it gladdens the world with an
  unflickering glow
Who will wrest it from Chandra·gupta, any more
  than the moonlight from the moon?

& 1.185

When the lion's mouth stretches in a yawn,
Who will extract the glittering fang
Ruddy as the crescent moon at twilight
That gleams with elephant's blood?

CHÁNDANA·DASA: *(to himself)* Your boasting is justified by the facts.

Offstage, a commotion.

KAUTÍLYA: Shárnga·rava, Shárnga·rava, find out what that is.

PUPIL: Yes, sir. *(going out and returning)* Sir, it is a traitor, the 1.190
Jain monk Jiva·siddhi: on His Majesty Chandra·gupta's orders he is being banished in disgrace from the city.

KAUTÍLYA: A Jain monk? Oh! But he must reap the reward of his treachery. Good master jeweler, you can see how severely His Majesty deals with traitors. Take a friend's good advice. Hand over Rákshasa's family. Enjoy for many years to come all the benefits that royal favor can bestow.

CANDANADĀSAḤ: ⌜ajja, gehe a|santaṃ kudo samappīadi.⌟

tato nepathye kalakalaḥ, punar utsāraṇā kriyate.

CĀṆAKYAḤ: Śārṅgarava, Śārṅgarava, jñāyatāṃ punaḥ kim etad iti.

I.195 ŚIṢYAḤ: yad ājñāpayaty upādhyāyaḥ. *(iti niṣkramya punaḥ praviśya)* upādhyāya, ayam asau rājñayā rāj'|âpathya|kārī kāyasthaḥ Śakaṭadāsaḥ śūlam āropayituṃ nīyate.

CĀṆAKYAḤ: sva|karma|phala|bhāg bhavatu. bhoḥ śreṣṭhin, Candanadāsa, evaṃ rāj'|âpathya|kāriṣu tīkṣṇa|daṇḍo rājā na marṣayiṣyati Rākṣasa|kalatra|pracchādanaṃ bhavataḥ. tad rakṣyatāṃ para|kalatreṇ' ātmanaḥ kalatraṃ jīvataṃ ca.

CANDANADĀSAḤ: ⌜ajja, kiṃ me bhaaṃ dāvesi? santaṃ pi ahaṃ gehe amacca|Rakkhasassa ghara|aṇaṃ ṇa samappemi kiṃ uṇa a|santaṃ.⌟

CĀṆAKYAḤ: Candanadāsa, eṣa te niścayaḥ?

CANDANADĀSAḤ: ⌜bāḍhaṃ. eso me thiro ṇiccao.⌟

I.200 CĀṆAKYAḤ: *(ātma|gatam)* sādhu, Candanadāsa, sādhu.

sulabheṣv artha|jāteṣu
  para|saṃvedane jane
ka idaṃ duṣkaraṃ kuryād
  idānīṃ Śibinā vinā?

(prakāśam) Candanadāsa, eṣa te niścayaḥ?

CANDANADĀSAḤ: ⌜bāḍhaṃ. eso thiro me ṇiccao.⌟

CHÁNDANA·DASA: I cannot hand over what I have not got.

Offstage, further commotion.

KAUTÍLYA: Shárnga·rava, Shárnga·rava, find out what THAT is.

PUPIL: Yes, sir. *(going out and returning)* Sir, it is another 1.195
traitor, the letter-writer Shákata·dasa: on His Majesty's orders he is being taken to be impaled.

KAUTÍLYA: Let him reap the reward of his actions. Good master jeweler, a king who is so severe toward traitors is not going to overlook your concealment of Rákshasa's wife. At the cost of the wife of another, save your own wife—and your own life.

CHÁNDANA·DASA: Why do you threaten me, Your Honor? Even if Rákshasa's family were in my house, I should not surrender them, and at any rate they are not.

KAUTÍLYA: Chándana·dasa, are you resolved?

CHÁNDANA·DASA: Yes, completely.

KAUTÍLYA: *(to himself)* Then bravo, Chándana·dasa— 1.200

When all the profit lies
In turning informer,
Who but another Shibi*
Would choose the difficult course?

(aloud) Chándana·dasa, are you resolved?

CHÁNDANA·DASA: Yes, completely.

CĀṆAKYAḤ: *(sa|krodham)* durātman duṣṭa|vaṇik, anubhūyatāṃ tarhi nara|pati|kopaḥ!

1.205 CANDANADĀSAḤ: ⌜sajjo mhi. aṇuciṭṭhadu ajjo attaṇo ahiārassa aṇurūvaṃ.⌟

CĀṆAKYAḤ: *(sa|krodham)* Śārṅgarava, Śārṅgarava, ucyatām asmad|vacanād daṇḍapāśikaḥ. śīghram ayaṃ duṣṭa|vaṇig nigṛhyatām. atha|vā tiṣṭha! ucyatām asmad|vacanād durga|pālo Vijayapālaḥ: gṛhīta|gṛha|sāram enaṃ sa|putra|kalatraṃ saṃyamya rakṣa tāvad yāvan mayā Vṛṣalāya kathyate. Vṛṣala ev' âsya prāṇa|haraṃ daṇḍam ājñāpayiṣyati.

ŚIṢYAḤ: yad ājñāpayaty upādhyāyaḥ. śreṣṭhin, ita itaḥ.

CANDANADĀSAḤ: *(utthāya)* ⌜aaṃ āacchāmi.⌟ *(ātma|gatam)* ⌜diṭṭhiā mitta|kajjeṇa me viṇāso ṇa uṇa purisa|doseṇa.⌟

parikramya ŚIṢYEṆA *saha niṣkrāntaḥ.*

1.210 CĀṆAKYAḤ: *(sa|harṣam)* hanta labdha idānīṃ Rākṣasaḥ. kutaḥ

tyajaty a|priyavat prāṇān
  yathā tasy' âyam āpadi
tath" âiv' âsy' āpadi prāṇā
  nūnaṃ tasy' âpi na priyāḥ.

nepathye kalakalaḥ.

ŚIṢYAḤ: *(praviśya)* upādhyāya, eṣa khalu Siddhārthakaḥ Śakaṭadāsaṃ vadhyamānaṃ vadhya|bhūmer ādāya samapakrāntaḥ!

KAUTÍLYA: *(angrily)* Villainous shopkeeper! Then suffer the Emperor's wrath.

CHÁNDANA·DASA: I am ready, sir. Live up to your office. 1.205

KAUTÍLYA: Shárnga·rava, tell the Chief of Police to have this villain arrested at once—no, wait! Tell the Governor of the Prison to seize this man and his goods, and hold him in jail with his wife and children until I have reported to Vríshala. Vríshala himself shall pass the sentence of death.

PUPIL: Yes, sir. This way, master jeweler.

CHÁNDANA·DASA: *(getting up)* I am coming. *(to himself)* Thank God I am dying for a friend, and not for any crime.

He walks about and goes out with the PUPIL.

KAUTÍLYA: *(in delight)* Now I have Rákshasa. For 1.210

> Just as one, when the other is in trouble,
> Gives up his life as something worthless,
> So assuredly when he is in trouble
> The other will not think of his own skin.

Offstage, a commotion.

PUPIL: *(entering)* Sir, it's Siddhárthaka! He has rescued Shákata·dasa from execution and escaped with him!

CĀṆAKYAḤ: *(ātma/gatam)* sādhu, Siddhārthaka, sādhu. kṛtaḥ kāry'|ārambhaḥ. *(prakāśam)* katham? apakrāntaḥ? *(sa/krodham)* vatsa, ucyatāṃ Bhāgurāyaṇo yathā «tvaritaṃ saṃbhāvay' âinam» iti.

1.215 ŚIṢYAḤ: *(niṣkramya praviśya ca)* upādhyāya, hā dhik kaṣṭam! apakrānto Bhāgurāyaṇa eva!

CĀṆAKYAḤ: *(ātma/gatam)* vrajatu kārya|siddhaye. *(prakāśaṃ sa/krodham)* vatsa, asmad|vacanād ucyantāṃ Bhadrabhaṭa|Puruṣadatta|Hiṅgurāta|Balagupta|Rājasena|Rohitākṣa|Vijayavarmāṇaḥ: «śīghram anusṛtya gṛhyatāṃ durātmā Śakaṭadāsa iti.»

ŚIṢYAḤ: yad ājñāpayaty upādhyāyaḥ. *(iti niṣkramya punaḥ praviśya sa/viṣādam)* upādhyāya, hā dhik kaṣṭam! sarvam eva tantram ākulī|bhūtam. te 'pi khalu Bhadrabhaṭa|prabhṛtayaḥ prathamataram a|prabhātāyām eva rajanyām apakrāntāḥ.

CĀṆAKYAḤ: *(sva/gatam)* sarveṣām eva panthānaḥ śivāḥ santu. *(prakāśam)* vatsa, kṛtaṃ viṣādena. paśya,

ye yātāḥ kim api pradhārya hṛdaye
    pūrvaṃ gatā eva te
  ye tiṣṭhanti bhavantu te 'pi gamane
    kāmaṃ sa|kām'|ôdyamāḥ
ekā kevalam artha|sādhana|vidhau
    senā|śatebhyo 'dhikā
  Nand'|ônmūlana|dṛṣṭa|vīrya|mahimā
    buddhis tu mā gān mama.

KAUTÍLYA: *(to himself)* Bravo, Siddhárthaka, the work is begun. *(aloud)* Escaped? *(angrily)* Tell Bhaguráyana to capture him at once.

PUPIL: *(going out and returning)* Oh sir, oh sir! Bhaguráyana 1.215
has run away as well!

KAUTÍLYA: *(to himself)* Success go with him. *(aloud, angrily)* Boy, take a message to Bhadra·bhata, Púrusha·datta, Hingu·rata, Bala·gupta, Raja·sena, Rohitáksha and Víjaya·varman: they are to go after the villain Bhaguráyana at once and catch him.

PUPIL: Yes, sir. *(going out and returning, in despair)* Oh sir, oh sir! Everything is upside down. All of them have run away already—they left before dawn.

KAUTÍLYA: *(to himself)* And let success attend every one of them. *(aloud)* Do not despair, my boy. Look,

> Those who have schemed and gone had left us
> long ago in their hearts.
> And those who stay may plot to go if they will.
> Let just one thing not desert me, for it can do more
> than a thousand armies—
> My mind, to whose power a dynasty destroyed
> bears witness.

1.220 *(utthāya)* tān eva Bhadrabhaṭa|prabhṛtīn durātmano grāhayāmi. *(ātma|gatam)* durātman Rākṣasa, kva yāsyāsi? eṣo 'ham acirād bhavantam:

svacchandam eka|caram ujjvala|dāna|śaktim
utsekinā bala|madena vidahyamānam
buddhyā nigṛhya Vṛṣalasya kṛte kriyāyām
āraṇyakaṃ gajam iva praguṇī|karomi.

iti niṣkrāntāḥ sarve.

(rising) I will go and catch your wicked fugitives. *(to himself)* 1.220
Wretched Rákshasa, where will you go? See, I will get you before long:

You are my wild elephant, self-willed and solitary,
Plunging through the jungle in rutting pride,
Whom I with guile will trap and then break in,
Making you apt for service under Vríshala.

All go out.

ACT II
RÁKSHASA RECEIVES THE RING

tataḥ praviśaty ĀHI|TUṆḌAKAḤ:

⌜jāṇanti tanta|juttiṃ
jaha|ṭṭhiaṃ maṇḍalaṃ ahilihanti
je manta|rakkhaṇa|parā
te sappa|ṇar'|âhive uvaaranti.⌟

(ākāśe) ⌜ajja, kiṃ bhaṇāsi? ko tumaṃ ti? ajja, ahaṃ khu āhituṇḍio Jiṇṇaviso ṇāma. kiṃ bhaṇāsi? ahaṃ pi ahiṇā khelidum icchāmi tti. adha kadaraṃ uṇa ajjo vuttiṃ uvajīvadi? kiṃ bhaṇāsi? rāa|kula|sevao mhi tti. ṇaṃ kheladi jjeva ajjo ahiṇā. kadhaṃ via,⌟

⌜vāla|ggāhi a|mant'|o-
sahi|kusalo matta|gaa|var'|āroho
rāa|kula|sevao tti a
vassaṃ tiṇṇi vi viṇāsam aṇuhonti.⌟

2.5 ⌜kadhaṃ? adikkanto eso.⌟ *(punar apy ākāśe)* ⌜ajja, tumaṃ kiṃ bhaṇāsi? kiṃ edesuṃ peḍāla|samuggaesuṃ ti? ajja, jīviā|saṃpādaā sappā sa|dāḍhā. kiṃ bhaṇāsi? pekkhidum icchāmi tti. pasīdadu pasīdadu ajjo. a|tthāṇaṃ khu edaṃ. tā jai kodūhalaṃ tā ehi. edassiṃ āvāse daṃsemi. kiṃ bhaṇāsi? edaṃ khu bhaṭṭhiṇo amacca|Rakkhasassa gehaṃ. ṇatthi amhārisāṇaṃ paveso tti? teṇa hi gacchadu ajjo. jīviāe pasāeṇa atthi me idha paveso tti. kadhaṃ, eso vi adikkanto!⌟

(diśo 'valokya Saṃskṛtam āśritya sva/gatam) aho āścaryam: Cāṇakya|mati|parigṛhītam Candraguptam avalokya viphalam iva Rākṣasa|prayatnam avagacchāmi. Rākṣasa|mati|parigṛhītaṃ Malayaketum avalokya calitam iv' ādhirājyāc Candraguptam avagacchāmi.

Enter a SNAKE CHARMER*:*

If you see a man who knows about administering,
Who cultivates the right circles.*
And likes to get in a good spell,
He must be a snake charmer, if he's not a politician.

(addressing the air) What's that you say, sir? Who am I? Sir, I am a snake charmer: Jirna·visha* is my name. What's that? You, too, would like to amuse yourself with snakes? Well, sir, what do you do for a living? You have a post in the palace? Then, my dear sir, you do play with snakes. Listen,

A snakeman that doesn't know his spells and herbs,
A rider that mounts an elephant in rut,
A palace official flushed with success—
All three of them are doomed.

Oh, the man's gone! *(addressing the air once more)* What's that, sir? What's in these boxes and hampers? Poisonous snakes! You want to see them, you say? Not here, sir, if you don't mind. If you're interested, come with me and I'll put on a show inside this house. This is Minister Rákshasa's house, you tell me, and no admission for the likes of us? Then you can be off, but I have a profession that will allow me in. Oh, he's gone, too! 2.5

(glancing about and then speaking in educated tones) Ah, it is extraordinary: I see Chandra·gupta with Kautílya to advise him, and despair of Rákshasa's chances—then I see Málaya·ketu with Rákshasa to advise him, and Chandra·gupta seems as good as toppled from his throne.

Kauṭilya|dhī|rajju|nibaddha|mūrtiṃ
  manye sthirāṃ Maurya|kulasya Lakṣmīm
upāya|hastair api Rākṣasena
  vyākṛṣyamāṇām iva lakṣayāmi.

tad evam anayoḥ sunaya|śālinoḥ susacivayor virodhe saṃśayit" êva Rājya|lakṣmīr lakṣyate. kutaḥ—

viruddhayor bhṛśam iha mantri|mukhyayor
  mahā|vane vana|gajayor iv' ântare
a|niścayād gaja|vaśay" êva bhītayā
  gat'|āgatair dhruvam iha khidyate Śriyā.

2.10 tad yāvad aham amātya|Rākṣasaṃ paśyāmi.

tataḥ praviśaty āsana/sthaḥ sva/bhavana/gataḥ PURUṢEṆ' *ânugamyamānaḥ sa/cinto* RĀKṢASAḤ.

RĀKṢASAḤ: *(sa/bāṣpam)* kaṣṭaṃ, bhoḥ kaṣṭam!

Vṛṣṇīnām iva nīti|vikrama|guṇa|
    vyāpāra|śānta|dviṣāṃ
  Nandānāṃ vipule kule 'karuṇayā
    nīte niyatyā kṣayam
cint"|āveśa|samākulena manasā
    rātriṃ|divaṃ jāgrataḥ
  s" âiv' êyaṃ mama citra|karma|racanā
    bhittiṃ vinā vartate.

Kautílya's wits had, I thought, roped and bound
Fortune to the Mauryan dynasty:
But Rákshasa's plotting seizes on the ropes
And seems to be loosening the knots again.

And as these two great statesmen dispute, Fortune seems perplexed—

The two ministers are violently disputing,
Like two wild elephants rampaging through the world.
And in her uncertainty, like a fearful she-elephant,
Fortune tires of running from one to the other.

Now I will call on Minister Rákshasa. 2.10

Enter, on a couch in his house and attended by a MANSERVANT, RÁKSHASA *in anxious thought.*

RÁKSHASA: *(weeping)* Alas, alas!

Once the Nandas had courage and skill to conquer all their foes,
But now Destiny has cruelly doomed them like Krishna's clan,*
And worn with care, sleepless by day or night,
I go on painting a picture on a nonexistent canvas.

atha|vā,

2.15 n' êdaṃ vismṛta|bhaktinā na viṣaya|
vyāsaṅga|mūḍh'|ātmanā
prāṇa|pracyuti|bhīruṇā na ca mayā
n' ātma|pratiṣṭh"|ârthinā
aty|arthaṃ para|dāsyam etya nipuṇaṃ
nītau mano dīyate
devaḥ svarga|gato 'pi śātrava|vadhen'
ārādhitaḥ syād iti.

(ākāśam avalokayan s'|âsram) Bhagavati kamal'|ālaye, bhṛśam a|guṇajñ" âsi. kutaḥ—

ānanda|hetum api devam apāsya Nandaṃ
rakt" âsi kiṃ, kathaya, dhik|kṛta|Maurya|putre?
dān'|âmbu|rājir iva gandha|gajasya nāśe
tatr' âiva kiṃ na, capale, pralayaṃ gat" âsi?

api ca, an|abhijāte!

pṛthivyāṃ kiṃ dagdhāḥ
prathita|kulajā bhūmi|patayaḥ
patiṃ, pāpe, Mauryaṃ
yad asi kula|hīnaṃ vṛtavatī?
prakṛtyā v" ākāśa|
prabhava|kusuma|prānta|capalā
purandhrīṇāṃ prajñā
puruṣa|guṇa|vijñāna|vimukhī.

2.20 api ca, a|vinīte, tad aham āśray'|ônmūlanen' âiva tvām a|kāmāṃ karomi.

(vicintya) mayā tāvat suhṛttamasya Candanadāsasya gṛhe gṛha|janaṃ nikṣipya nagarān nirgacchatā nyāyyam anu-

But,

> It is not that I have forgotten my loyalty, or steeped my mind in worldly things, 2.15
> Not that I fear for my life or seek my own security,
> If I now enslave myself to another and plunge into politics—
> It is only so that my master in heaven may be avenged.

(gazing up, with tears) Blessed Goddess of Fortune, truly you ignore merit.

> Why did you forsake your joy the Nanda monarch
> For that cursed son of the Mauryas, oh why?
> Why, fickle one, did you not vanish on the spot,
> Like the streak of ichor when the musk elephant dies?

Base creature!

> Are kings of noble line all dead and burned
> That you have chosen the Mauryan upstart for your consort?
> But fickle by nature as the petal of a full-blown flower
> Is the mind of woman, and loath to judge men aright.

Very well, my wench. I shall frustrate you by robbing you of him you lean on. 2.20

(reflectively) I did well to leave my family in my dear friend Chándana·dasa's house before I left Pátali·putra. My lord's dependents who are working there in our cause

ṣṭhitam. kiṃ kāraṇam iti? Kusumapur'|âbhiyogaṃ praty an|udāsīno Rākṣasa iti tatrasthānām asmābhiḥ sah' âika|kāryāṇāṃ deva|pād'|ôpajīvināṃ n' ôdyamaḥ śithilī|bhaviṣyati. Candragupta|śarīram abhidrogdhum asmat|prayuktānāṃ tīkṣṇa|rasa|dāyinām upasaṃgrah'|ârthaṃ prakṛty|upajāp'|ârthaṃ ca mahatā koṣa|saṃcayena sthāpitaḥ Śakaṭadāsaḥ. prati|kṣaṇam arāti|vṛttānt'|ôpalabdhaye tat|saṃghāta|bhedāya ca vyāpāritāḥ suhṛdo Jīvasiddhi|prabhṛtayaḥ. tat kim atra bahunā?

iṣṭ'|ātmajaḥ sapadi s'|ânvaya eva devaḥ
 śārdūla|potam iva yaṃ paripuṣya naṣṭaḥ
tasy' âiva buddhi|viśikhena bhinadmi marma
 varmī|bhaved yadi na daivam a|dṛśyamānam.

tataḥ praviśati KAÑCUKĪ.

KAÑCUKĪ:

2.25 kāmaṃ Nandam iva pramathya jarayā
 Cāṇakya|nītyā yathā
dharmo Maurya iva krameṇa nagare
 nītaḥ pratiṣṭhāṃ mayi
taṃ sampraty upacīyamānam api me
 labdh'|ântaraḥ sevayā
lobho Rākṣasavaj jayāya yatate
 jetuṃ na śaknoti ca.

idam amātya|Rākṣasa|gṛham. yāvat praviśāmi. *(parikramy' ôpasṛtya ca)* svasti bhavate!

RĀKṢASAḤ: ārya, abhivādaye. Priyaṃvadaka, āsanam ānīyatām.

will know that I am committed to taking the city, and will not slacken in their efforts. I have put large resources at Shákata·dasa's disposal to encourage the poisoners we are employing against Chandra·gupta, and also for use in propaganda. And I have set Jiva·siddhi and other friends to the hourly collecting of information about the enemy and the undermining of their unity. In fact,

That tiger cub which my dear lord cherished as
the son he longed for,
Only to be struck down with all his kin,
I will in turn strike down with the arrow of my
thought,
Unless he has an invisible shield of fate about him.

Enter a CHAMBERLAIN.

CHAMBERLAIN:

Old age has killed desire in me, and strengthened virtue, 2.25
As it might be Kautílya establishing the Mauryan
where Nanda ruled.
Now virtue nourishes like the Mauryan, and greed
like Rákshasa
Seizes its chance to strike but cannot win.

Here is Minister Rákshasa's house. I will go in. *(walking about and approaching)* Greetings to you, sir.

RÁKSHASA: Sir, I salute you. Priyam·vádaka, a seat!

PURUṢAḤ: ⌜edaṃ āsaṇaṃ. uvavisadu ajjo.⌟

KAÑCUKĪ: *(nāṭyen' ôpaviśya)* amātya, kumāro Malayaketur amātyaṃ vijñāpayati: «cirāt|prabhṛty āryaḥ ‹parityakt'|ôcita|śarīra|saṃskāra iti› pīḍyate me hṛdayam. yady api svāmi|guṇā na śakyante vismartuṃ tath" âpi mad|vijñāpanāṃ mānayitum arhaty āryaḥ.» *(ity ābharaṇaṃ darśayitvā)* amātya, idam ābharaṇaṃ kumāreṇa sva|śarīrād avatārya preṣitaṃ dhārayitum arhaty āryaḥ.

2.30 RĀKṢASAḤ: ārya Jājale, vijñāpyatām asmad|vacanāt kumāraḥ. «vismṛtā bhavad|guṇa|pakṣa|pātinā mayā svāmi|guṇāḥ. kiṃ tu,

na tāvan nirvīryaiḥ
    para|paribhav'|ākrānti|kṛpaṇaiḥ
  vahāmy aṅgair ebhiḥ
    pratanum api saṃskāra|racanām
na yāvan niḥśeṣa|
    kṣayita|ripu|cakrasya nihitaṃ
  Sugāṅge hem'|âṅkaṃ
    nṛ|vara tava siṃh'|āsanam idam.»

KAÑCUKĪ: amātye netari sulabham etat kumārasya. tat pratimānyatāṃ kumārasya prathamaḥ praṇayaḥ.

RĀKṢASAḤ: ārya, kumāra iv' ân|atikramaṇīya|vacano bhavān api. tad anuṣṭhīyatāṃ kumārasy' ājñā.

KAÑCUKĪ: *(nāṭyena bhūṣaṇāni paridhāpya)* svasti bhavate. sādhayāmy aham.

2.35 RĀKṢASAḤ: ārya, abhivādaye.

MANSERVANT: Here you are, sir. Please sit down.

CHAMBERLAIN: *(sitting down)* Minister, His Highness Prince Málaya·ketu begs to say that he has long grieved in his heart to see Your Honor without proper adornment of your person. Though your former master's virtues can never be forgotten, he begs you to honor his request. *(producing decorations)* His Highness, sir, has taken these decorations from his own person and sent them for you to wear.

RÁKSHASA: Noble Jájali, please take this answer to His High- 2.30
ness: "In my admiration of Your Highness's virtues I have forgotten the virtues of my former Lord. But,

This feeble and humiliated body
Shall bear no trace of adornment
Until the circle of your foes is laid low
And your gold throne, great hero, set in the River
Palace."

CHAMBERLAIN: Now that you, sir, are guiding him, that is easy for His Highness to achieve. Therefore I ask you to honor the first request His Highness has ever made of you.

RÁKSHASA: Noble sir, I can offend you no more than I can His Highness: I will do as the Prince commands.

CHAMBERLAIN: *(after arranging the decorations on him)* Thank you, sir, I will take my leave.

RÁKSHASA: Sir, I salute you. 2.35

KAÑCUKĪ *niṣkrāntaḥ.*

RĀKṢASAḤ: Priyaṃvadaka, jñāyatāṃ ko 'smad|darśan'|ârthī dvāri tiṣṭhati.

PURUṢAḤ: ⌜jaṃ ajjo āṇavedi.⌟ *(iti niṣkramya* ĀHITUṆḌIKAṂ *dṛṣṭvā)* ⌜ajja, ko tumaṃ?⌟

ĀHI|TUṆḌIKAḤ: ⌜bhadda, ahaṃ khu āhituṇḍio Jiṇṇaviso ṇāma. icchāmi amacca|Rakkhasassa purado sappehiṃ khelidum.⌟

2.40 PURUṢAḤ: ⌜ciṭṭha tāva jāva amaccassa ṇivedemi.⌟ *(Rākṣasam upasṛtya)* ⌜ajja, eso kkhu sappa|jīvī icchadi amaccassa purado sappehiṃ khelidum.⌟

RĀKṢASAḤ: *(vām'|âkṣi|spandaṃ sūcayitvā ātma|gatam)* katham, prathamam eva sarpa|darśanam? *(prakāśam)* Priyaṃvadaka, na naḥ kutūhalaṃ sarpeṣu. tat paritoṣya visarjay' âinam.

PURUṢAḤ: ⌜jaṃ ajjo āṇavedi.⌟ *(niṣkramya* ĀHITUṆḌAKAM *upasṛtya)* ⌜ajja, a|daṃsaṇeṇ' âvi ajjo pasādaṃ karedi ṇa uṇa daṃsaṇeṇa.⌟

ĀHI|TUṆḌIKAḤ: ⌜bhadda, viṇṇavehi maha vaaṇeṇa amaccaṃ: ṇa kevalaṃ ahaṃ sappa|jīvī. pāüḍa|kavi kkhu ahaṃ. tā jaï me daṃsaṇeṇa amacco pasādaṃ ṇa karedi tā edaṃ pi pattaaṃ vācedum pasīdadu tti.⌟ *(pattram arpayati.)*

PURUṢAḤ: *(pattraṃ gṛhītvā Rākṣasam upasṛtya)* ⌜amacca, eso kkhu sappa|jīvī viṇṇavedi: ṇa kevalaṃ ahaṃ sappa|jīvī. pāüḍa|kavi kkhu ahaṃ. tā jaï me daṃsaṇeṇa amacco pasādaṃ ṇa karedi tā edaṃ pi pattaaṃ vācedum pasīdadu tti.⌟

The CHAMBERLAIN *withdraws.*

RÁKSHASA: Priyam·vádaka, find out who is waiting at the door to see me.

MANSERVANT: Yes, sir. *(going out and seeing the* SNAKE CHARMER*)* Who are you, sir?

SNAKE CHARMER: I am Jirna·visha, a snake charmer, my dear man. I should like to perform with my snakes before the Minister.

MANSERVANT: Wait here while I tell the Minister. *(approaching* RÁKSHASA*)* A snake charmer, sir, who wants to perform before you. 2.40

RÁKSHASA: *(indicating an inauspicious throbbing of the left eye, to himself)* What! See snakes now?* *(aloud)* I don't feel interested in snakes, Priyam·vádaka. Give him something and send him away.

MANSERVANT: Yes, sir. *(going out and approaching the* SNAKE CHARMER*)* My master thanks you without seeing the snakes, sir, and would prefer not to see them.

SNAKE CHARMER: Tell your master from me that I'm not just a snake charmer. I'm also a poet in the common tongue. If he won't favor me with an audience, perhaps he will be so good as to read this. *(He hands over a sheet of paper.)*

MANSERVANT: *(taking it and going up to* RÁKSHASA*)* Sir, he says he is a poet as well as a snake charmer, and would you be so good as to read this.

2.45 RĀKṢASAḤ: *(pattraṃ gṛhītvā vācayati)*

⌜«pāūṇa ṇir|avasesaṃ
kusuma|rasaṃ attaṇo kusalaāe
jaṃ uggirei bhamaro
taṃ aṇṇāṇaṃ kuṇaï kajjaṃ.»⌟

(vicintya, ātma|gatam) aye «Kusumapura|vṛttānta|jño 'haṃ bhavat|praṇidhiś c' êti» gāth"|ârthaḥ. kārya|vyagratvān manasaḥ prabhūtatvāc ca praṇidhīnāṃ vismṛtam. idānīṃ smṛtir upalabdhā. vyaktam āhituṇḍika|cchadmanā Virādhagupten' ânena bhavitavyam. *(prakāśam)* Priyaṃvadaka, praveśay' âinaṃ. su|kavir eṣaḥ. śrotavyam asmāt subhāṣitam.

PURUṢAḤ: ⌜jaṃ ajjo āṇavedi.⌟ (ĀHITUṆḌIKAM *upasṛtya)* ⌜uvasappadu ajjo.⌟

ĀHI|TUṆḌIKAḤ: *(nāṭyen' ôpasṛty' âvaloky' ātma|gatam)* aye, ayam amātya|Rākṣasas tiṣṭhati. sa eṣaḥ,

2.50 vāmāṃ bāhu|latāṃ niveśya śithilāṃ
kaṇṭhe vivṛtt"|ānanā
skandhe dakṣiṇayā balān nihitay" â-
py aṅkaṃ patantyā muhuḥ
gāḍh'|āliṅgana|saṅga|pīḍita|mukhaṃ
yasy' ôdyam'|āśaṅkinī
Mauryasy' ôrasi n' âdhun" âpi kurute
vām'|êtaraṃ Śrīḥ stanam.

(prakāśam) ⌜jaadu, jaadu ajjo.⌟

RÁKSHASA: *(takes the paper and reads it out)* 2.45

> "The probing bee has used his power
> To drink the nectar of the flower.
> The honey that he makes of it
> Is work for others' benefit."

(after reflection, to himself) This verse must mean that the writer has news of the Flower City, Pátali·putra, and is an agent of mine. I have so much on my mind, and so many agents, that I was forgetting. But I remember now. It must be Virádha·gupta disguised as a snake charmer. *(aloud)* Priyam·vádaka, show him in. He is a good poet, and I want to hear more from him.

MANSERVANT: Yes, sir. *(approaching the* SNAKE CHARMER*)* Come in, sir.

SNAKE CHARMER: *(approaching and looking at* RÁKSHASA*, to himself)* Here is Minister Rákshasa,

> Whom Fortune turns anxiously to watch, as she lies in the Mauryan's embraces, 2.50
> With one arm loosely placed around her lover.
> Though he draws her other arm about him, it always falls away
> And even now she will not let him crush her other breast against him.

(aloud) Victory, sir, victory!

RĀKṢASAḤ: *(vilokya)* aye Virādha—*(ity ardh'|ôkte)* virūḍha|śmaśruḥ. Priyaṃvadaka, bhujaṅgair idānīṃ vinodaḥ. tad viśramyatāṃ parijanena. tvam api svam adhikāram a|śūnyaṃ kuru.

PURUṢAḤ: ⌜jaṃ amacco āṇavedi.⌟ *(iti sa|parijano niṣkrāntaḥ.)*

RĀKṢASAḤ: sakhe Virādhagupta, idam āsanam. āsyatām.

2.55 VIRĀDHAGUPTAḤ: yad ājñāpayaty āryaḥ. *(iti nāṭyen' ôpaviṣṭaḥ.)*

RĀKṢASAḤ: *(nirvarṇya)* aho deva|pāda|padm'|ôpajīvino janasy' âvasthā. *(iti rodati.)*

VIRĀDHAGUPTAḤ: amātya, alaṃ śokena. n' âticirād amātyo 'smān purātanīm avasthām āropayiṣyati.

RĀKṢASAḤ: sakhe Virādhagupta, varṇay' êdānīṃ Kusumapura|vṛttāntam.

VIRĀDHAGUPTAḤ: amātya, vistīrṇaḥ Kusumapura|vṛttāntaḥ. tat kutaḥ prabhṛti kathayāmi?

2.60 RĀKṢASAḤ: sakhe, Candraguptasy' âiva tāvan nagara|praveśāt prabhṛti mat|prayuktais tīkṣṇa|rasad'|ādibhiḥ kim anuṣṭhitam iti śrotum icchāmi.

VIRĀDHAGUPTAḤ: eṣa kathayāmi. asti tāvac Chaka|Yavana|Kirāta|Kāmboja|Pārasīka|Bāhlīka|prabhṛtibhiś Cāṇakya|mati|parigṛhītaiś Candragupta|Parvateśvara|balair udadhibhir iva pralaya|kāla|calita|salila|gambhīraiḥ samantād uparuddhaṃ Kusumapuram.

RÁKSHASA: *(seeing him)* Why, good Vi—*(breaking off)* good vigorous growth of beard you've got there, my man! Priyam·vádaka, there's no snake-show for the moment. The servants can take a rest. And you, too, go about your work.

MANSERVANT: Yes, sir. *(He withdraws with the attendants.)*

RÁKSHASA: My dear Virádha·gupta. Here, sit down.

VIRÁDHA·GUPTA: * Thank you, Minister. *(He seats himself.)* 2.55

RÁKSHASA: *(taking in his appearance)* What a state we loyal subjects of His Majesty are reduced to! *(He weeps.)*

VIRÁDHA·GUPTA: Do not grieve, Minister. You will soon restore our former glory.

RÁKSHASA: Virádha·gupta, my dear friend. Tell me what has been happening in Pátali·putra.

VIRÁDHA·GUPTA: Much has been happening, Minister. Where shall I begin?

RÁKSHASA: I want to know how the poisoners and others 2.60
I employed have been faring since Chandra·gupta first entered the city.

VIRÁDHA·GUPTA: Well, then: with Pátali·putra now besieged on all sides by the great horde of Scythians, Greeks, Hill Tribesmen, Cambodians, Persians, Bactrians and all the others, numberless as the ocean waters at Doomsday, that make up the forces of Chandra·gupta and Párvataka under Kautílya's guidance—

RĀKṢASAḤ: *(sa/sambhramaṃ śastram ākṛṣya)* āḥ mayi sthite kaḥ Kusumapuram avarotsyati? Pravīraka, Pravīraka, kṣipram idānīm!

prākārān paritaḥ śarāsana|dharaiḥ
  kṣipraṃ parikṣipyatāṃ
dvāreṣu dviradaiḥ prati|dvipa|ghaṭā|
  bheda|kṣamaiḥ sthīyatām
muktvā mṛtyu|bhayaṃ prahartu|manasaḥ
  śatror bale durbale
te niryāntu mayā sah' âika|manaso
  yeṣām abhīṣṭaṃ yaśaḥ.

VIRĀDHAGUPTAḤ: amātya, alam āvegena. vṛttam idaṃ varṇyate.

2.65 RĀKṢASAḤ: katham? vṛttam idam? mayā punar jñātaṃ sa ev' âyaṃ kālo vartate. *(śastram utsṛjya s'/âsram)* hā deva Nanda, smarati te Rākṣasaḥ prasādānāṃ yas tvam atra kāle,

«yatr' âiṣā megha|nīlā calati gaja|ghaṭā
  Rākṣasas tatra yāyād»
«etat pāriplav'|âmbhaḥ|pluti turaga|balaṃ
  dhāryatāṃ Rākṣasena»
«pattīnāṃ Rākṣaso 'ntaṃ nayatu balam iti»
  preṣayan mahyam ājñām
ajñāsīḥ prīti|yogāt sthitam iha nagare
  Rākṣasānāṃ sahasram.

tatas tataḥ.

RÁKSHASA: *(in agitation, drawing his sword)* What, who threatens the city while I am alive? Quick, Pravíraka, quick now!

Man the ramparts at once with archers!
Put elephants at the gates to break the enemy elephants' attack!
Lay fear of death aside, resolve to strike our nerveless foe,
March out with me, all you who look for glory!

VIRÁDHA·GUPTA: Minister, calm yourself. We are talking of the past.

RÁKSHASA: The past? To me it all seemed to be happening again. *(relinquishing his sword and weeping)* Oh, Nanda, my beloved Emperor! Well do I remember how you favored me at such times. 2.65

"There are elephants massing like a storm cloud," you would say—"send Rákshasa there!"
"Rákshasa must stem the tidal wave of cavalry!"
"Rákshasa shall destroy their infantry!" Such were your orders,
For you loved me so well you thought the city had a thousand Rákshasas.

Well, go on.

VIRĀDHAGUPTAḤ: tataḥ samantād uparuddhaṃ Kusumapuram avalokya bahu|divasa|pravṛttam atimahad uparodha|vaiśasam upari paurāṇāṃ vartamānam a|sahamāne tasyām avasthāyāṃ paura|jan'|âpekṣayā suruṅgām ety' âpakrānte tapo|vanāya deve Sarvārthasiddhau svāmi|virahāt praśithilī|kṛta|prayatneṣu yuṣmad|baleṣu ghoṣaṇā|vyāghāt'|ādi|sāhas'|ânumiteṣv antar|nagara|nivāsiṣu punar api Nanda|rājya|pratyānayanāya suruṅgām adhigateṣu yuṣmāsu Candragupta|nidhanāya yuṣmat|prayuktayā viṣa|kanyayā ghātite tapasvini Parvateśvare.

RĀKṢASAḤ: sakhe paśy' āścaryam,

2.70 Karṇen' êva viṣ'|âṅgan" âika|puruṣa|
vyāpādinī rakṣitā
hantuṃ śaktir iv' Ârjunaṃ balavatī
yā Candraguptaṃ mayā
sā Viṣṇor iva Viṣṇugupta|hatakasy'
ātyantika|śreyase
Haiḍimbeyam iv' êtya Parvata|nṛpaṃ
tad vadhyam ev' âvadhīt.

VIRĀDHAGUPTAḤ: amātya, daivasy' âtra kāma|cāraḥ. kim atra kriyate?

RĀKṢASAḤ: tatas tataḥ.

VIRĀDHAGUPTAḤ: tataḥ pitṛ|vadha|paritrāsād apakrānte kumāre Malayaketau, viśvāsite Parvataka|bhrātari Vairodhake, prakāśite Candraguptasya Nanda|bhavana|praveśe, Cāṇakyen' āhūy' âbhihitāḥ Kusumapura|nivāsinaḥ

VIRÁDHA·GUPTA: With Pátali·putra now besieged on all sides and the privations of the siege continuing day after day, His Majesty the Emperor Sarvártha·siddhi could not bear to let the people go on suffering, and for their sake made his escape through the secret passage and retired to a hermitage. The loss of their lord dampened the enthusiasm of your own forces, and when the boldness of the resistance to Chandra·gupta's victory proclamation revealed your presence in the city, you yourself left by the secret passage to work for the later restoration of Nanda rule. It was then that the poison-girl you engaged to kill Chandra·gupta brought about the death of poor Párvataka—

RÁKSHASA: How strange that was, friend!

She was like the once-and-for-all weapon* that Karna kept to kill Árjuna, 2.70
Which instead helped Krishna by killing Hidímba's son.
I had been keeping her for Chandra·gupta, but, alas,
She did Kautílya's work by killing Párvataka.

VIRÁDHA·GUPTA: It was the sport of fate, Minister. What can one do?

RÁKSHASA: Go on.

VIRÁDHA·GUPTA: His father's death frightened Prince Málaya·ketu into escaping, but his uncle, Párvataka's brother Vairódhaka, was given assurances of safety. It was proclaimed that Chandra·gupta would enter the Nanda Palace, and Kautílya called all the carpenters in the city

sarva eva sūtra|dhārā yathā «sāṃvatsarika|datta|lagna|vaśād ady' âiv' ârdha|rātra|samaye Candraguptasya Nanda|bhavana|praveśo bhaviṣyat' îti.» ataḥ «prathama|dvārāt prabhṛti saṃskriyatāṃ rāja|bhavanam iti.» tataḥ sūtra|dhārair abhihitam: «ārya, prathamam eva devasya Candraguptasya Nanda|bhavana|praveśam upalabhya sūtra|dhāreṇa Dāruvarmaṇā kanaka|toraṇa|nyās'|ādibhiḥ saṃskāra|viśeṣaiḥ saṃskṛtaṃ rāja|bhavana|dvāram. idānīm asmābhir abhyantare saṃskāro vidheya iti.» tataś Cāṇakya|vaṭun" «ân|ādiṣṭen' âiva Dāruvarmaṇā saṃskṛtaṃ rāja|bhavana|dvāram» iti parituṣṭena suciraṃ Dāruvarmaṇa dākṣyam abhipraśasy' âbhihitam: «acirād asya dākṣyasy' ânurūpaṃ phalaṃ Dāruvarm" âdhigamiṣyat' îti.»

RĀKṢASAḤ: *(s'|ôdvegam)* sakhe, kutaś Cāṇakya|vaṭoḥ paritoṣaḥ? a|phalam an|iṣṭa|phalaṃ vā Dāruvarmaṇaḥ prayatnam adhigacchāmi yad anena buddhi|mohād atha|vā rāja|bhakti|prakarṣān niyoga|kālam a|pratīkṣamāṇena janitaś Cāṇakya|vaṭoś cetasi balavān vikalpaḥ. tatas tataḥ?

2.75 VIRĀDHAGUPTAḤ: tataś Cāṇakya|hataken' «ânukūla|lagna|vaśād ardha|rātra|samaye Candraguptasya Nanda|bhavana|praveśo bhaviṣyat' îti» śilpinaḥ paurāṃś ca gṛhīt'|ârthān kṛtvā tasminn eva kṣaṇe Parvateśvara|bhrātaraṃ Vairodhakam ek'|āsane Candraguptena sah' ôpaveśya kṛtaḥ pṛthvī|rājya|vibhāgaḥ.

together and told them that because of a favorable astrological juncture the entry into the Palace would take place at midnight on that same day, and that they were to decorate the whole royal palace beginning with the Eastern Gate. The carpenters informed him that one of their number, Daru·varman, had contrived sumptuous decorations for the royal gateway, including a golden triumphal arch, as soon as he had heard that Chandra·gupta would enter the palace, and it remained only for them to decorate the interior. That fellow Kautílya seemed delighted to hear that Daru·varman had decorated the palace gateway without waiting to be asked, praised his talents at considerable length and said that it wouldn't be long before he earned a reward in keeping with his enterprise.

RÁKSHASA: *(disturbed)* Why should the fellow be so pleased, friend? I can guess that Daru·varman's efforts were not rewarded, at least not in the way he intended: he was mad to act before being commissioned, and make Kautílya suspicious—or, rather, he was too zealous in the service of his rightful king. What happened?

VIRÁDHA·GUPTA: Kautílya made sure that the craftsmen and the citizens at large knew that because of a favorable astrological juncture Chandra·gupta was due to enter the palace at midnight. Then, on the stroke of the hour, he set Párvataka's brother Vairódhaka on the throne with Chandra·gupta and divided the empire between them. 2.75

RĀKṢASAḤ: kiṃ c' âtisṛṣṭaḥ Parvateśvara|bhrātre Vairodhakāya pūrva|pratiśruto rājy'|ârdhaḥ?

VIRĀDHAGUPTAḤ: amātya, atha kim.

RĀKṢASAḤ: *(ātma|gatam)* niyatam atidhūrtena vaṭunā tasy' âpi tapasvinaḥ kam apy upāṃśu|vadham ākalayya Parvateśvara|vināśa|janitasy' â|yaśasaḥ parihār'|ârtham eṣā loka|bhaktir uparacitā. *(prakāśam)* tatas tataḥ.

VIRĀDHAGUPTAḤ: tataḥ prathamam eva prakāśite rātrau Candraguptasya Nanda|bhavana|praveśe, kṛt'|âbhiṣeke ca, hima|vimala|muktā|guṇa|parikṣep'|ôparacita|paṭṭamaya|vāravāṇa|pracchādita|śarīre maṇimaya|mukuṭa|niyamita|rucira|tara|maulau surabhi|kusuma|vaikakṣik'|âvabhāsita|vakṣaḥ|sthale paricita|janair apy an|abhijñāyamān'|ākṛtau, Cāṇakya|hatakasy' ājñayā Candragupt'|ôpavāhyāṃ Candralekhāṃ nāma gaja|vaśām āruhya, Candragupt'|ânuyāyinā rāja|loken' ânugamyamāne devasya Nandasya bhavanaṃ praviśati Vairodhake yuṣmat|prayuktena sūtra|dhāreṇa Dāruvarmaṇā «Candragupto 'yam» iti manyamānena Vairodhakasy' ôpari pātanāya sajjī|kṛtaṃ yantra|toraṇam. atr' ântare bahir|nigṛhīta|vāhaneṣu sthiteṣu Candragupt'|ânuyāyiṣu bhūmi|pāleṣu yuṣmat|prayukten' âiva Candralekhā|niṣādinā Varvarakeṇa kanaka|daṇḍik"|ântar|nihitām asi|putrikām ākraṣṭu|kāmen' âvalambitā kareṇa kanaka|śṛṅkhalā|mukh'|âvalambinī kanaka|daṇḍikā.

RÁKSHASA: He gave away to Vairódhaka the half-share in the empire which had been promised to Vairódhaka's brother?

VIRÁDHA·GUPTA: Exactly.

RÁKSHASA: *(to himself)* Then the cunning villain can only have been plotting to have the poor wretch quietly killed, and contrived this act of public good faith to wipe out the unpopularity that Párvataka's murder was earning him. *(aloud)* Go on.

VIRÁDHA·GUPTA: It had already been proclaimed that Chandra·gupta would enter the palace that night. The ceremony of consecration was performed and the Emperor was robed in a silk corselet encrusted with strings of snow-white pearls. A jeweled crown fitted closely around his gleaming head. His chest glowed with a fragrant mantle of flower garlands. His closest friends would not have recognized him. On the accursed Kautílya's orders, he was mounted on Chandra·gupta's own mount, the she-elephant Chandra·lekha, and attended by Chandra·gupta's own vassal princes; but the Emperor who entered the Nanda Palace was not Chandra·gupta but Vairódhaka. Supposing him to be Chandra·gupta, your agent the carpenter Daru·varman set the mechanism of the arch in motion to fall on him. The vassal princes reined in their mounts outside the gateway, but Chandra·lekha's driver Várvaraka, who was also your agent, reached for his gold staff, hanging on a gold chain, intending to take out the dagger he had concealed within.

2.80 RĀKṢASAḤ: kaṣṭam! ubhayor apy a|sthāne yatnaḥ! tatas tataḥ.

VIRĀDHAGUPTAḤ: atha jaghan'|âbhighātam utprekṣamāṇā gaja|vadhūr atijavatayā gaty|antaram ārūḍhavatī. tataḥ prathama|gaty|anurodha|pratyākalita|muktena prabhraṣṭa|lakṣyaṃ patatā yantra|toraṇen' ākṛṣṭa|kṛpāṇī|vyagra|pāṇir an|āsādayann eva Candragupt'|āśayā Vairodhakaṃ Dāruvarmaṇā hatas tapasvī Varvarakaḥ. tato Dāruvarmaṇā yantra|toraṇa|nipātam ātma|vināśa|phalam ākalayya pūrvam ev' ôttuṅga|toraṇa|sthalam ārūḍhena yantra|ghaṭana|bījaṃ loha|kīlakam ādāya hastinī|gata eva hatas tapasvī Vairodhakaḥ.

RĀKṢASAḤ: kaṣṭam! anartha|dvayam āpatitam. na hataś Candragupto, hatau Vairodhaka|Varvarakau. atha sūtra|dhāro Dāruvarmā katham?

VIRĀDHAGUPTAḤ: Vairodhaka|puraḥ|sareṇa padāti|lokena loṣṭa|ghātaṃ hataḥ.

RĀKṢASAḤ: *(s'|âsram)* kaṣṭam! aho vatsalena suhṛdā viyuktāḥ smaḥ. atha tatra tena bhiṣaj" Âbhayadattena kim anuṣṭhitam?

2.85 VIRĀDHAGUPTAḤ: amātya, sarvam anuṣṭhitam.

RĀKṢASAḤ: *(sa|harṣam)* api, sakhe, hataś Candraguptaḥ?

VIRĀDHAGUPTAḤ: daivān na hataḥ.

RĀKṢASAḤ: tat kim iti parituṣṭaḥ kathayasi «sarvam anuṣṭhitam» iti?

RÁKSHASA: Alas! It was not the moment for either attempt! Yes? 2.80

VIRÁDHA·GUPTA: The elephant expected a blow on the rump, and quickened her pace. The release of the mechanical arch had been calculated on her previous speed and when it fell it missed its target and instead killed poor Várvaraka while his hands were occupied with the dagger he had drawn, and before he could reach Vairódhaka—whom he supposed to be Chandra·gupta. Daru·varman knew that the release of the arch had signed his own death warrant, and since he was already perched on top of it he seized the iron bolt that had triggered the mechanism and killed Vairódhaka where he was on the elephant.

RÁKSHASA: Alas, two equal disasters—Chandra·gupta still alive, Vairódhaka and Várvaraka killed! The carpenter Daru·varman, what happened to him?

VIRÁDHA·GUPTA: Stoned to death by Vairódhaka's infantry.

RÁKSHASA: *(weeping)* We have lost a loving friend! And the doctor, Abhaya·datta, what of his work?

VIRÁDHA·GUPTA: It is done. 2.85

RÁKSHASA: *(in delight)* He has killed Chandra·gupta?

VIRÁDHA·GUPTA: As fate would have it, he has not.

RÁKSHASA: Then why tell me his work is done?

VIRĀDHAGUPTAḤ: amātya, kalpitam anena yoga|cūrṇa|miśram auṣadhaṃ Candraguptāya. tac ca pratyakṣī|kurvatā Cāṇakya|hatakena kanaka|bhājane varṇ'|ântaram upalabhy' âbhihitaś Candraguptaḥ: «Vṛṣala, Vṛṣala, sa|viṣam auṣadham, na pātavyam iti.»

2.90 RĀKṢASAḤ: śaṭhaḥ khalv asau vaṭuḥ. atha sa vaidyaḥ katham?

VIRĀDHAGUPTAḤ: sa khalu vaidyas tad ev' āuṣadhaṃ pāyitaś c' ôparataś ca.

RĀKṢASAḤ: *(sa/viṣādam)* aho, mahān vijñāna|rāśir uparataḥ. atha tasya śayan'|âdhikṛtasya Pramodakasya kiṃ vṛttam?

VIRĀDHAGUPTAḤ: ārya, yad itareṣām.

RĀKṢASAḤ: *(s'/ôdvegam)* katham iva?

2.95 VIRĀDHAGUPTAḤ: sa khalu mūrkhas taṃ yuṣmābhir atisṛṣṭaṃ prabhūtam artha|rāśim avāpya mahatā vyayen' ôpabhoktum ārabdhavān. tataḥ «kutas tav' âyaṃ bhūyān dhan'|āgama iti» pṛcchyamāno yadā bahu|vākya|bhedam ākulam akathayat tadā Cāṇakya|hatak'|ādeśād vicitreṇa vadhena vyāpāditaḥ.

RĀKṢASAḤ: *(s'/ôdvegam)* katham? atr' âpi vayam ev' ôpahatā daivena. atha śayitasya Candraguptasya śarīre prahartum asmat|prayuktānāṃ narapati|śayana|gṛhasy' ântaḥ|suruṅgāyām etya prathamam eva nivasatāṃ Bībhatsak'|ādīnāṃ ko vṛttāntaḥ?

VIRĀDHAGUPTAḤ: amātya, dāruṇo vrttāntaḥ.

RĀKṢASAḤ: kathaṃ dāruṇo vṛttāntaḥ? na khalu viditās te tatra nivasantaś Cāṇakya|hatakena?

VIRĀDHAGUPTAḤ: atha kim. prāk Candragupta|praveśāt praviṣṭa|mātreṇ' âiva śayana|gṛhaṃ durātmanā Cāṇakya|ha-

VIRÁDHA·GUPTA: He prepared medicine for Chandra·gupta containing a fatal powder. When the accursed Kautílya inspected it, he saw that the gold cup it was in had changed color, and he said, "Vríshala, don't drink it, it's poisoned."

RÁKSHASA: He's a cunning villain. What happened to the 2.90
doctor?

VIRÁDHA·GUPTA: The doctor was made to drink his own medicine, and died.

RÁKSHASA: *(despondently)* The world has lost a very learned man. What has happened to Pramódaka, the steward of the bedchamber?

VIRÁDHA·GUPTA: The same as to the others, sir.

RÁKSHASA: *(alarmed)* How do you mean?

VIRÁDHA·GUPTA: When he got the huge sum of money you 2.95
allowed him, the fool began spending extravagantly. On being asked to account for his wealth he told a confused variety of stories—and on Kautílya's orders he was put to death by torture.

RÁKSHASA: *(in despair)* Does fate strike us down yet again? And those we employed to kill the Emperor in bed, who were already living in a secret passage inside the bedchamber—Bibhátsaka and the others, what news of them?

VIRÁDHA·GUPTA: Grim news, I fear.

RÁKSHASA: Grim? Did Kautílya discover they were there?

VIRÁDHA·GUPTA: He did. Before Chandra·gupta occupied the bedchamber, Kautílya entered it and made a sudden

taken' âvalokitam. tata ekasmād bhitti|cchidrād gṛhīta|bhakt'|âvayavānāṃ pipīlikānāṃ niṣkrāmantīnāṃ paṅktim avalokya «puruṣa|garbham etad gṛham iti» gṛhīt'|ârthena dāhitaṃ tad eva śayana|gṛham. tasmin dahyamāne dhūma|nivaha|niruddha|dṛṣṭi|viṣayāḥ prathama|pihitam an|avagamya nirgamana|pathaṃ Bībhats'|ādayas tatr' âiva jvalita|jvalana|patham upagatāḥ.

2.100 RĀKṢASAḤ: *(s'|âsram)* sakhe, paśya daiva|saṃpadaṃ durātmanaś Candraguptasya. kutaḥ:

kanyā tasya vadhāya yā viṣamayī
gūḍhaṃ prayuktā mayā
daivāt Parvatakas tayā vinihato
yas tasya rājy'|ârdha|bhāk
ye śastreṣu raseṣu ca praṇihitās
tair eva te ghātitāḥ
Mauryasy' âiva phalanti hanta
vividhaṃ śreyaḥ sunītāni me.

VIRĀDHAGUPTAḤ: amātya, tath" âpi prārabdham a|parityājyam eva. paśyatv amātyaḥ.

ārabhyate na khalu vighna|bhayena nīcaiḥ
prārabhya vighna|vihatā viramanti madhyāḥ
vighnaiḥ punaḥ punar api pratihanyamānāḥ
prārabdham uttama|guṇās tvam iv' ôdvahanti.

inspection. He saw a column of ants emerging with bits of food from a crack in the wall, and, realizing there were men in the room, had the place fired. As it was burning, Bibhátsaka and his companions were blinded by the thick smoke and could not find the way out, which they had closed behind them, and they perished in the flames.

RÁKSHASA: *(weeping)* See, friend, that accursed Chandra·gupta's luck: 2.100

The poison-girl I secretly engaged to kill him
By chance killed Párvataka, who would have taken half his empire.
My agents die themselves by the knives and poisons that they use.
It is the Mauryan who reaps the benefit of every plan I make.

VIRÁDHA·GUPTA: Even so, Minister, you must not give up. Think, sir.

Obstacles deter the worst from starting
And turn the mediocre from what they have begun.
But the best and noblest like yourself will persevere
Though obstacles beset them time and time again.

api ca, kiṃ Śeṣasya bhara|vyathā na vapuṣi
kṣmāṃ na kṣipaty eṣa yat?
kiṃ vā n' âsti pariśramo dina|pater
āste na yan niścalaḥ?
kiṃ tv aṅgī|kṛtam utsṛjan kṛpaṇavat
ślāghyo jano lajjate?
nirvyūḍhiḥ pratipanna|vastuṣu satām
ekaṃ hi gotra|vratam.

2.105 RĀKṢASAḤ: sakhe, prārabdham a|parityājyam iti pratyakṣam ev' âitad bhavataḥ. tatas tataḥ.

VIRĀDHAGUPTAḤ: tataḥ prabhṛti Candragupta|śarīre saha-sra|guṇam apramattaś Cāṇakya|hataka «ebhya etādṛśaṃ bhavat' îty» anviṣy' ânviṣya nigṛhītavān Kusumapura|ni-vāsino yuṣmadīyān āpta|puruṣān.

RĀKṢASAḤ: *(s'|āvegam)* vayasya, ke ke nigṛhītāḥ?

VIRĀDHAGUPTAḤ: ādāv eva Kṣapaṇako Jīvasiddhiḥ sa|ni-kāraṃ nagarān nirvāsitaḥ.

RĀKṢASAḤ: *(ātma|gatam)* etat tāvat sahyam. na niṣ|pari-grahaṃ sthāna|bhraṃśaḥ pīḍayiṣyati. *(prakāśam)* sakhe, kam aparādham uddiśya nirvāsitaḥ?

2.110 VIRĀDHAGUPTAḤ: «eṣa Rākṣasa|prayukto viṣa|kanyayā Par-vateśvaraṃ ghātitavān» iti.

RĀKṢASAḤ: sādhu, Kauṭilya, sādhu.

parihṛtam a|yaśaḥ pātitam
asmāsu ca ghātito 'rdha|rājya|haraḥ
ekam api nīti|bījaṃ
bahu|phalatām eti yasya tava.

Does the Serpent feel no ache, that he does not throw off the earth?
Has the sun no weariness that it does not pause to rest?
A great man is ashamed to give up like a commoner.
The noble have one family law, to do what they have promised.

RÁKSHASA: My friend, you see for yourself that I cannot give up. Continue. 2.105

VIRÁDHA·GUPTA: Thereafter Kautílya became a thousand times more vigilant for Chandra·gupta's safety, and by tracking everything that happened to its source he uncovered your most trusted agents in the city.

RÁKSHASA: *(in alarm)* Whom did he discover?

VIRÁDHA·GUPTA: First the Jain monk Jiva·siddhi, whom he banished in disgrace from the city.

RÁKSHASA: *(to himself)* That at least is endurable: loss of home will not bear hard on a man without ties. *(aloud)* Friend, for what offense was he banished?

VIRÁDHA·GUPTA: For being employed by you to have Párvataka killed by a poison-girl. 2.110

RÁKSHASA: Bravo, Kautílya!

You avoid unpopularity, transfer it to me,
And dispose of a claimant to half the empire.
You sow one seed of policy
And harvest many fruits.

(prakāśam) tatas tataḥ.

VIRĀDHAGUPTAḤ: «Candragupta | śarīram abhidrogdhum anena vyāpāritā Dāruvarm'|ādaya iti» nagare prakhyāpya Śakaṭadāsaḥ śūlam āropitaḥ.

2.115 RĀKṢASAḤ: *(s'|âsram)* hā, sakhe Śakaṭadāsa! ayuktas tav' âyam īdṛśo mṛtyuḥ. atha|vā svāmy|artham uparato na śocyas tvam asi. vayam ev' âtra nanu śocyā ye Nanda|kula|vināśe 'pi jīvitum icchāmaḥ.

VIRĀDHAGUPTAḤ: amātya, mā m" âivam! svāmy|artha eva sādhayitavya iti.

RĀKṢASAḤ: sakhe,

asmābhir amum ev' ârtham
  avalambya jijīviṣām
para|loka|gato devaḥ
  kṛtaghnair n' ânugamyate.

VIRĀDHAGUPTAḤ: amātya, n' âitad evam—

2.120 yuṣmābhir amum ev' ârtham
  ālambya na jijīviṣām
para|loka|gato devaḥ
  kṛtajñair n' ânugamyate.

RĀKṢASAḤ: sakhe, kathyatām. aparasy' âpi suhṛd|vyasanasya śravaṇe sajjo 'smi.

VIRĀDHAGUPTAḤ: tata etad upalabhya Candanadāsen' âpavāhitaṃ sauhārden' âmātya|kalatram.

(aloud) What then?

VIRÁDHA·GUPTA: Then Shákata·dasa was publicly proclaimed to have employed Daru·varman and others in plots against Chandra·gupta, and was impaled.

RÁKSHASA: *(weeping)* Oh, Shákata·dasa, dearest friend, you 2.115
did not deserve such a death. But you died in your master's cause: it is not you who should be mourned, but I, who think of living when the House of Nanda has perished.

VIRÁDHA·GUPTA: No, Minister, no! You must live to serve our master's cause.

RÁKSHASA: Friend,

It is because of that cause
That I still love life,
And am so disloyal
As not to follow my lord into the next world.

VIRÁDHA·GUPTA: You put it wrongly, Minister—

It is because of that cause, 2.120
Not because you love life,
That you are loyal to your Lord
And keep from following him into the next world.

RÁKSHASA: Speak on, my friend. I am waiting to hear of other disasters to those I love.

VIRÁDHA·GUPTA: Hearing the news, Chándana·dasa, out of the love he bears you, got your wife safely away.

RĀKṢASAḤ: sakhe, krūrasya Cāṇakya|vaṭor viruddham ayuktam anuṣṭhitaṃ Candanadāsena.

VIRĀDHAGUPTAḤ: amātya, na yuktataraḥ suhṛd|drohaḥ.

2.125 RĀKṢASAḤ: tatas tataḥ?

VIRĀDHAGUPTAḤ: tato yācyamānen' ânen' âpi yadā na samarpitam amātya|kalatraṃ tataḥ kupitena Cāṇakya|vaṭunā—

RĀKṢASAḤ: *(s'|āvegam)* na khalu vyāpāditaḥ?

VIRĀDHAGUPTAḤ: amātya, na khalu vyāpāditaḥ. kiṃ tu gṛhīta|gṛha|sāraḥ sa|putra|kalatro bandhane nikṣiptaḥ.

RĀKṢASAḤ: tat kiṃ parituṣṭaḥ kathayasi: «apavāhitam anena Rākṣasa|kalatram» iti? nanu vaktavyaṃ: «saṃyato 'nena sa|putra|kalatro Rākṣasa iti.»

2.130 *(praviśya)* PURUṢAḤ: ⌜jaadu, jaadu ajjo. ajja, eso kkhu Saaḍadāso paḍihāra|bhūmīe uvatthido.⌟

RĀKṢASAḤ: api satyam?

PURUṢAḤ: ⌜kiṃ aliaṃ amacca|pād'|ôvajīviṇo mantiduṃ jāṇanti?⌟

RĀKṢASAḤ: sakhe Virādhagupta, katham etat?

VIRĀDHAGUPTAḤ: amātya, syād evam. rakṣati khalu bhavyaṃ bhavitavyatā.

RÁKSHASA: He did ill to oppose one so merciless as Kautílya.

VIRÁDHA·GUPTA: Would he have done better to betray a friend?

RÁKSHASA: What happened? 2.125

VIRÁDHA·GUPTA: When he was pressed to hand her over and refused, Kautílya grew angry—

RÁKSHASA: *(in alarm)* And had him killed?

VIRÁDHA·GUPTA: No, sir, not that. His goods were confiscated and he was thrown into jail with his wife and son.

RÁKSHASA: Then why tell me in pleased tones that he got my wife safely away? Tell me, rather, that I am in jail with my wife and son.

(Enter the) MANSERVANT: Victory, sir. Sir, Shákata·dasa is 2.130
waiting in the entrance hall.

RÁKSHASA: Is this true?

MANSERVANT: Can Your Honor's own household lie to you?

RÁKSHASA: What can this mean, Virádha·gupta?*

VIRÁDHA·GUPTA: It may be true, sir. Destiny looks to what must be.

2.135 RĀKṢASAḤ: Priyaṃvadaka, yady evaṃ tat kiṃ cirayasi? kṣipraṃ praveśya samāśvāsaya mām.

PURUṢAḤ: ⌜jaṃ amacco āṇavedi.⌟ *(iti niṣkrāntaḥ.)*

tataḥ praviśati SIDDHĀRTHAKEN' *ânugamyamānaḥ* ŚAKAṬADĀSAḤ.

ŚAKAṬADĀSAḤ: *(ātma|gatam)*

dṛṣṭvā Mauryam iva pratiṣṭhita|padaṃ
śūlaṃ dharitryās tale
tal|lakṣmīm iva cetasaḥ pramathinīm
ūḍhvā ca vadhya|srajam
śrutvā svāmy|uparodha|raudra|viṣamān
āghāta|tūrya|svanān
na dhvastaṃ pratham'|âbhighāta|kaṭhinaṃ
manye madīyaṃ manaḥ.

2.140 *(nāṭyen' âvalokya sa|harṣam)* ayam amātya|Rākṣasas tiṣṭhati ya eṣaḥ:

a|kṣīṇa|bhaktiḥ kṣīṇe 'pi
Nande svāmy|artham udvahan
pṛthivyāṃ svāmi|bhaktānāṃ
pramāṇe parame sthitaḥ.

(upasṛtya) jayatv amātyaḥ.

RĀKṢASAḤ: *(nāṭyen' âvalokya sa|harṣam)* sakhe Śakaṭadāsa, diṣṭyā dṛṣṭo 'si. tat pariṣvajasva mām. *(pariṣvajya)* idam āsanam. āsyatām.

ŚAKAṬADĀSAḤ: yad ājñāpayaty amātyaḥ. *(iti nāṭyen' ôpaviṣṭaḥ.)*

RÁKSHASA: If it is true, then hurry, Priyam·vádaka! Show him in at once and put new heart in me. 2.135

MANSERVANT: Yes, sir. *(He goes out.)*

Enter, with SIDDHÁRTHAKA *in attendance,* SHÁKATA·DASA.

SHÁKATA·DASA: *(to himself)*

When I saw the stake set firm as the Mauryan in
the earth,
When I felt the garland as heavy on my heart as
his royal glory,
When I heard the trumpet of execution as harsh
as my lord's defeat,
My mind held firm only because it was hardened
by earlier blows.

(looking joyfully) There stands Minister Rákshasa: 2.140

He goes on serving his master's cause,
His devotion alive though Nanda is dead.
He stands as the supreme example
Of all on earth who are loyal to a master.

(approaching) Victory to you, Minister.

RÁKSHASA: *(seeing him, joyfully)* Dearest Shákata·dasa, thank God I see you! Embrace me! *(after embracing him)* Here, sit down.

SHÁKATA·DASA: Yes, sir. *(He sits down.)*

2.145 RĀKṢASAḤ: sakhe Śakaṭadāsa, ko 'sya mama hṛday'|ānandasya hetuḥ?

ŚAKAṬADĀSAḤ: (SIDDHĀRTHAKAṂ *nirdiśya)* anena priya|suhṛdā Siddhārthakena ghātakān vidrāvya vadhya|sthānād upahṛto 'smi.

RĀKṢASAḤ: *(sa|harṣam)* bhadra Siddhārthaka, kāmam a|paryāptam idam asya priyasya. tath" âpi gṛhyatām. *(iti sva|gātrād avatārya bhūṣaṇāni prayacchati.)*

SIDDHĀRTHAKAḤ: *(gṛhītvā pādayor nipatya sva|gatam)* ⌜aaṃ khu ajj' | ôvadeso. bhodu. tadhā karissaṃ.⌟ *(prakāśam)* ⌜amacca, ettha me paḍhamaṃ paviṭṭhassa ṇatthi ko vi paricido jahiṃ edaṃ amaccassa pasādaṃ ṇikkhivia ṇivvudo bhavissaṃ. tā icchāmi ahaṃ imāe muddiāe muddia amaccassa jjeva bhaṇḍāāre ṇikkhividuṃ. jadā me ediṇā paoaṇaṃ bhavissadi tadā geṇhissaṃ.⌟

RĀKṢASAḤ: bhadra, ko doṣaḥ? Śakaṭadāsa, evaṃ kriyatām.

2.150 ŚAKAṬADĀSAḤ: yad ājñāpayaty amātyaḥ. *(iti jan' | ântikaṃ mudrāṃ vilokya)* amātya|nām'|âṅkit" êyaṃ mudrā.

RĀKṢASAḤ: *(viloky' ātma|gatam)* satyam. asmad|utkaṇṭhā|vinod'|ârthaṃ nagarān niṣkrāmato mama hastād brāhmaṇyā gṛhītā. tat katham asya hastam upagatā? *(prakāśam)* bhadra Siddhārthaka, kutas tvay" êyam adhigatā?

SIDDHĀRTHAKAḤ: ⌜amacca, atthi Kusumaüre maṇi|āra|seṭṭhī Candaṇadāso ṇāma. tassa geha|duvāre paḍidā mae laddhā.⌟

RĀKṢASAḤ: yujyate.

RÁKSHASA: Shákata·dasa, dear friend, what have I to thank for this happiness? 2.145

SHÁKATA·DASA: *(indicating* SIDDHÁRTHAKA*)* My dear friend Siddhárthaka here frightened off the executioners and rescued me from the Execution Ground.

RÁKSHASA: *(joyfully)* Good Siddhárthaka, this is nothing, I know, for such a service, but take it. *(He removes Málaya·ketu's decorations from his body and offers them.)*

SIDDHÁRTHAKA: *(taking them and going down on his knees, to himself)* My master Kautílya has given me my instructions: I will carry them out. *(Aloud)* Minister, I am a newcomer here, and I don't know anyone I would be happy to entrust with your generous gift. May I seal it with this signet ring and deposit it in Your Honor's own strong room? Then I can take it when I have need of it.

RÁKSHASA: My dear man, why not? See to it, Shákata·dasa.

SHÁKATA·DASA: Yes, sir. *(looking at the signet ring, aside)* This signet ring has Your Honor's name engraved on it. 2.150

RÁKSHASA: *(looking at it, to himself)* So it has. My wife took this ring from my finger as a keepsake when I was leaving the city. How has it fallen into his hands? *(aloud)* Siddhárthaka, my dear fellow, where did you get this from?

SIDDHÁRTHAKA: Minister, there is a master jeweler called Chándana·dasa in Pátali·putra and I found it lying at the gate of his house.

RÁKSHASA: That certainly fits.

SIDDHĀRTHAKAḤ: ⌜amacca, kiṃ ettha jujjadi?⌟

2.155 RĀKṢASAḤ: bhadra, yan mahā|dhanānāṃ gṛha|dvāri patitasy' âivaṃ|vidhasy' ôpalabdhir iti.

ŚAKAṬADĀSAḤ: sakhe Siddhārthaka, amātya | nām' | âṅkit" êyaṃ mudrā. tad ito bahutareṇ' ârthena bhavantam amātyas toṣayiṣyati. tad dīyatām eṣā mudrā.

SIDDHĀRTHAKAḤ: ⌜ajja, ṇaṃ eso jjeva me parioso jaṃ imāe muddāe amacco pariggahaṃ karedi.⌟ *(iti mudrāṃ samarpayati.)*

RĀKṢASAḤ: Śakaṭadāsa, anay" âiva mudrayā sv'|âdhikāre vyavahartavyaṃ bhavatā.

ŚAKAṬADĀSAḤ: yad ājñāpayaty amātyaḥ.

2.160 SIDDHĀRTHAKAḤ: ⌜amacca, viṇṇavemi kiṃ pi.⌟

RĀKṢASAḤ: brūhi viśrabdham.

SIDDHĀRTHAKAḤ: ⌜jāṇadi jjeva amacco jadhā Cāṇakka|hadaassa vippiaṃ kadua ṇatthi me Pāḍaliutte paveso tti. tā icchāmi ahaṃ amaccassa jjeva suppasaṇṇassa calaṇesuṃ sevidum.⌟

RĀKṢASAḤ: bhadra, priyaṃ naḥ. kiṃ tu tvad|abhiprāy'|â|parijñānena corito 'smākam anunayaḥ. tad evaṃ kriyatām.

SIDDHĀRTHAKAḤ: *(sa|harṣam)* ⌜aṇuggihido mhi.⌟

2.165 RĀKṢASAḤ: sakhe Śakaṭadāsa, viśrāmaya Siddhārthakam.

SIDDHÁRTHAKA: What fits, Minister?

RÁKSHASA: Finding such a thing lying at the gate of such a rich man's house. 2.155

SHÁKATA·DASA: Siddhárthaka, my friend, the ring has the Minister's name engraved on it, and he will give you much more than it is worth. So let him have it.

SIDDHÁRTHAKA: I shall be well rewarded, Minister, if you will do me the honor of accepting it. *(He hands over the ring.)*

RÁKSHASA: Use this ring, Shákata·dasa, in your administrative duties.

SHÁKATA·DASA: Yes, sir.

SIDDHÁRTHAKA: May I say something, sir? 2.160

RÁKSHASA: Speak freely.

SIDDHÁRTHAKA: Your Honor knows that as one who has given offense to Kautílya I cannot return to Pátali·putra. I should like to enter Your Honor's service if Your Honor would be so kind.

RÁKSHASA: My dear man, I should be delighted. I did not know how you would feel about it, or I should have had the politeness to ask you myself. Let it be so.

SIDDHÁRTHAKA: *(delighted)* I am honored.

RÁKSHASA: Shákata·dasa, my friend, see that Siddhárthaka is made comfortable. 2.165

ŚAKAṬADĀSAḤ: yad ājñāpayaty amātyaḥ. *(iti* SIDDHĀRTHAKENA *saha niṣkrāntaḥ.)*

RĀKṢASAḤ: sakhe Virādhagupta, varṇay' êdānīṃ Kusumapura|vṛttānta|śeṣam. api kṣamante 'smad|upajāpaṃ Candragupta|prakṛtayaḥ?

VIRĀDHAGUPTAḤ: amātya, bāḍhaṃ kṣamante. nanu yathā|pradhānam anugacchanty eva.

RĀKṢASAḤ: sakhe, kiṃ tatra kāraṇam?

2.170 VIRĀDHAGUPTAḤ: amātya, etat kāraṇam. Malayaketor apakramaṇāt prabhṛti pīḍitaś Candraguptena Cāṇakya iti Cāṇakyo 'py ati|jita|kāśitayā tais tair ājñā|bhaṅgaiś Candraguptasya citta|pīḍām upacinoti. ayam api mam' ânubhavaḥ.

RĀKṢASAḤ: *(sa|harṣam)* sakhe Virādhagupta, tvam anen' âiv' āhituṇḍika|cchadmanā punaḥ Kusumapuram eva gaccha. tatra hi me priya|suhṛd vaitālika|vyañjanaḥ Stanakalaśo nāma prativasati. sa tvay" âsmad|vacanād vācyaḥ: «Cāṇakyena kriyamāṇeṣv ājñā|bhaṅgeṣu Candraguptas tvayā samuttejana|samarthaiḥ śokair upaślokayitavyaḥ kāryaṃ c' âtinibhṛtaṃ Karabhaka|hastena saṃdeṣṭavyam» iti.

VIRĀDHAGUPTAḤ: yad ājñāpayaty amātyaḥ. *(iti niṣkrāntaḥ.)*

praviśya PURUṢAḤ. ⌜jaadu, jaadu amacco. amacca, Saaḍadāso viṇṇavedi: Ede kkhu tiṇṇi alaṃkārā vikkāanti. tā paccakkhīkaredu amacco.⌟

RĀKṢASAḤ: *(viloky' ātma|gatam)* aho mah"|ârghyāṇy ābharaṇāni. *(prakāśam)* bhadra, ucyatāṃ Śakaṭadāsaḥ: «paritoṣya vikretāraṃ gṛhyatām» iti.

SHÁKATA·DASA: Yes, sir. *(He goes out with* SIDDHÁRTHAKA.*)*

RÁKSHASA: And now, dear Virádha·gupta, the rest of the news from the city. Are Chandra·gupta's subjects responding to our overtures?

VIRÁDHA·GUPTA: Indeed they are, sir. In fact, they are increasingly coming over to our side.

RÁKSHASA: Why is that, my friend?

VIRÁDHA·GUPTA: Ever since Málaya·ketu's escape, Chandra· 2.170
gupta has been putting pressure on Kautílya, and Kautílya, flushed with success, has increased Chandra·gupta's irritation by defying him on a number of occasions. This is something I myself can confirm.

RÁKSHASA: *(delighted)* Virádha·gupta, my friend, keep your disguise as a snake charmer and go back to Pátali·putra. I have a good friend called Stana·kálasha living there disguised as a bard. Tell him in my name that when Kautílya defies Chandra·gupta's commands he should address the Emperor in stanzas calculated to inflame him further. And he should report progress very discreetly via Kárabhaka.

VIRÁDHA·GUPTA: As you command, Minister. *(He goes out.)*

Enter the MANSERVANT. Victory to you, sir. Shákata·dasa begs to say that these three ornaments are being offered for sale, and would you examine them.

RÁKSHASA: *(looking at them, to himself)* Why, what valuable jewels! *(aloud)* Tell Shákata·dasa to give the trader a good price for them and accept them.

2.175 PURUṢAḤ: ⌜jaṃ amacco āṇavedi.⌟ *(iti niṣkrāntaḥ.)*

RĀKṢASAḤ: *(ātma|gatam)* yāvad ahaṃ Kusumapurāya Karabhakaṃ preṣayāmi. *(ity utthāya)* api nāma durātmanaś Cāṇakyāc Candragupto bhidyeta! atha|vā siddham eva samīhitaṃ paśyāmi. kutaḥ—

Mauryas tejasi sarva|bhū|tala|bhujām
ājñāpako vartate
Cāṇakyo 'pi «mad|āśrayād ayam abhūd
rāj" êti» jāta|smayaḥ
rājya|prāpti|kṛt'|ârtham ekam aparaṃ
tīrṇa|pratijñ"|ârṇavaṃ
sauhārdāt kṛta|kṛtyat" âiva niyataṃ
labdh'|ântarā bhetsyati.

iti niṣkrāntāḥ sarve.

MANSERVANT: Yes, sir. *(He goes out.)* 2.175

RÁKSHASA: *(to himself)* I must send Kárabhaka to Pátali·putra. *(getting up)* Ah, if Chandra·gupta can just be split from the cursed Kautílya! But I see that the thing has been done for me—

> The Mauryan is supreme ruler of all the monarchs of the earth,
> And Kautílya swells with pride at having made him so.
> One has achieved his kingly ambitions, the other has fulfilled his vow:
> Success in itself will be enough to break their friendship.

All withdraw.

ACT III
KAUTÍLYA RESIGNS

tataḥ praviśati KAÑCUKĪ.

KAÑCUKĪ:

rūp'|ādīn viṣayān nirūpya karaṇair
yair ātma|lābhas tvayā
labdhas teṣv api cakṣur|ādiṣu hatāḥ
sv'|ârth'|âvabodha|kriyāḥ
aṅgāni prasabhaṃ tyajanti paṭutām
ājñā|vidheyāni me
nyastaṃ mūrdhni padaṃ tav' âiva jarayā
tṛṣṇe mudhā tāmyasi.

(parikramy' ākāśe) bho bhoḥ Sugāṅga | prāsād' | âdhikṛtāḥ puruṣāḥ! sugṛhīta | nāmā devaś Candraguptaḥ samājñāpayati: «pravṛtta|Kaumudī|mah"|ôtsava|ramaṇīyaṃ Kusuma | puram avalokayitum icchāmi. tat kriyantām asmad|darśana|yogyāḥ Sugāṅga|prāsādasy' ôpari|bhūmaya iti.» *(ākāśe ākarṇya)* kiṃ kathayanti bhavantaḥ? «ārya, kim avidita ev' âyaṃ devasya Candraguptasya Kaumudī | mah" | ôtsava | pratiṣedha iti?» āḥ daiv' | ôpahatāḥ! kim anena vaḥ prāṇa | hareṇa kath" | ôddhātena. śīghram idānīm,

3.5 āliṅgantu gṛhīta|dhūpa|surabhīn
stambhān pinaddha|srajaḥ
saṃpūrṇ'|êndu|mayūkha|saṃhati|rucāṃ
sac|cāmarāṇāṃ śriyaḥ
siṃh'|âṅk'|āsana|dhāraṇāc ca su|ciraṃ
saṃjāta|mūrchām iva
kṣipraṃ candana|vāriṇā su|kusumaḥ
seko 'nugṛhṇātu gām.

Enter a CHAMBERLAIN.

CHAMBERLAIN:

> It was the use of my senses that gave you birth,
> But now my senses are dull and tell me little,
> While my limbs that were your servants have lost
> their cunning:
> Desire, old age has beaten you and you repine in
> vain.

(walking about, and addressing the air) Ho there, officials of the River Palace! His Majesty the Emperor Chandra·gupta of auspicious name has declared his intention of enjoying the spectacle of the city celebrating the Full Moon Festival, and desires that the upper terrace of the Palace be made ready for him to watch from. *(listening)* What's that you say? Does His Majesty not know that the Full Moon Festival has been canceled? Doomed fools! Such talk will cost you your lives. Quick now,

> Let yak-tail plumes lustrous as moonbeams be 3.5
> massed
> About pillars fragrant with incense and wreathed
> in garlands.
> Too long the earth has languished beneath a heavy
> throne:
> Revive it with flower-strewn water of sandalwood.

(ākāśe) kiṃ kathayanti bhavantaḥ? «ete tvarāmaha iti.» bhadrās, tvaryatāṃ tvaryatām. ayam āgata eva devaś Candraguptaḥ. ya eṣa,

su|viśrabdhair aṅgaiḥ
pathiṣu viṣameṣv apy acalatā
ciraṃ dhuryeṇ' ōḍhā
gurur api bhuvo y" âsya guruṇā
dhuraṃ tām ev' ôccair
nava|vayasi voḍhuṃ vyavasito
manasvī damyatvāt
skhalati na na duḥkhaṃ vahati ca.

PRATĪHĀRĪ *nepathye:* ⌜ido ido devo.⌟

tataḥ praviśati RĀJĀ PRATĪHĀRĪ *ca.*

3.10 RĀJĀ: *(svagatam)* rājyaṃ hi nāma rāja|dharm'|ânuvṛtti|para-tantrasya nṛpater mahad a|prīti|sthānam. kutaḥ:

par'|ârth'|ânuṣṭhāne
ślathayati nṛpaṃ sv'|ârtha|paratā
parityakta|sv'|ârtho
niyatam a|yath"|ârthaḥ kṣiti|patiḥ
par'|ârthaś cet sv'|ârthād
abhimatataro hanta paravān
par'|āyattaḥ prīteḥ
katham iva rasaṃ vettu puruṣaḥ?

api ca: durārādhā rāja|lakṣmīr ātmavadbhir api rājabhiḥ. kutaḥ:

(addressing the air) What do you say? "At once, sir!" Well, be quick, be quick. Here comes His Majesty the Emperor:

The heavy yoke his elder bore so long and confidently,
Trained in the task, sure-footed in the roughest ground,
He is resolved to bear aloft now in his time of youth,
And though new to the yoke and headstrong, he does not stumble or feel distress.

Voice of FEMALE GUARD *offstage:* This way, sire, this way.

Enter the EMPEROR *and a* FEMALE GUARD.

EMPEROR: *(to himself)* A kingdom brings little pleasure if the king is intent on doing his duty. 3.10

In seeing to others' interests a king loses sight of his own.
And a sovereign whose interests are unregarded is surely no sovereign.
For if he puts another's good before his, why, he is in bondage.
And how is a man in bondage to know what pleasure means?

And even where a king is his own master, success is a hard mistress:

tīkṣṇād udvijate mṛdau paribhava|
trāsān na saṃtiṣṭhate
mūrkhān dveṣṭi na gacchati praṇayitām
atyanta|vidvatsv api
śūrebhyo 'bhyadhikaṃ bibhety upahasaty
ekānta|bhīrūn aho
Śrīr labdha|prasar" êva veśa|vanitā
duḥkh'|ôpacaryā bhṛśam.

anyac ca: «kṛtaka|kalahaṃ kṛtvā sva|tantreṇa tvayā kiṃ cit kāl'|ântaraṃ vyavahartavyam ity» āry'|ôpadeśaḥ. sa ca katham api mayā pātakam iv' âbhyupagataḥ. atha|vā śaśvad|āry'|ôpadeśa|saṃskriyamāṇa|matayaḥ sarvad" âiva sva|tantrā vayam. kutaḥ:

3.15 iha viracayan sādhvīṃ śiṣyaḥ
kriyāṃ na nivāryate
tyajati tu yadā mārgaṃ mohāt
tadā gurur aṅkuśaḥ
vinaya|rucayas tasmāt santaḥ
sad" âiva niraṅkuśāḥ
padam api yataḥ svātantryebhyo
na yānti parāṅ|mukhāḥ.

(prakāśam) ārya Vaihīnare, Sugāṅga|prāsāda|mārgam ādeśaya.

KAÑCUKĪ: ita ito devaḥ. *(parikramya)* ayaṃ Sugāṅga|prāsādaḥ. śanaiḥ|śanair ārodhum arhati devaḥ.

RĀJĀ: *(nāṭyen' āruhya diśo 'valokya)* aho śarat|samaya|saṃbhṛta|śobhā|vibhūtīnāṃ diśām atiśaya|ramaṇīyatā. saṃprati hi:

If he is stern, she recoils; if he is mild, she fears
contempt and shuns him.
Fools she can't stand, yet never loves the
over-learned.
A hero she is afraid of, a coward she despises—
Success is as hard to please as a capricious whore.

And now my revered preceptor tells me I must pretend to quarrel with him and rule for a time on my own account. I have agreed reluctantly, as to something sinful. And yet I have always ruled by myself, while his guidance has illuminated all my decisions.

While he acts well, a pupil is never checked: 3.15
It is when his wits go wandering that he feels the
goad.
And therefore, self-disciplined, the good are never
curbed,
For they never wish to stray beyond the limits of
their independence.

(aloud) Noble Vaihínari, lead me to the River Palace.

CHAMBERLAIN: This way, sire. *(They walk about.)* Here is the River Palace, Your Majesty. Have a care as you ascend.

EMPEROR: *(acting the ascent and gazing at the heavens)* How lovely the skies are in the rich splendor of autumn:

śanaiḥ śānt'|ākūtāḥ
sita|jala|dhara|ccheda|pulināḥ
samantād ākīrṇāḥ
kala|virutibhiḥ sārasa|kulaiḥ
citāś citr'|ākārair
niśi vikaca|nakṣatra|kumudaiḥ
nabhastaḥ syandante
sarita iva dīrghā daśa diśaḥ.

3.20 api ca: apām udvṛttānāṃ
nijam upadiśantyā sthiti|padaṃ
dadhatyā śālīnām
avanatim udāre sati phale
mayūrāṇām ugraṃ
viṣam iva harantyā madam aho
kṛtaḥ kṛtsnasy' âyaṃ
vinaya iva lokasya śaradā.

imām api: bhartus tathā kaluṣitāṃ bahu|vallabhasya
mārge kathaṃ cid avatārya tanū|bhavantīm
sarv'|ātmanā rati|kathā|catur" êva dūtī
Gaṅgāṃ śaran nayati Sindhu|patiṃ prasannām.

(samantān nāṭyen' âvalokya) aye, katham a|pravṛtta|Kaumudī|mah"|ôtsavaṃ Kusumapuraṃ paśyāmi? ārya Vaihīnare, ath' âsmad|vacanād āghoṣitaḥ Kusumapure Kaumudī|mah"|ôtsavaḥ?

KAÑCUKĪ: deva, atha kim. āghoṣito devasy' ājñayā Kusumapure Kaumudī|mah"|ôtsavaḥ.

RĀJĀ: ārya, tat kiṃ na parigṛhītam asmad|vacanaṃ paura|janena?

Now they are calm, with sandbanks of scattered
cloud,
And strewn with flocks of softly calling cranes.
At night they fill with stars like blossoming water
lilies:
The skies are like rivers flowing away into the
distance.

The rains are gone, and autumn corrects the world, 3.20
Teaching the swollen waters their proper limits,
Making the rice bow down in its time of richness,
Drawing from peacocks like venom their fierce
passion.

Though Ganga was swollen with rage at her
faithless spouse,
Autumn has brought her back to her true self,
And like a go-between skilled in love's adventures
Has led her sweet and calm to her lord the Ocean.

(looking all around) What is this? Is the city not celebrating the Full Moon Festival? Vaihínari, was my proclamation of a holiday made known in the city?

CHAMBERLAIN: Assuredly, sire. On Your Majesty's orders a Full Moon Festival was proclaimed in Pátali·putra.

EMPEROR: Then, have the citizens rejected my orders, sir?

3.25 KAÑCUKĪ: *(karṇau pidhāya)* deva, śāntaṃ pāpam! a|skhalita|pūrvaṃ pṛthivyāṃ devasya śāsanaṃ, kathaṃ paureṣu skhalitum arhati?

RĀJĀ: ārya Vaihīnare, yady evaṃ tat kim a|pravṛtta|Kaumudī|mah"|ôtsavam ady' âpi Kusumapuraṃ paśyāmi? paśya:

dhūrtair anvīyamānāḥ
sphuṭa|catura|kathā|kovidair veśa|nāryo
n' âlaṃkurvanti rathyāḥ
pṛthu|jaghana|bhar'|ākrānti|mandaiḥ prayātaiḥ
anyonyaṃ spardhamānā
na ca gṛha|vibhavaiḥ svāmino mukta|śaṅkāḥ
sākaṃ strībhir bhajante
vidhim abhilaṣitaṃ pārvaṇaṃ paura|mukhyāḥ.

KAÑCUKĪ: deva, evam etat. . .

RĀJĀ: kim etat?

3.30 KAÑCUKĪ: āṃ idaṃ.

RĀJĀ: ārya, sphuṭam abhidhīyatām.

KAÑCUKĪ: deva, pratiṣiddhaḥ Kaumudī|mah"|ôtsavaḥ.

RĀJĀ: *(sa|krodham)* āḥ! kena?

KAÑCUKĪ: n' âtaḥ param asmābhir devo vijñāpayituṃ śakyate.

3.35 RĀJĀ: na khalv āryeṇa Cāṇakyen' âpahṛtaḥ prekṣakāṇām atiśaya|ramaṇīyaś cakṣuṣo viṣayaḥ.

KAÑCUKĪ: deva, jīvitu|kāmaḥ ko 'nyo devasya śāsanam ullaṅghayiṣyati?

CHAMBERLAIN: *(stopping his ears)* Perish the thought, sire! 3.25
Till now Your Majesty's command has prevailed throughout the earth: could it fail among your own citizens?

EMPEROR: In that case, sir, why do I see even now no sign of holiday-making in the city?

> The streets are not thronged with harlots,
> broad-hipped and walking slow,
> Pursued by rakes that flirt and joke with them.
> Nor have the solider citizens, vying with each other
> in the splendor of their houses,
> Put aside cares to enjoy with their wives the
> longed-for holiday.

CHAMBERLAIN: The fact is, sire...

EMPEROR: Is what?

CHAMBERLAIN: It's this. 3.30

EMPEROR: Speak out, sir.

CHAMBERLAIN: The Full Moon Festival has been canceled, Your Majesty.

EMPEROR: *(angrily)* What! By whom?

CHAMBERLAIN: I can tell Your Majesty no more than that.

EMPEROR: Can the revered Kautílya have robbed us of this beautiful spectacle? 3.35

CHAMBERLAIN: Sire, who else who valued his life would dare transgress Your Majesty's orders?

RĀJĀ: Śoṇottare, upaveṣṭum icchāmi.

PRATĪHĀRĪ: ⌜deva, edaṃ sīh'|āsaṇaṃ. uvavisadu devo.⌟

RĀJĀ: *(nāṭyen' ôpaviṣya)* ārya Vaihīnare, ārya|Cāṇakyaṃ draṣṭum icchami.

3.40 KAÑCUKĪ: yad ājñāpayati devaḥ. *(iti niṣkrāntaḥ.)*

tataḥ praviśati kop'|ânuviddhāṃ cintāṃ nāṭayan sva|bhavana|gataḥ kṛt'|āsana|parigrahaś CĀṆAKYAḤ.

CĀṆAKYAḤ: *(ātma|gatam)* kathaṃ spardhate mayā saha durātmā Rākṣasa|hatakaḥ? kutaḥ:

«kṛt'|āgāḥ Kauṭilyo
bhujaga iva niryāya nagarād
yathā Nandaṃ hatvā
nṛpatim akaron Maurya|Vṛṣalam
tath" âhaṃ Maury'|êndoḥ
śriyam apaharām' îti» kṛta|dhīḥ
prabhāvaṃ mad|buddher
atiśayitum eṣa vyavasitaḥ.

(pratyakṣavad ākāśe lakṣyaṃ baddhvā) Rākṣasa Rākṣasa, viramyatām asmād durvyavasitāt.

3.45 utsiktaḥ ku|saciva|dṛṣṭa|rājya|tantro
Nando 'sau na bhavati Candragupta eṣaḥ
Cāṇakyas tvam api na c' âiva kevalaṃ te
sādharmyaṃ mad|anukṛteḥ pradhāna|vairam.

(vicintya) atha|vā n' âtimātram asmin vastuni mayā manaḥ khedayitavyam. kutaḥ:

EMPEROR: Shonóttara, a seat.

FEMALE GUARD: Here is the throne, sire: be seated.

EMPEROR: *(sitting)* Vaihínari, I wish to see the revered Kautílya.

CHAMBERLAIN: Yes, Your Majesty. *(He goes out.)* 3.40

Enter in angry thought, seated and in his house, KAUTÍLYA.

KAUTÍLYA: *(to himself)* Does the wretched Rákshasa dare fight me?

He thinks that, as Kautílya left the city like a wounded snake,
Then slew the Nandas and made the Mauryan king,
He in his turn can dim the light of this Mauryan moon—
He is determined to be cleverer than I!

(gazing into the air as if he could see him) Rákshasa, Rákshasa, give up this obstinate attempt.

Chandra·gupta is no Nanda, 3.45
Ruling arrogantly with the aid of incompetent ministers,
And you are no Kautílya—the comparison holds
In one point alone, in our hatred of the ruler.

(on reflection) But I need not be too concerned.

mad|bhṛtyaiḥ kila nāma Parvata|suto
vyāptaḥ pradiṣṭ'|ântaraiḥ
udyuktāḥ sva|niyoga|sādhana|vidhau
Siddhārthak'|ādyāḥ spaśāḥ
kṛtvā saṃprati kaitavena kalahaṃ
Maury'|êndunā Rākṣasaṃ
bhetsyāmi sva|matena bheda|kuśalo
deva|pratīpaṃ dviṣaḥ.

praviśya KAÑCUKĪ: kaṣṭā khalu sevā nāma. kutaḥ:

bhetavyaṃ nṛpates tataḥ sacivato
rājñas tato vallabhād
anyebhyaś ca bhavanti ye 'sya bhavane
labdha|prasādā viṭāḥ
dainyād unmukha|darśan'|ôpalapanaiḥ
piṇḍ'|ârtham āyasyataḥ
sevāṃ lāghava|kāriṇīṃ kṛta|dhiyaḥ
sthāne ‹śva|vṛttiṃ› viduḥ.

3.50 *(parikramy' âvalokya ca)* idam ārya|Cāṇakyasya gṛham. yāvat praviśāmi. *(nāṭyena praviśy' âvalokya ca)* aho rāj'|âdhirāja|mantriṇo gṛha|vibhūtiḥ! kutaḥ:

upala|śakalam etad bhedakaṃ gomayānāṃ
vaṭubhir upahṛtānāṃ barhiṣāṃ stūpam etat
śaraṇam api samidbhiḥ śuṣyamāṇābhir ābhiḥ
vinamita|paṭal'|āntaṃ dṛśyate jīrṇa|kuḍyam.

tataḥ sthāne 'sya Vṛṣalo devaś Candraguptaḥ. kutaḥ:

My agents are all about Párvataka's son, and waiting for their chance;
Siddhárthaka and other spies are working keenly at their tasks.
Now I shall feign a quarrel with the King, and use my talents
To split off his opponent from mine.

Enter the CHAMBERLAIN*:* It is hard to be in service!

One has the King to fear, his ministers, his favorites,
And all the court parasites that have chanced to catch his ear.
The obsequious fawning, the struggling for scraps—
"A dog's life" is just the name for such degrading service.

(walking about and looking) Here is the revered Kautílya's 3.50
house. I'll go in. *(entering and looking)* Why, this man, minister of the King of Kings, lives in extraordinary luxury!—

Here is a piece of stone for breaking cow dung,
Here is a heap of grass collected by his pupils for the sacrifice.
And the house itself, I can see, is broken-walled,
For the drying firewood makes the gables sag.

No wonder that His Majesty Chandra·gupta is simply "Vríshala" to him.

stuvanty a|śrānt'|āsyāḥ
kṣiti|patim abhūtair api guṇaiḥ
pravācaḥ kārpaṇyād
yad avitatha|vāco 'pi kṛtinaḥ
prabhāvas tṛṣṇāyāḥ
sa khalu sakalaḥ syād itarathā
nirīhāṇām īśas
tṛṇam iva tiraskāra|viṣayaḥ.

(vilokya sabhayam) aye, tad ayam amātyaś Cāṇakyas tiṣṭhati. sa eṣaḥ:

3.55 yo Nanda|Maurya|nṛpayoḥ paribhūya lokam
ast'|ôdayāv upadiśann avibhinna|kālam
paryāya|pātita|him'|ôṣṇam a|sarva|gāmi
dhāmn" âtiśāyayati dhāma sahasra|dhāmnaḥ.

(jānubhyāṃ bhūmau nipatya) jayatu jayatv āryaḥ.

CĀṆAKYAḤ: *(nāṭyen' âvalokya)* Vaihīnare, kim āgamana|prayojanam?

KAÑCUKĪ: ārya, praṇati|saṃbhrama|calita|bhūmi|pāla|mauli|maṇi|śikhā|piśaṅgī|kṛta|pāda|padma|yugalaḥ pādayor āryaṃ praṇipatya devaś Candragupto vijñāpayati: «a|kṛta|kriy"|ântarāyam āryaṃ draṣṭum icchām' îti.»

CĀṆAKYAḤ: Vṛṣalo māṃ draṣṭum icchati? Vaihīnare, na khalu Vṛṣalasya śravaṇa|patham upagato 'yaṃ mayā kṛtaḥ Kaumudī|mah"|ôtsava|pratiṣedhaḥ?

3.60 KAÑCUKĪ: ārya, atha kim.

When even honest, clever men, ignobly eloquent,
Praise a king for nonexistent virtues till their jaws
break,
It shows what power greed has—for otherwise
In their indifference they would treat him as a wisp
of straw.

(looking, in awe) Oh, here he is, Kautílya—

Who vanquished the world, and ordained with no pause between 3.55
The setting of Nanda and the rise of the Mauryan
king.
His splendor outshines the splendor of the shining
sun,
Which must shift its realm and vary heat with cold.

(falling on his knees to the ground) Victory to Your Honor!

KAUTÍLYA: *(seeing him)* Vaihínari, what brings you here?

CHAMBERLAIN: Sir, His Majesty the Emperor Chandra·gupta, whose feet are dappled by the light of jewels in the crowns of princes that bow down in homage to him, worships at Your Honor's feet and begs to say that he would like to see you at the earliest moment convenient to yourself.

KAUTÍLYA: Vríshala wants to see me? Can it be, Vaihínari, that my cancellation of the Full Moon Festival has come to his ears?

CHAMBERLAIN: It has, my lord. 3.60

CĀṆAKYAḤ: *(sa|krodham)* āḥ! kena kathitam?

KAÑCUKĪ: *(bhayaṃ nāṭayati)* prasīdatv āryaḥ. svayam eva Sugāṅga|prāsāda|gatena deven' âvalokitam a|pravṛtta|Kaumudī|mah"|ôtsavaṃ Kusumapuraṃ.

CĀṆAKYAḤ: āṃ jñātam. duṣṭa, tato bhavadbhir eva mad|antareṇa protsāhya kopito Vṛṣalaḥ. kim anyat?

KAÑCUKĪ: *(sa|bhayaṃ tūṣṇīm adho|mukhas tiṣṭhati)*

3.65 CĀṆAKYAḤ: aho rāja|parijanasya Cāṇakyasy' ôpari pradveṣe pakṣa|pātaḥ! atha kva Vṛṣalas tiṣṭhati?

KAÑCUKĪ: ārya, Sugāṅga|prāsāda|gatena deven' âham āryasya pāda|mūlaṃ preṣitaḥ.

CĀṆAKYA: *(utthāya)* Sugāṅga|prāsāda|mārgam ādeśaya.

KAÑCUKĪ: ita ita ārya.

ubhau parikrāmataḥ.

3.70 KAÑCUKĪ: ayaṃ Sugāṅga|prāsādaḥ. śanaiḥ|śanair āroḍhum arhaty āryaḥ.

CĀṆAKYAḤ: *(nāṭyen' āruhy' âvalokya ca sa|harṣam ātma|gatam)* aye siṃh'|āsanam adhyāste Vṛṣalaḥ. sādhu sādhu.

Nandair vimuktam an|apekṣita|rāja|vṛttaiḥ
adhyāsitaṃ ca Vṛṣalena vṛṣeṇa rājñām
siṃh'|āsanaṃ sa|dṛṣa|pārthiva|sat|kṛtaṃ ca
prītiṃ trayas tri|guṇayanti guṇā mam' âite.

KAUTÍLYA: *(angrily)* Ha! Who told him?

CHAMBERLAIN: *(terrified)* May it please Your Honor, His Majesty observed for himself from the River Palace that Pátali·putra was not celebrating the Festival.

KAUTÍLYA: I see! Whereupon in my absence you inflamed Vríshala against me. Of course!

CHAMBERLAIN: *(stands in terrified silence with face bent down)*

KAUTÍLYA: How the Court loves to see Kautílya in disgrace! 3.65
Where is Vríshala?

CHAMBERLAIN: His Majesty was in the River Palace when he sent me to Your Honor.

KAUTÍLYA: *(rising)* Conduct me there.

CHAMBERLAIN: This way, my lord.

Both walk about.

CHAMBERLAIN: Here is the River Palace. Have a care, my 3.70
lord, as you ascend.

KAUTÍLYA: *(ascending and looking, with pleasure to himself)* Ah, Vríshala is seated on the throne! That is well.

> The throne is rid of Nandas, who took no thought
> of their duty,
> And occupied by Vríshala, Bull* of Kings.
> At last it is graced by a monarch worthy of it.
> This threefold good thrice multiplies my joy.

(upasṛtya) vijayatāṃ Vṛṣalaḥ.

RĀJĀ: *(āsanād utthāya* CĀṆAKYASYA *pādau gṛhītvā)* ārya, Candraguptaḥ praṇamati.

3.75 CĀṆAKYAḤ: *(pāṇau gṛhītvā)* uttiṣṭh' ôttiṣṭha, Vatsa.

ā Śail'|êndrāc chil"|ântaḥ|skhalita|Sura|dhunī|
  śīkar'|āsāra|śītād
ā tīrān n' âika|rāga|sphurita|maṇi|ruco
  dakṣiṇasy' ârṇavasya
āgaty' āgatya bhīti|praṇata|nṛpa|śataiḥ
  śaśvad eva kriyantāṃ
cūḍā|ratn'|âṃśu|garbhās tava caraṇa|yugasy'
  âṅgulī|randhra|bhāgāḥ.

RĀJĀ: ārya|prasādād anubhūyata ev' âitat. n' āśāsyate. upaviśatv āryaḥ.

ubhau yath"|āsanam upaviṣṭau.

CĀṆAKYAḤ: Vṛṣala, kim|artham vayam āhūtāḥ?

3.80 RĀJĀ: āryasya darśanen' ātmānam anugrahītum.

CĀṆAKYAḤ: *(smitaṃ kṛtvā)* Vṛṣala, alam anena praśrayeṇa. na niṣ|prayojanam adhikāravantaḥ prabhubhir āhūyante. tat prayojanam abhidhīyatām.

RĀJĀ: ārya, Kaumudī|mah"|ôtsava|pratiṣedhasya kiṃ phalam āryaḥ paśyati?

CĀṆAKYAḤ: *(smitaṃ kṛtvā)* Vṛṣala, upālabdhuṃ tarhi vayam āhūtāḥ.

RĀJĀ: ārya, n' ôpālabdhum.

(approaching) Victory to you, Vríshala.

EMPEROR: *(rising from his throne and clasping* KAUTÍLYA*'s feet)* Chandra·gupta salutes you, sir.

KAUTÍLYA: *(taking him by the hand)* Rise, dear child, rise. 3.75

From Himálaya, cooled by the Sacred River's spray,
To the shore of the southern ocean, lit by its jewels
of many flashing hues,
May awestruck princes come to do you homage in
their hundreds,
Forever bathing your feet in the jeweled radiance
of their crowns.

EMPEROR: By Your Honor's favor the wish is already granted. Let Your Honor be seated.

Both sit in their respective seats.

KAUTÍLYA: Why did you summon me, Vríshala?

EMPEROR: To favor myself with your sight. 3.80

KAUTÍLYA: *(smiling grimly)* Enough of these courtesies. Masters do not summon their stewards without a reason. Let me know the reason.

EMPEROR: What good does Your Honor see in canceling the Full Moon Festival?

KAUTÍLYA: *(again smiling grimly)* So, Vríshala, I have been summoned to be reprimanded!

EMPEROR: Not to be reprimanded, no.

CĀṆAKYAḤ: kiṃ tarhi?

RĀJĀ: vijñāpayitum.

CĀṆAKYAḤ: Vṛṣala, yady evaṃ tarhi vijñāpanīyānām avaśyaṃ śiṣyeṇa rucayo 'nuroddhavyāḥ.

RĀJĀ: ārya, kaḥ saṃdehaḥ? kiṃ tu «na kadā cid apy āryasya niṣ|prayojanā ruciḥ pravartiṣyata ity» asti naḥ praśnasy' âvakāśaḥ.

CĀṆAKYAḤ: Vṛṣala, samyag gṛhītavān asi. «na prayojanam an|apekṣamāṇaḥ svapne 'pi Cāṇakyaś ceṣṭata iti.»

RĀJĀ: ata eva māṃ prayojana|śuśrūṣā mukharayati.

CĀṆAKYAḤ: Vṛṣala, śrūyatām. iha khalv artha|śāstra|kārās tri|vidhāṃ siddhim upavarṇayanti tad yathā: «rāj'|āyattāṃ saciv'|āyattām ubhay'|āyattāṃ c' êti.» tat saciv'|āyatta|siddher bhavataḥ kiṃ prayojan'|ânveṣaṇena vāṅ|manasayoḥ khedam utpādayituṃ yato vayam ev' âtra niyuktā vartāmahe.

RĀJĀ: *(sa|kopa iva mukhaṃ parivartayati)*

tato nepathye VAITĀLIKAU *paṭhataḥ.*

EKAḤ:

ākāśaṃ kāśa|tūla|cchavim abhibhavatā
    bhasmanā śuklayantī
  śīt'|âṃśor aṃśu|jālair jala|dhara|malināṃ
    kliśnatī kṛttim aibhīm
 kāpālīm udvahantī srajam iva dhavalāṃ
    kaumudīm ity apūrvā
  hāsa|śrī|rāja|haṃsā haratu tanur iva
    kleśam Aiśī śarad vaḥ.

KAUTÍLYA: What, then?

EMPEROR: To be questioned politely.

KAUTÍLYA: In that case, Vríshala, the whims of those he must "question politely" are surely bound to be respected by a pupil?

EMPEROR: Of course they are, sir. But the fact that Your Honor's whim could never operate without a motive gives me some excuse for my question.

KAUTÍLYA: You understand well, Vríshala—even in dreams my actions are always motivated.

EMPEROR: And it is my wish to know your motive which makes me so persistent.

KAUTÍLYA: Listen, Vríshala. Textbooks on statecraft distinguish three types of government—monarchical, or ministerial, or monarchical and ministerial. You have a ministerial government—no need to tire your tongue and brain with searching after reasons: that is my job.

EMPEROR: *(hides away his face in a show of anger)*

Offstage, two BARDS *recite.*

FIRST BARD:

> As the sky is lit with an ash whiter than *kasha* down,
> And moonbeams banish the elephant gray of rain clouds,
> Dressed in bright moonlight like a garlanding of skulls,
> With a smile of geese in flight may autumn like Shiva ease your cares.

api ca: pratyagr'|ônmeṣa|mandā kṣaṇam an|abhimukhī
ratna|dīpa|prabhāṇām
ātma|vyāpāra|gurvī janita|jala|lavā
jṛmbhitaiḥ s'|âṅga|bhaṅgaiḥ
nāg'|âṅgaṃ moktum icchoḥ śayanam uru phaṇā|
cakravāl'|ôpadhānaṃ
nidrā|cched'|âbhitāmrā ciram avatu Harer
dṛṣṭir ākekarā vaḥ.

DVITĪYAḤ:

sattv'|ôtkarṣasya Dhātrā nidhaya iva kṛtāḥ
ke 'pi kasy' âpi hetoḥ
jetāraḥ svena dhāmnā mada|salila|mucāṃ
nāga|yūth'|ēśvarāṇām
daṃṣṭrā|bhaṅgaṃ mṛgāṇām adhipataya iva
vyaktamān'|âvalepāḥ
n' ājñā|bhaṅgaṃ sahante nṛ|vara nṛpatayas
tvādṛśāḥ sārva|bhaumāḥ.

api ca: bhūṣaṇ'|ādy|upabhogena
prabhur bhavati na prabhuḥ
parair a|paribhūt'|ājñas
tvam iva prabhur ucyate.

3.100 CĀṆAKYAḤ: *(ākarṇy' ātma/gatam)* prathamaṃ tāvad iṣṭa|devatā|rūpakeṇa pravṛtta|śarad|guṇa|prakhyāpanam āśīr|vacanam. idam aparaṃ kim iti n' âvadhārayāmi. *(vicintya)* āṃ jñātam. Rākṣasasy' âyaṃ prayogaḥ. durātman Rākṣasa, dṛśyase. jāgarti khalu Kauṭilyaḥ.

When in the first moment he screws his face against
the brightness of the jewel-lamps,
While body-racking yawns bring tears to his
languorous eyes,
And he makes to rise from his broad serpent's
couch, where his pillow is the serpent's hood,
May Vishnu's glance still dazed and red with sleep
be your salvation.

SECOND BARD:

Some men for some reason the Creator has filled
with his glory,
To outshine in power the rutting lords of the herd.
As is the breaking of his fang to the fierce pride of
the king of beasts,
So is the breaking of his command to a monarch
of the earth, great king, like you.

It is not luxury and pomp
That make a king a king.
It is when his orders are never disobeyed
That he has earned a title such as yours.

KAUTÍLYA: *(listening, to himself)* The earlier recitation was a blessing, and described the present season of autumn in terms of a particular god—but what is the point of the other? *(on reflection)* Ah, I see! This is Rákshasa's doing. Villain, you are detected! Kautílya is awake. 3.100

RĀJĀ: ārya Vaihīnare, dīyatām ābhyāṃ vaitālikābhyāṃ suvarṇa|śata|sahasram.

KAÑCUKĪ: yad ājñāpayati devaḥ. *(iti utthāya parikrāmati)*

CĀṆAKYAḤ: *(sa|krodham)* Vaihīnare, tiṣṭha tiṣṭha. na gantavyam. Vṛṣala, kim ayam a|sthāna eva mahān arth'|ôtsargaḥ kriyate?

RĀJĀ: āryeṇ' âivaṃ sarvato niruddha|ceṣṭā|prasarasya mama bandhanam iva rājyaṃ na rājyam iva.

3.105 CĀṆAKYAḤ: Vṛṣala, svayam an|abhiyuktānāṃ rājñām ete doṣā bhavanti. tad yadi na sahase tadā svayam ev' âbhiyujyasva.

RĀJĀ: ete sva|karmaṇy abhiyujyāmahe vayam.

CĀṆAKYAḤ: priyaṃ naḥ. vayam api sva|karmaṇy abhiyujyāmahe.

RĀJĀ: yady evaṃ tarhi Kaumudī|mah"|ôtsava|pratiṣedhasya phalaṃ śrotum icchāmi.

CĀṆAKYAḤ: Vṛṣala, Kaumudī|mah"|ôtsav'|ânuṣṭhānasya kiṃ prayojanam ity aham api śrotum icchāmi.

3.110 RĀJĀ: prathamaṃ tāvan mam' ājñ"|âvyāghātaḥ.

CĀṆAKYAḤ: Vṛṣala, mam' âpi khalu tvad|ājñā|vyāghāta eva Kaumudī|mah"|ôtsava|pratiṣedhasya prathamaṃ prayojanam. kutaḥ:

EMPEROR: Vaihínari, give these bards a hundred thousand gold pieces.

CHAMBERLAIN: Yes, Your Majesty. *(He gets up and moves away.)*

KAUTÍLYA: *(angrily)* One moment, Vaihínari, one moment—don't go. Vríshala, what is this ludicrous piece of extravagance?

EMPEROR: If you are going to thwart my every action like this, sir, it will make me feel more like a prisoner than a king.

KAUTÍLYA: A natural affliction for a king that does not see 3.105
to his own affairs. If you don't like it, do the job yourself.

EMPEROR: That is exactly what I am doing now.

KAUTÍLYA: Excellent! And I shall do my job.

EMPEROR: Then tell me why you should want to cancel the Full Moon Festival.

KAUTÍLYA: You just tell me why you should want to celebrate it.

EMPEROR: To see my command obeyed, for a start. 3.110

KAUTÍLYA: And for a start I want it canceled to see your command disobeyed—

ambho|dhīnāṃ tamāla|prabhava|kisalaya|
śyāma|velā|vanānām
ā pārebhyaś caturṇāṃ caṭula|timi|kula|
kṣobhit'|ântar|jalānām
māl" êv' âmlāna|puṣpā nata|nṛpati|śatair
uhyate yā śirobhiḥ
sā mayy eva skhalantī prathayati vinay'|â-
laṃkṛtaṃ te prabhutvam.

RĀJĀ: ath' âparam api prayojanaṃ śrotum icchāmi.

CĀṆAKYAḤ: tad api kathayāmi.

3.115 RĀJĀ: kathyatām.

CĀṆAKYAḤ: Śoṇottare, mad|vacanāt kāyastham Acalaṃ brūhi: «yat tad Bhadrabhaṭa|prabhṛtīnāṃ lekhya|pattraṃ tat tāvad dīyatām iti.»

PRATĪHĀRĪ: ⌜jaṃ ajjo āṇavedi.⌟ *(iti niṣkramya punaḥ praviśya)* ⌜ajja, edaṃ pattaṃ.⌟

CĀṆAKYAḤ: *(gṛhītvā)* Vṛṣala, śrūyatām.

RĀJĀ: datt'|âvadhāno 'smi.

3.120 CĀṆAKYAḤ: *(vācayati)* «sugṛhīta|nāmadheyasya devasya Candraguptasya sah'|ôtthāyināṃ pradhāna|puruṣāṇām ito 'pakramya Malayaketum āśritānāṃ parimāṇa|lekhya|pattram. atra prathamaṃ tāvat gaj'|âdhyakṣo Bhadrabhaṭaḥ; aśv'|âdhyakṣaḥ Puruṣadattaḥ; mahā|pratīhārasya Candrabhānor bhāgineyo Hiṅgurātaḥ; devasya sva|jana|gandhir mahā|rāja|Balaguptaḥ; devasy' âiva kumāra|sevako

As far as the ocean's edge where the jungle is dark
with flowering blackwood
And the waters teem with darting whale,
Your command is worn like an ever-blooming
garland by countless princes:
That it cannot encompass me gives a becoming
modesty to your kingship.

EMPEROR: And what other reason have you?

KAUTÍLYA: I will tell you.

EMPEROR: Do so. 3.115

KAUTÍLYA: Shonóttara, tell Áchala the letter-writer that I should like to have that list of Bhadra·bhata and the others.

FEMALE GUARD: Yes, Your Honor. *(going out and returning)* Here is the list, Your Honor.

KAUTÍLYA: *(taking it)* Hear this, Vríshala.

EMPEROR: I am listening.

KAUTÍLYA: *(reads out)* "A list of eminent associates of His 3.120
Majesty the Emperor Chandra·gupta who have defected to Málaya·ketu:

(1) Bhadra·bhata, superintendent of elephants
(2) Púrusha·datta, superintendent of horse
(3) Hingu·rata, nephew of Chandra·bhanu, the Chief Equerry
(4) Prince Bala·gupta, His Majesty's connection by marriage
(5) Raja·sena, His Majesty's own former tutor
(6) Bhaguráyana, younger brother of General Símhala

Rājasenaḥ; senā|pateḥ Siṃhalasya kanīyān bhrātā Bhāgurāyaṇaḥ; Mālava|rāja|putro Rohitākṣaḥ; kṣatra|gaṇa|mukhyo Vijayavarm" êti.» etāvad etat pattram.

RĀJĀ: ārya, eteṣām aparāga|hetuṃ śrotum icchāmi.

CĀṆAKYAḤ: Vṛṣala, śrūyatām. atra yāv etau gaj'|âdhyakṣ'|âśv'|âdhyakṣau Bhadrabhaṭa|Puruṣadatta|nāmanāv etau khalu strī|madya|mṛgayā|śīlau hasty|aśv'|âvekṣaṇe 'n|abhiyuktāv ity adhikārābhyām avaropya mayā sva|jīvana|mātra eva sthāpitāv ity aparaktau svena sven' âdhikāreṇa Malayaketum āśritau.

yāv etau Hiṅgurāta|Balaguptau tāv apy atyanta|lobh'|âbhibhūtau tvad|dattaṃ jīvanam a|bahu manyamānau tatra bahu labhyata iti Malayaketum āśritau.

yo 'py asau bhavataḥ kumāra|sevako Rājasenaḥ so 'pi tava prasādād atiprabhūta|koṣa|hasty|aśvaṃ sahas" âiva su|mahad aiśvaryam avāpya punar|uccheda|śaṅkay" âpakramya Malayaketum āśritaḥ.

3.125 yo 'yam aparaḥ senā|pateḥ Siṃhalasya kanīyān bhrātā Bhāgurāyaṇo 'sāv api tatra kāle Parvatakena saha samutpanna|sauhārdas tat|prītyā ca «pitā te Cāṇakyeṇa ghātita ity» utpādya Malayaketum apavāhitavān. tato bhavad|a|pathya|kāriṣu Candanadāsa|pramukheṣu nigṛhyamāṇeṣu sva|doṣ'|āśaṅkay" âpakramya Malayaketum ev' āśritaḥ. ten' âpy asau «mam' ânena prāṇāḥ parirakṣitā iti» kṛta|jñatām anuvartamānena paitṛkaṃ ca paricayaṃ jñātv" ātmano 'nantaram amātya|padam āropitaḥ.

(7) Rohitáksha, son of the King of Malwa
(8) Víjaya·varman, head of a warrior family."

EMPEROR: I should like to know their reasons for defection.

KAUTÍLYA: Then listen: Bhadra·bhata and Púrusha·datta, the superintendent of elephant and horse, were given over to women, drinking and hunting, neglected their duties and accordingly were removed from their posts by me and put on subsistence pay. In their indignation they have now defected to Málaya·ketu, each to serve in his own capacity.

As for Hingu·rata and Bala·gupta, being excessively greedy they were dissatisfied with the pay they got from you and defected to Málaya·ketu in the expectation of greater rewards.

Your old tutor Raja·sena by your favor found himself in sudden possession of vast resources of money, elephants and horses. He defected for fear of being deprived of this wealth with equal abruptness.

General Símhala's younger brother Bhaguráyana was very close to King Párvataka, and on the strength of this he told Málaya·ketu some tale of my being responsible for his father's death, and got him away from the city. Later, when other malefactors such as Chándana·dasa were being arrested for treason against you, the guilty knowledge of his own offense led him to defect to Málaya·ketu, who, in gratitude to him for saving his life and in memory of his friendship with his father, has admitted him to his closest personal counsels. 3.125

yāv etau Rohitākṣa|Vijayavarmāṇau tāv apy atyanta|mānitvāt sva|dāy'|ādebhyas tvayā dīyamānaṃ samānam a|sahamānau Malayaketum āśritau. ity eteṣām aparāga|hetavaḥ.

RĀJĀ: ārya, evam eteṣu parijñāt'|âparāga|hetuṣv api kṣipram eva kasmān na prativihitam āryeṇa?

CĀṆAKYAḤ: Vṛṣala, na pāritaṃ pravidhātum.

RĀJĀ: kim a|kauśalād uta prayojan'|âpekṣay" âiva vā?

3.130 CĀṆAKYAḤ: katham a|kauśalaṃ bhaviṣyati? niyataṃ prayojan'|âpekṣayā.

RĀJĀ: prayojanam a|pratividhānasy' êdānīṃ śrotum icchāmi.

CĀṆAKYAḤ: Vṛṣala, śrūyatām avadhāryatāṃ ca.

RĀJĀ: ubhayam api kriyate. kathyatām.

CĀṆAKYAḤ: Vṛṣala, nanv ih' âparaktānāṃ prakṛtīnāṃ dvi|vidhaṃ pratividhānaṃ tad yath" ânugraho nigrahaś c' êti. anugrahas tāvat. ākṣipt'|âdhikārayor Bhadrabhaṭa|Puruṣadattayoḥ punar adhikār'|āropaṇam eva. adhikāraś ca tādṛśeṣu vyasana|doṣād an|abhiyukteṣu punar āropyamāṇaḥ sakalam eva rājyasya mūlaṃ hasty|aśvam avasādayati. Hiṅgurāta|Balaguptayor atyanta|lubdha|prakṛtyoḥ sakala|rājya|pradānen' âpy a|parituṣyator anugrahaḥ kathaṃ kartuṃ śakyate? Rājasena|Bhāgurāyaṇayos tu dhana|prāṇa|nāśa|bhītayoḥ kuto 'nugrahasy' âvakāśaḥ?

Finally, Rohitáksha and Víjaya·varman defected because in their vanity they could not bear your awarding equal shares to their kinsmen. Those were the motives for the various defections.

EMPEROR: Why, sir, did you not take action against them at once, knowing those motives?

KAUTÍLYA: I could not, Vríshala.

EMPEROR: You mean you lacked the skill, or you had some reason?

KAUTÍLYA: How could I lack the skill? I had a reason, of course. 3.130

EMPEROR: Then I should like to hear what this reason can have been for your failing to take action.

KAUTÍLYA: Hear what I have to say, my child, and mark it well.

EMPEROR: I am doing both. Continue.

KAUTÍLYA: There are two kinds of action, Vríshala, that one can take against subjects with a grievance—reward them, or punish them. We will take reward first. In the case of Bhadra·bhata and Púrusha·datta, dismissed from their posts, this would have meant reinstating them. And to reinstate men whom their vices have made so incompetent would be to strike at the very foundations of government, our forces of elephant and horse. Rewarding Hingu·rata or Bala·gupta was an impossibility—they were so greedy that giving them the whole empire would not have satisfied them. Rewarding Raja·sena or Bhaguráyana would have been an irrelevance: they were afraid, one

Rohitākṣa|Vijayavarmaṇor api dāyāda|samāna|dāna|pīḍitayor atyanta|māninor anugrahaḥ kīdṛśaḥ prītiṃ janayiṣyat' îti parihṛtaḥ pūrvaḥ pakṣaḥ.

3.135 uttaro 'pi khalu vayam acirād adhigata|Nand'|āiśvaryāḥ sah'|ôtthāyinaṃ pradhāna|puruṣa|vargam ugreṇa daṇḍena pīḍayanto Nanda|kul'|ânuraktānāṃ prakṛtīnām a|viśvāsyā mā bhūm' êty ataḥ parihṛta eva. evam upagṛhīt'|âsmad|bhṛtya|pakṣo Rākṣas'|ôpadeśa|pravaṇo mahīyasā mleccha|rāja|balena parivṛtaḥ pitṛ|vadh'|āmarṣitaḥ Parvataka|putro Malayaketur asmān abhiyoktum udyataḥ. «so 'yaṃ vyāyāma|kālo n' ôtsava|kāla iti.» «ato durga|saṃskāra ārabdhavye kiṃ Kaumudī|mah"|ôtsaven' êti» pratiṣiddhaḥ.

RĀJĀ: ārya, bahu praṣṭavyam atra.

CĀṆAKYAḤ: Vṛṣala, viśrabdhaṃ pṛccha. may" âpi bahv ākhyeyam atra.

RĀJĀ: eṣa pṛcchāmi.

CĀṆAKYAḤ: aham apy eṣa kathayāmi.

3.140 RĀJĀ: yo 'sya sarvasy' âiv' ân|arthasya hetur Malayaketuḥ sa āryeṇ' âpakrāman kasmād upekṣitaḥ?

CĀṆAKYAḤ: Vṛṣala Malayaketāv an|upekṣit'|âpakramaṇe dvayī gatiḥ syāt: nigṛhyeta vā pūrva|pratiśrutaṃ rājy'|ârdhaṃ vā pratipādyeta. nigrahe tāvad asya Parvatako

of losing his wealth, the other of losing his life. And if Rohitáksha and Víjaya·varman were so vain that having the same share as their kinsmen vexed them, what reward would have been big enough to give them positive pleasure? So the former alternative was ruled out.

But so was the latter. If we who have just taken over power 3.135
from the Nandas start severely punishing our own most prominent supporters, how could we avoid losing the confidence of citizens who previously supported the House of Nanda? Thus Málaya·ketu has acquired these former servants of ours. He lends an ear to Rákshasa's schemes. He has the large forces of the barbarian chieftains to support him. He is incensed at his father Párvataka's murder. And he is poised to attack us. This is a time for work, not play. What place has a Full Moon Festival, when we should be looking to our defenses? There you have the reason that I canceled it.

EMPEROR: There is much, sir, to question in this.

KAUTÍLYA: Question away, Vríshala. I have much to reply.

EMPEROR: Then I will ask.

KAUTÍLYA: And I will answer.

EMPEROR: Málaya·ketu, the cause of all the trouble—why 3.140
did you let him get away?

KAUTÍLYA: If I had not let him get away, Vríshala, I could have done one of two things: suppress him, or give him half the empire as promised. By suppressing him we would have put our signatures to a confession that we treacherously murdered Párvataka. By giving him half

'smābhir vyāpādita iti kṛta|ghnatāyāḥ svayaṃ hasto dattaḥ syāt. pratiśruta|rājy'|ârdha|pradānen' âpi Parvataka|vināśaḥ kevalaṃ kṛta|ghnatā|mātra|phalaṃ syād iti Malayaketur apakrāmann upekṣitaḥ.

RĀJĀ: ārya, astu tāvad evam. Rākṣasas tu punar ih' âiv' ântar|nagare vartamāna āryeṇ' âpekṣita ity atra kim uttaram āryasya?

CĀṆAKYAḤ: Vṛṣala, Rākṣaso 'pi khalu svāmini sthir'|ânurāgitvāt suciram ekatra saṃvāsāc ca śīla|jñānāṃ Nand'|ânuraktānāṃ prakṛtīnām atyanta|viśvāsyaḥ prajñā|puruṣakārābhyām upetaḥ sahāya|saṃpadā yuktaḥ koṣavān ih' âiv' ântar|nagare vartamānaḥ khalu mahāntam antaḥ|kopam utpādayet. dūrī|kṛtas tu bāhya|kopam utpādayann api na duḥkha|sādhyo bhaviṣyat' îty ato 'pakrāmann upekṣitaḥ.

RĀJĀ: tat kim artham atra|stha ev' ôpāyair n' ôpakrāntaḥ?

3.145 CĀṆAKYAḤ: atha katham an|upakrānto bhaviṣyati? nan' ûpāyair ev' âsau hṛdaye|śayaḥ śaṅkur iv' ôddhṛtya dūrī|kṛtaḥ.

RĀJĀ: ārya, kasmād vikramya na gṛhītaḥ?

CĀṆAKYAḤ: Vṛṣala, Rākṣasaḥ khalv asau vikramya gṛhyamāṇaḥ svayaṃ vā vinaśyed yuṣmad|balāni vā vināśayet. evaṃ saty ubhayath" âpi doṣaḥ. paśya:

the empire, we should have avoided the charge of treachery but gained nothing else. And that is why I let Málaya·ketu get away.

EMPEROR: Granted that is so, sir; but you also let Rákshasa himself go on living here right in the heart of the city. What answer have you to that?

KAUTÍLYA: Rákshasa had the full confidence of the citizens who supported Nanda: they knew his character through his steadfast devotion to his master and through his staying with them for so long. He had brains and courage, a wealth of allies, plenty of money. If he had gone on living here he would have stirred up a lot of internal disorder. But if removed to a distance, though he might stir up external disorders, he would not be difficult to deal with. These were my reasons for letting him escape.

EMPEROR: Why did you not find means to defeat him while he was still here?

KAUTÍLYA: Isn't that what I did? I found the means to 3.145
pluck him out like a rankling dart and remove him to a distance—and I've already told you why he had to be removed.

EMPEROR: But why not have seized him by force?

KAUTÍLYA: Vríshala, you are speaking of Rákshasa. If he had been seized by force, either he would have died himself or he would have destroyed your forces. Either way it would have been a misfortune.

sa hi bhṛśam abhiyukto yady upeyād vināśaṃ
nanu Vṛṣala viyuktas tādṛśen' âsi puṃsā
atha tava bala|mukhyān nāśayet s" âpi pīḍā
vana|gaja iva tasmāt so 'bhyupāyair vineyaḥ.

RĀJĀ: na śaknumo vayam āryasya vācā vācam atiśayitum. sarvath" âmātya|Rākṣasa eva praśasyataraḥ.

3.150 CĀṆAKYAḤ: *(sa/krodham)* «na bhavān iti» vākya|śeṣaḥ. mā tāvat! bho Vṛṣala, tena kiṃ kṛtam?

RĀJĀ: yadi na jñāyate tadā śrūyatām. tena khalu mah"|ātmanā:

labdhāyāṃ puri yāvad iccham uṣitaṃ
kṛtvā padaṃ no gale
vyāghāto jaya|ghoṣaṇ'|ādiṣu balād
asmad|balānāṃ kṛtaḥ
atyarthaṃ vipulaiś ca nīti|vibhavaiḥ
saṃmoham āpāditāḥ
viśvāsyeṣv api viśvasanti matayo
na sveṣu vargeṣu naḥ.

CĀṆAKYAḤ: *(vihasya)* Vṛṣala, etat kṛtaṃ Rākṣasena?

RĀJĀ: atha kim.

3.155 CĀṆAKYAḤ: Vṛṣala, mayā punar jñātaṃ: «Nandam iva bhavantam uddhṛtya bhavān iva bhū|tale Malayaketur adhirājyam āropita iti.»

RĀJĀ: anyen' âiv' êdam anuṣṭhitaṃ: kim atr' āryasya?

If such a competent minister had perished,
You, Vríshala, would have lost a great man.
If he had killed the flower of your forces, an equal blow.
He had, then, to be managed like a wild elephant, with cunning.

EMPEROR: I cannot defeat you in argument, sir, but at all events it is Minister Rákshasa whom one must admire.

KAUTÍLYA: *(angrily)* Rather than me, you mean? Never! Vrí- 3.150
shala, what has he done?

EMPEROR: I'll tell you, if you don't know. That great man:

When the city was taken, stayed as long as he liked, putting his foot on our neck;
He created resistance to our army—for instance in the victory proclamation;
And by a wealth of stratagems he has so bemused our wits
That we don't trust even our most loyal supporters.

KAUTÍLYA: *(with a laugh)* So, Vríshala, that is what Rákshasa has done?

EMPEROR: Yes.

KAUTÍLYA: I really thought he must have overthrown you 3.155
and crowned Málaya·ketu Emperor of the World, as I overthrew Nanda and crowned you.

EMPEROR: That was another's doing—what did it have to do with you?

CĀṆAKYAḤ: he mat|sarin!

āruhy' ārūḍha|kopa|sphuraṇa|viṣamit'|â-
gr'|âṅgulī|mukta|cūḍāṃ
loka|pratyakṣam ugrāṃ sakala|ripu|kul'|ôc-
cheda|dīrghāṃ pratijñām
ken' ânyen' âvaliptā nava|navati|śata|
dravya|koṭ"|īśvarās te
Nandāḥ paryāya|śūrāḥ paśava iva hatāḥ
paśyato Rākṣasasya?

api ca: gṛdhrair ābaddha|cakraṃ viyati valanayā
dīrgha|niṣkampa|pakṣaiḥ
dhūmair dhvast'|ârka|bhāsāṃ sa|ghanam iva diśāṃ
maṇḍalaṃ darśayantaḥ
Nandānāṃ nandayantaḥ pitṛ|vana|nilayān
prāṇinaḥ paśya caityāḥ
nirvānty ady' âpi n' âite sruta|vahala|vasā|
gandhino havya|vāhāḥ.

3.160 RĀJĀ: Nanda|kula|vidveṣiṇā Daiven' êdam anuṣṭhitam.

CĀṆAKYAḤ: Daivam a|vidvāṃsaḥ pramāṇayanti.

RĀJĀ: vidvāṃso 'py a|vikatthanā bhavanti.

CĀṆAKYAḤ: *(kopaṃ nāṭayan)* Vṛṣala, bhṛtyam iva mām āro-
ḍhum icchasi!

KAUTÍLYA: Oh, envious one!

Who was it loosed his topknot with fingers that shook with rage
And swore before the world the long and dreadful oath to kill the whole race of his foes?
Who took the proud Nandas, owners of wealth untold,
And slew them one by one like sacrificial beasts, under the very eyes of Rákshasa?

With a ring of vultures slowly wheeling in the sky above,
And smoke that kills the sunlight and clouds the heavens,
Look, the funeral fires still burn with a reek of melting fat,
Delighting the beasts that prowl in the Nandas' cemetery.

EMPEROR: That was the doing of Destiny that hated the Nandas. 3.160

KAUTÍLYA: The stupid always appeal to Destiny.

EMPEROR: While the wise are duly modest.

KAUTÍLYA: *(showing anger)* Vríshala, you want to degrade me to a servant!

śikhāṃ moktuṃ muktām
    api punar ayaṃ dhāvati karaḥ

3.165 *bhūmau pāda|prahāraṃ dattvā.*

pratijñām ārodhuṃ
    punar api calaty eṣa caraṇaḥ
  praṇāśān Nandānāṃ
    praśamam upayātaṃ tvam adhunā
parītaḥ kālena
    jvalayasi punaḥ kopa|dahanam.

RĀJĀ: *(s'|āvegaṃ sva|gatam)* aye, tat kathaṃ satyam ev' āryaḥ kupitaḥ? tathā hi:

saṃrambha|spandi|pakṣma|kṣarad|amala|jala|
    kṣālana|kṣāmay" âpi
  bhrū|bhaṅg'|ôdbhūta|dhūmaṃ jvalitam iva puraḥ
    piṅgayā netra|bhāsā
manye Rudrasya raudraṃ rasam abhinayatas
    Tāṇḍave saṃsmarantyā
  saṃjāt'|ôdagra|kampaṃ katham api dharayā
    dhāritaḥ pāda|ghātaḥ.

CĀṆAKYAḤ: *(kṛtaka|kopaṃ saṃhṛtya)* Vṛṣala Vṛṣala, alam uttar'|ôttareṇa. yady asmatto garīyān Rākṣaso 'vagamyate tad" âsmākam idaṃ śastraṃ tasmai dīyatām. *(iti śastram utsṛjy' ôtthāya ca pratyakṣavad ākāśe lakṣyaṃ baddhvā sva|gatam)* Rākṣasa Rākṣasa, eṣa eva bhavataḥ Kauṭilya|buddhi|vijigīṣor buddheḥ prakarṣaḥ.

This hand flies to loose my bound hair yet again.

Stamping the ground with his foot. 3.165

This foot runs to embrace my vow again.
My wrath was extinguished when the Nandas were destroyed,
But you, doomed fool, are kindling it again.

EMPEROR: *(in alarm, to himself)* What, can His Honor be genuinely angry?

Though tears of emotion from his quivering eyelids seek to quench it,
The tawny blaze of his eyes bursts into flame beneath his smoking brow.
And as if remembering Shiva in his Terror Dance,
The earth trembles violently and scarcely bears the stamping of his foot.

KAUTÍLYA: *(checking his show of anger)* Vríshala, enough of recriminations. If you respect Rákshasa more than me, here, let him have my sword of office. *(relinquishing his sword and rising; then to himself, gazing into the air as if he could see him)* Rákshasa, Rákshasa, so much for your superior wisdom, which you hope will defeat me!

3.170 «Cāṇakyataḥ skhalita|bhaktim ahaṃ sukhena
jeṣyāmi Mauryam iti» samprati yaḥ prayuktaḥ
bhedaḥ kil' âiṣa bhavatā sakalaḥ sa eva
saṃpatsyate śaṭha tav' âiva hi dūṣaṇāya.

iti niṣkrāntaś CĀṆAKYAḤ.

RĀJĀ: ārya Vaihīnare, «adya|prabhṛty an|ādṛtya Cāṇakyaṃ Candraguptaḥ svayam eva rāja|kāryāṇi kariṣyat' îti» gṛhīt'|ârthāḥ kriyantāṃ prakṛtayaḥ.

KAÑCUKĪ: *(sva|gatam)* kathaṃ nir|upapadam eva Cāṇakyo n' ārya|Cāṇakya iti. hanta, satyam eva hṛto 'dhikāraḥ. atha|vā na khalv atra vastuni devaṃ doṣeṇ' âvamantum arhāmi. kutaḥ:

sa doṣaḥ sacivasy' âiva
yad asat kurute nṛpaḥ
yāti yantuḥ pramādena
gajo vyālatva|vācyatām

3.175 RĀJĀ: ārya, kiṃ vicārayasi?

KAÑCUKĪ: deva, na kiṃ cid vicārayāmi. kiṃ tv etac cintayāmi: «diṣṭyā, deva, idānīṃ devaḥ saṃvṛtta iti.»

RĀJĀ: *(ātma|gatam)* evam asmāsu nigṛhyamāṇeṣu sva|kārya|siddhi|kāmaḥ sa|kāmo bhavatv āryaḥ. *(prakāśam)* Śoṇottare, anena śuṣka|kalahena śiro|vedanā māṃ bādhate. tac chayana|gṛham ādeśaya.

PRATĪHĀRĪ: ⌜edu edu devo.⌟

"When the Mauryan loses the loyalty of Kautílya," 3.170
You tell yourself, "I can beat him easily."
Well, here is the split between us that you planned,
But it will only redound to your own undoing.

He goes out.

EMPEROR: Vaihínari, let the people be told that from now on the Emperor will administer the affairs of state in person, without reference to Kautílya.

CHAMBERLAIN: *(to himself)* Plain "Kautílya," with no title of honor? Alas, he really has been dismissed. But in truth I cannot blame His Majesty for this.

It is the minister's fault
If the king acts ill,
As it is the driver's incompetence
That makes a rogue elephant.

EMPEROR: What is keeping you, sir? 3.175

CHAMBERLAIN: Nothing, Your Majesty. I was only thinking how glad I am that Your Majesty has now become a true king.

EMPEROR: *(to himself)* While they view me in this light, let His Honor achieve the success he wants. *(aloud)* This arid dispute has given me a headache, Shonóttara. Conduct me to my bedchamber.

FEMALE GUARD: This way, sire.

RĀJĀ: *(āsanād utthāya sva|gatam)*

3.180 ārySecret'|ājñay" âiva mama laṅghita|gauravasya
buddhiḥ praveṣṭum avaner vivaraṃ pravṛttā
ye satyam eva na guruṃ pratimānayanti
teṣāṃ kathaṃ nu hṛdayaṃ na bhinatti lajjā?

iti niṣkrāntāḥ sarve.

EMPEROR: *(rising from his throne, to himself)*

At his own bidding I have slighted my teacher, 3.180
And I feel that I want to sink into the ground.
When others commit such impiety in earnest
Why do their hearts not split in two with shame?

All go out.

ACT IV
DISSENSION

tataḥ praviśaty adhvaga|veśaḥ PURUṢAḤ.

PURUṢAḤ: ⌜hī māṇahe.⌟

⌜⌜joaṇa|saaṃ samahiaṃ
ko ṇāma ga'|āgaaṃ karejja jaṇo
a|ṭṭhāṇa|gamaṇa|garuī
pahuṇo āṇā jaï ṇa hojja.⌟

⌜tā jāva amacca|Rakkhasassa jjeva gehaṃ pavisāmi.⌟ *(pariśrāntavat parikramya)* ⌜edaṃ bhaṭṭiṇo amacca|Rakkhasassa gehaṃ. ko ettha dovāriāṇaṃ? ṇivededha dāva bhaṭṭiṇo amacca|Rakkhasassa: eso kkhu Karahao karahao via tuvaranto Pāḍaliuttādo āado tti.⌟

4.5 *praviśya* DAUVĀRIKAḤ: ⌜bhadda bhadda, mā uccaṃ mantehi. eso kkhu bhaṭṭā amacca|Rakkhaso kajja|cintā|jaṇideṇa jāareṇa samuppaṇṇa|sīsa|veaṇo ajja vi ṇa dāva saaṇa|dalaṃ muñcadi. tā ciṭṭha muhuttaaṃ jāva se laddh'|âvasaro bhavia bhavado āgamaṇaṃ ṇivedemi.⌟

PURUṢAḤ: ⌜bhadda|muha, jadhā de roadi.⌟

tataḥ praviśati śayana|gata āsana|gatena ŚAKAṬADĀSENA *saha sa|cinto* RĀKṢASAḤ.

RĀKṢASAḤ: *(ātma|gatam)*

mama vimṛśataḥ kāry'|ārambhe
Vidher a|vidheyatām
sahaja|kuṭilāṃ Kauṭilyasya
pracintayato matim
api ca vihite tat|kṛtyānāṃ
nikāmam upagrahe
«katham idam ih' êty» unnidrasya
prayānty aniśaṃ niśāḥ.

Enter someone dressed as a TRAVELER.

TRAVELER: Oh, heavens above!

> A thousand miles or more there and back!
> Who would ever make such journeys?—
> Except when his master's orders
> Mean more than the discomfort of travel.

So now I have to call on Minister Rákshasa. *(walking about wearily)* Here is my master the Minister Rákshasa's house. Ho there, doormen! Tell your master that Kárabhaka has come like a camel* from Pátali·putra!

Enter a DOORKEEPER*:* Hey, good sir, not so loud! Our master Minister Rákshasa has a headache brought on by overwork and insomnia, and he hasn't yet left his bed. Wait a minute while I pick the right moment to let him know you've come. 4.5

TRAVELER: Right you are, then.

Enter, in his bed with SHÁKATA·DASA *seated beside him,* RÁKSHASA, *careworn.*

RÁKSHASA: *(to himself)*

> When I think how little Fate has been my ally in
>   the struggle
> And how devious has been the plotting of
>   Kautílya,
> For all my successful winning of his subordinates,
> My nights pass in sleepless bewilderment.

4.10 api ca: kāry'|ôpakṣepam ādau tanum api racayaṃs
tasya vistāram icchan
bījānāṃ garbhitānāṃ phalam atigahanaṃ
gūḍham udbhedayaṃś ca
kurvan buddhyā vimarśaṃ prasṛtam api punaḥ
saṃharan kārya|jātaṃ
kartā vā nāṭakānām imam anubhavati
kleśam asmad|vidho vā.

tad api nāma durātmā Cāṇakya|vaṭuḥ—

(upasṛtya DAUVĀRIKAḤ:*)* ⌜jaadu jaadu—⌟

RĀKṢASAḤ: —abhisaṃdhātuṃ śakyaḥ syāt.

DAUVĀRIKAḤ: ⌜—amacco.⌟

4.15 RĀKṢASAḤ: *(vām'|âkṣi|spandaṃ sūcayitvā ātma|gatam)* Cāṇakya|vaṭur jayati. abhisaṃdhātuṃ śakyaḥ syād amātya iti. *(prakāśam)* bhadra, kim asi vaktu|kāmaḥ?

DAUVĀRIKAḤ: ⌜amacca, eso kkhu Karahao Pāḍaliuttādo āado icchadi amaccaṃ pekkhiduṃ.⌟

RĀKṢASAḤ: bhadra, a|vilambitaṃ praveśaya.

DAUVĀRIKAḤ: ⌜jaṃ amacco āṇavedi.⌟ *(iti niṣkramya puruṣam upasṛtya)* ⌜bhadda, eso amacco ciṭṭhadi. uvasappehi ṇaṃ.⌟

iti niṣkrānto DAUVĀRIKAḤ.

4.20 KARABHAKAḤ: *(*RĀKṢASAM *upasṛtya)* ⌜jaadu jaadu amacco.⌟

RĀKṢASAḤ: *(nāṭyen' âvalokya)* bhadra Karabhaka, sv|āgatam. upaviśyatām.

Contriving the first faint outlines of a plot, and then elaborating, 4.10
Causing the hidden seeds to germinate unsuspected,
Cleverly managing the crisis, drawing together all the sprawling threads—
In these painful anxieties of creation I am working like a playwright.

I pray, then, that Kautílya may know—

DOORKEEPER: *(approaching)* Victory—

RÁKSHASA: —the bitterness of defeat!

DOORKEEPER: —be yours, Minister!

RÁKSHASA: *(indicating an inauspicious throbbing of his left* 4.15 *eye, to himself)* Must Kautílya, then, know victory, and the bitterness of defeat be mine? *(aloud)* What do you want to tell me?

DOORKEEPER: Minister, Kárabhaka has arrived from Pátali·putra and is asking to see you.

RÁKSHASA: Show him in at once.

DOORKEEPER: Yes, sir. *(withdrawing and approaching the traveler)* There is the Minister, friend. You may approach him.

He goes out.

KÁRABHAKA: *(going up to* RÁKSHASA*)* Victory, sir, victory! 4.20

RÁKSHASA: *(seeing him)* Good Kárabhaka, welcome! Sit down.

KARABHAKAḤ: ⌜jaṃ amacco āṇavedi.⌟ *(iti bhūmāv upaviṣṭaḥ)*

RĀKṢASAḤ: *(sva|gatam)* atha «kasmin prayojane mam' âyaṃ praṇidhiḥ prahita iti» prabhūtatvāt prayojanānāṃ na khalv avadhārayāmi. *(cintāṃ nāṭayati)*

tataḥ praviśati vetra|pāṇir aparaḥ PURUṢAḤ

4.25 PURUṢAḤ: ⌜ośaladha ayyā ośaladha. avedha, māṇahe, avedha. kiṃ ṇa peskadha—⌟

⌜dūle paccā|śattī daṃśaṇam avi dullahaṃ a|dhaññehiṃ kallāṇa|maṇahalāṇaṃ devāṇa va bhūmi|devāṇaṃ.⌟

(ākāśe) ⌜ayyā, kiṃ bhaṇādha? kiṃ ṇimittaṃ eśā ośālaṇā kalīadi tti? ayyā, eśe kkhu kumāle Malaakedū śamuppaṇṇa|śīśa|veaṇaṃ amacca|Lahkaśaṃ śuṇia peskiduṃ ido yyeva āaścadi. tā ediṇā kālaṇeṇa ośālaṇā kalīadi.⌟ *(iti niṣkrāntaḥ* PURUṢAḤ*)*

tataḥ praviśati BHĀGURĀYAṆENA *saha* KAÑCUKIN' *ânugamyamāno* MALAYAKETUḤ.

MALAYAKETUḤ: *(niśvasy' ātma|gatam)* adya daśamo māsas tātasy' ôparatasya na c' asmābhir vṛthā|puruṣ'|âbhimānam udvahadbhis tam uddiśya toy'|âñjalir apy āvarjitaḥ. pratijñātam etat purastāt:

KÁRABHAKA: Yes, sir. *(He seats himself on the floor.)*

RÁKSHASA: *(to himself)* I have so many affairs on hand I can't remember what it was I sent this agent to do. *(He acts anxious thought.)*

Enter a MAN *bearing an official staff.*

MAN: Make way, sirs, make way! Be off, you people, be off! 4.25
Do you not realize—

Like the fair lords of the heavens,
The fair lords of this world
Are hard for those less fortunate
Even to see, let alone come near to.

(addressing the air) What's that you say, sirs? Why are we clearing the road? Sirs, His Highness Prince Málaya·ketu is coming this way, to see Minister Rákshasa, having heard that he has a headache. That's why we're clearing the road. *(He goes out.)*

Enter, with BHAGURÁYANA *and attended by his* CHAMBERLAIN, MÁLAYA·KETU.

MÁLAYA·KETU: *(with a sigh, to himself)* It's ten months now since father died, and in a vain act of manly pride I have not offered even a handful of water in his memory. I have sworn an oath that first:

4.30 vakṣas|tāḍana|bhinna|ratna|valayaṃ
bhraṣṭ'|ôttarīy'|âṃśukaṃ
«hā h" êty» uccarit'|ārta|nāda|karuṇaṃ
bhū|reṇu|rūkṣ'|âlakam
yādrṅ mātṛ|janasya śoka|janitaṃ
saṃpraty avasth"|ântaraṃ
śatru|strīṣu mayā vidhāya gurave
deyo jalasy' âñjaliḥ.

tat kiṃ bahunā?

udyacchatā dhuram a|kā|puruṣ'|ânurūpāṃ
gantavyam āji|vihitena pituḥ pathā vā
ācchidya vā sva|jananī|jana|locanebhyo
neyo mayā ripu|vadhū|nayanāni bāṣpaḥ.

(prakāśam) ārya Jājale, ucyantām asmad|vacanād anuyāyino rājānaḥ: «eka ev' âham amātya|Rākṣasasy' âtarkit'|āgamanena prītim utpādayitum icchāmi. ataḥ kṛtam anugamana|kleśen' êti.»

KAÑCUKĪ: yad ājñāpayati kumāraḥ. *(parikramy' ākāśe)* bho bho rājānaḥ, kumāraḥ samājñāpayati: «na khalv ahaṃ kena cid anugantavya iti.» *(vilokya sa|harṣam)* kumāra, ete kumārasy' ājñ"|ânantaram eva pratinivṛttāḥ sarva eva rājānaḥ. paśyatu hi kumāraḥ—

My enemies' wives shall beat their breasts till their bangles break and their garments fall apart, 4.30
Piteous in their cries of woe, dust roughening their hair,
And they shall know all the grief my mother knows
Before I make the offering of water to my sire.

In short,

I must bear the hero's yoke,
And either tread my father's fatal path in battle
Or snatch the tears from my mother's eyes
And put them in the eyes of the enemy's womenfolk.

(aloud) Noble Jájali, tell the princes in my name that I want to go on alone and give Minister Rákshasa the pleasure of a surprise visit. So they need not trouble to attend me.

CHAMBERLAIN: Yes, Your Highness. *(walking about and addressing the air)* Princes! His Highness states that he does not wish you to attend him! *(looking, with pleasure)* See, Your Highness: they have all turned back as soon as they learned of Your Highness's command—

4.35 s'|ôtsedhaiḥ skandha|deśaiḥ khara|kavika|kaś"|ā-
karṣaṇ'|âtyartha|bhugnaiḥ
aśvāḥ kaiś cin niruddhāḥ kham iva khura|puṭaiḥ
khaṇḍayantaḥ purastāt
ke cin mātaṅga|mukhyair vihata|javatayā
mūka|ghaṇṭair nivṛttāḥ
maryādāṃ bhūmi|pālā jala|dhaya iva te
deva n' ôllaṅghayanti.

MALAYAKETUḤ: ārya Jājale, tvam api sa|parijano nivartasva. Bhāgurāyaṇa ev' âiko mām anugacchatu.

KAÑCUKĪ: yad ājñāpayati kumāraḥ. *(iti sa|parijano niṣkrāntaḥ)*

MALAYAKETUḤ: sakhe Bhāgurāyaṇa, vijñāpito 'ham ih' āgacchadbhir Bhadrabhaṭa|prabhṛtibhir yathā «na vayam amātya|Rākṣasa|dvāreṇa kumāram āśrayāmahe. kiṃ tu kumārasya senā|patiṃ Śikharasenaṃ dvārī|kṛtya duṣṭ'|amātya|parigṛhītāc Candraguptād aparaktāḥ kumāram ābhigāmika|guṇa|yogād āśrayaṇīyam āśrayāmaha iti.» tan mayā su|ciram api vicārayatā teṣāṃ vāky'|ârtho n' âvadhāritaḥ.

BHĀGURĀYAṆAḤ: kumāra, n' âiv' âyaṃ durbodhaḥ. paśya. «vijigīṣur ātma|guṇa|saṃpannaḥ priya|hita|dvāreṇ' āśrayaṇīya iti» nanu nyāyyam ev' êdam.

Some, pulling hard on the reins, have checked their steeds, 4.35
Which rear with necks arched back, breaking thin air with their hoofs.
Others turn their stately elephants about, bells faltering into silence.
These princes respect your command as the sea respects the shore.

MÁLAYA·KETU: Noble Jájali, you too go back with my servants. No one but Bhagaráyana need attend me.

CHAMBERLAIN: Certainly, Your Highness. *(He goes out with the servants.)*

MÁLAYA·KETU: Bhaguráyana, my friend, when Bhadra·bhata and his companions arrived here, they said to me, "We are not seeking asylum with Your Highness through Minister Rákshasa: it was Your Highness's general Shíkhara·sena who, when we sickened of seeing Chandra·gupta in the clutches of an evil minister, enabled us to take refuge with Your Highness, as your amiable qualities had made us long to do." I have been turning their words over in my mind for a long time, but I can't decide what they were getting at.

BHAGURÁYANA: It is simple enough, Your Highness. It is natural, surely, to wish to turn to a master who is both determined and talented, and to do so through a dear and good friend of that master.

4.40 MALAYAKETUḤ: sakhe Bhāgurāyaṇa, nanv asmākam amātya|Rākṣasaḥ priyatamo hitatamaś ca.

BHĀGURĀYAṆAḤ: kumāra, evam etat. «kiṃ tu amātya|Rākṣasaś Cāṇakye baddha|vairo na Candragupte. tad yadi kadā cic Candraguptaś Cāṇakyam ati|jita|kāśinam a|sahamānaḥ sācivyād avaropayet tato Nanda|kula|bhaktyā ‹Nand'|ânvaya ev' âyam iti› saṃjāta|suhṛj|jan'|âpekṣayā c' âmātya|Rākṣasaś Candraguptena saha saṃdadhīta. Candragupto 'pi ‹pitṛ|paryāy'|āgata ev' âyam› ity aṅgī|kuryāt. evaṃ saty asmāsv api kumāro na viśvased» ity ayam eṣāṃ vāky'|ârthaḥ.

MALAYAKETUḤ: yujyate. amātya|Rākṣasasya gṛham ādeśaya.

BHĀGURĀYAṆAḤ: ita itaḥ kumāraḥ.

iti ubhau parikrāmataḥ.

4.45 BHĀGURĀYAṆAḤ: kumāra, idam amātya|Rākṣasasya gṛham. praviśatu kumāraḥ.

MALAYAKETUḤ: eṣa praviśāmi.

praveśanaṃ nāṭayataḥ.

RĀKṢASAḤ: āṃ smṛtam. *(prakāśam)* bhadra, api dṛṣṭas tvayā Kusumapure vaitālikaḥ Stanakalaśaḥ?

KARABHAKAḤ: ⌜amacca, adha iṃ.⌟

4.50 MALAYAKETUḤ: sakhe Bhāgurāyaṇa, Kusumapura|vṛtt'|ântaḥ prastutaḥ. tatas tāvan n' ôpasarpāvaḥ. śṛṇuvas tāvat. kiṃ kāraṇam iti.

MÁLAYA·KETU: But Bhaguráyana, Minister Rákshasa him- 4.40
self is the dearest and best of friends.

BHAGURÁYANA: No doubt, Your Highness. But their reasoning is as follows. Minister Rákshasa is fighting Kautílya, not Chandra·gupta. Suppose by some chance Chandra·gupta were to find Kautílya's arrogance impossible to bear, and were to dismiss him from his post. Out of his loyalty to the House of Nanda, since Chandra·gupta is after all of Nanda stock, or else for the sake of his friends in prison, Minister Rákshasa might come to terms with Chandra·gupta—who for his part might accept him, as being his minister by family tradition. Now, in such circumstances Your Highness might suspect their own loyalty as well.

MÁLAYA·KETU: Yes, I see what you mean. Lead the way to Minister Rákshasa's house.

BHAGURÁYANA: This way, Your Highness.

They both walk about.

BHAGURÁYANA: Here is the house. Enter, Your Highness. 4.45

MÁLAYA·KETU: I do so.

They act entering.

RÁKSHASA: Ah, I remember! *(aloud)* Did you see Stana·kálasha the bard in Pátali·putra, my dear man?

KÁRABHAKA: Certainly, sir.

MÁLAYA·KETU: Bhaguráyana, my friend, they are discussing 4.50
events in Pátali·putra. Let's not interrupt, but simply listen.

sattva|bhaṅga|bhayād rājñāṃ
kathayanty anyathā puraḥ
anyathā vivṛtt'|ârtheṣu
svair'|ālāpeṣu mantriṇaḥ.

BHĀGURĀYAṆAḤ: yad ājñāpayati kumāraḥ.

RĀKṢASAḤ: bhadra, api tat kāryaṃ siddham?

KARABHAKAḤ: ⌜amaccassa pasāeṇa siddham.⌟

4.55 MALAYAKETUḤ: Bhāgurāyaṇa, kiṃ tat kāryam?

BHĀGURĀYAṆAḤ: kumāra, gahanaḥ khalu saciva|vṛtt'|ântaḥ. n' âitāvatā paricchettuṃ śakyate. avahitas tāvac chrotum arhati kumāraḥ.

RĀKṢASAḤ: bhadra, vistareṇa śrotum icchāmi.

KARABHAKAḤ: ⌜suṇādu amacco. atthi dāva ahaṃ amacceṇ' āṇatto jadhā: «Karahaa, Kusumaüraṃ gacchia mama vaaṇeṇa bhaṇidavvo tae vedālio Thaṇaalaso jadhā Cāṇakka|hadaeṇa tesuṃ tesuṃ āṇā|bhaṅgesuṃ aṇuciṭṭhīamāṇesuṃ Candaütto tae samutteaṇa|samatthehiṃ siloehiṃ uvasiloaïdavvo tti.»⌟

RĀKṢASAḤ: bhadra, tatas tataḥ.

4.60 KARABHAKAḤ: ⌜tado mae Pāḍaliuttaṃ gacchia suṇāvido amacca|saṃdesaṃ thaṇa|alaso.⌟

RĀKṢASAḤ: bhadra, tatas tataḥ.

KARABHAKAḤ: ⌜etth' | antare Ṇanda | kula | viṇāsa | dūsidassa pora | jaṇassa paridosaṃ uppādaanteṇa Candaütteṇa āghosido Kusumaüre komudī|mah'|ûsavo. so a cira|āla|ppavattaṇa|jaṇida|paridoso ahimada|bandhu|aṇa|samāgamo via sa|sinehaṃ bahu|māṇido ṇāara|aṇeṇa.⌟

For fear of destroying his resolve
Ministers say one thing to a prince's face,
And quite another when they are speaking freely
And saying what they mean.

BHAGURÁYANA: By all means, Your Highness.

RÁKSHASA: Was your mission successful, my dear man?

KÁRABHAKA: Quite successful, if it pleases Your Honor.

MÁLAYA·KETU: What mission, Bhaguráyana? 4.55

BHAGURÁYANA: A minister's affairs are complicated, Your Highness. This is hardly enough to go on. Just listen attentively.

RÁKSHASA: Tell me in detail what happened.

KÁRABHAKA: You had instructed me, sir, to go to Pátali·putra and tell Stana·kálasha the bard in your name that when the accursed Kautílya infringed some command or other of the Emperor he should address inflammatory stanzas to the Emperor.

RÁKSHASA: Yes?

KÁRABHAKA: So I went to Pátali·putra and gave Stana·kála-sha your message, sir. 4.60

RÁKSHASA: Go on.

KÁRABHAKA: At this point, to dispel the gloom that the destruction of the House of Nanda has cast over the city, Chandra·gupta proclaimed that Pátali·putra should celebrate the Full Moon Festival. The return of this festival after so long an absence delighted the people and they greeted it as affectionately as a long-lost relative.

RĀKṢASAḤ: *(sa|bāṣpam)* hā deva Nanda!

Kaumudī kumud'|ānande
jagad|ānanda|hetunā
kīdṛśī sati candre 'pi
nṛpa|candra tvayā vinā?

4.65 bhadra, tatas tataḥ.

KARABHAKAḤ: ˹amacca, tado so loaṇ'|āṇanda|bhūdo aṇicchantassa jjeva ṇāara|aṇassa ṇivārido Cāṇakka|hadaeṇa komudī|mah'|ûsavo. etth'|antare Thaṇaalaseṇa paüttā Candaütta|samutteaṇa|samatthā siloa|parivāḍī.˼

RĀKṢASAḤ: *(sa|harṣam)* sādhu, sakhe Stanakalaśa, sādhu! kāle bheda|bījam uptam avaśyaṃ phalam upadarśayati. kutaḥ:

sadyaḥ krīḍā|rasa|cchedaṃ
prākṛto 'pi na marṣayet
kim u lok'|âdhikaṃ dhāma
bibhrāṇāḥ pṛthivī|bhujaḥ?

MALAYAKETUḤ: evam etat.

4.70 RĀKṢASAḤ: bhadra, tatas tataḥ.

KARABHAKAḤ: ˹tado Candaütteṇa āṇā|bhaṅga|kalusida|hiaeṇa su|iraṃ amacca|guṇaṃ pasaṃsia ṇibbhacchido ahiārādo Cāṇakka|hadao.˼

MALAYAKETUḤ: sakhe Bhāgurāyaṇa, guṇa|praśaṃsayā darśitaś Candraguptena Rākṣase bhakti|pakṣa|pātaḥ.

RÁKSHASA: *(weeping)* Alas, Nanda, my emperor!

> What Full Moon Festival can there be today
> Though the moon shine never so full?
> For it was you, great king,
> Who were the full moon of this world.

Go on, my dear fellow, go on. 4.65

KÁRABHAKA: Then this glorious spectacle was canceled by the accursed Kautílya against the Emperor's wishes. Upon which Stana·kálasha addressed two inflammatory stanzas to Chandra·gupta. *(He repeats the two stanzas of the* SECOND BARD *(Act 3.98 and 3.99).)*

RÁKSHASA: *(delightedly)* Bravo, Stana·kálasha, my friend! This seed of dissension so opportunely sown is sure to bear fruit:

> When his pleasure is rudely shattered,
> Even a common man will not endure it—
> What then of emperors, lords of the earth,
> Men of no common splendor?

MÁLAYA·KETU: He is right there.

RÁKSHASA: And what then? 4.70

KÁRABHAKA: Then Chandra·gupta, furious at being disobeyed, praised Your Honor's ability at some length and stripped Kautílya of his powers.

MÁLAYA·KETU: Friend Bhaguráyana, if he praised his ability, it shows that Chandra·gupta is sympathetic toward Rákshasa.

BHĀGURĀYAṆAḤ: kumāra, na tathā guṇa|praśaṃsayā yathā Cāṇakya|vaṭor nirākaraṇena.

RĀKṢASAḤ: bhadra, kim ayam ev' âikaḥ Kaumudī|mah"|ôtsava|pratiṣedhaś Candraguptasya Cāṇakyaṃ prati kopa|kāraṇam ut' ânyad apy asti?

4.75 MALAYAKETUḤ: sakhe Bhāgurāyaṇa, Candraguptasya kopa|kāraṇ'|ânveṣaṇe kiṃ phalam eṣa paśyati?

BHĀGURĀYAṆAḤ: kumāra, etat phalaṃ paśyati. matimāṃś Cāṇakyas tucche prayojane kim iti Candraguptaṃ kopayiṣyati? na ca kṛta|vedī Candragupta etāvatā gauravam ullaṅghayiṣyati. sarvathā Cāṇakya|Candraguptayoḥ puṣkalāt kāraṇād yo viśleṣa utpadyate sa ātyantiko bhavat' îti.

KARABHAKAḤ: ⌜amacca, atthi aṇṇāiṃ pi Candaüttassa kova|kāraṇāiṃ Cāṇakke. uvekkhido aṇeṇa avakkamanto kumāro Malaakedū amacca|Rakkhaso a.⌟

RĀKṢASAḤ: *(sa|harṣam)* sakhe Śakaṭadāsa, hasta|tala|gato me saṃprati Candragupto bhaviṣyati. idānīṃ Candanadāsasya bandhanān mokṣas tava ca putra|dāreṇa saha samāgamaḥ.

MALAYAKETUḤ: sakhe Bhāgurāyaṇa, «hasta|tala|gato me saṃprati Candragupta iti» vyāharataḥ ko 'yam asy' âbhiprāyaḥ?

4.80 BHĀGURĀYAṆAḤ: kumāra, kim anyat? Cāṇakyād apakṛṣṭasya Candraguptasy' ôddharaṇe saukaryam avaśyaṃ paśyati.

RĀKṢASAḤ: bhadra, hṛt'|âdhikāraḥ kva sāṃpratam asau vaṭuḥ?

BHAGURÁYANA: Yes, but not so much because he praised him, Your Highness, as because he dismissed Kautílya.

RÁKSHASA: Tell me, was this cancellation of the Festival the sole reason for Chandra·gupta's displeasure at Kautílya, or was there something else as well?

MÁLAYA·KETU: Bhaguráyana, what point does he see in look- 4.75
ing into the reasons for Chandra·gupta's displeasure?

BHAGURÁYANA: I will explain, Your Highness. Since Kautílya is a sensible man, why should he anger Chandra·gupta over such a trivial matter? And since Chandra·gupta knows what he owes him, why should he offer Kautílya disrespect just over this? At all events, if there is rich cause for their estrangement, it will then be lasting.

KÁRABHAKA: Yes, Minister, Chandra·gupta does have other grievances against Kautílya. He allowed Prince Málaya·ketu and yourself to escape.

RÁKSHASA: *(delightedly)* Dear Shákata·dasa, now I know I have Chandra·gupta in the palm of my hand! This means Chándana·dasa's release from prison, and your own reunion with your wife and children.

MÁLAYA·KETU: What does he mean, Bhaguráyana—he has Chandra·gupta in the palm of his hand?

BHAGURÁYANA: He must think it will be easier to defeat 4.80
Chandra·gupta now that he is without Kautílya, Your Highness—I'm sure it can't be anything else.

RÁKSHASA: Now that the fellow's lost his post, where is he?

KARABHAKAḤ: ⌜amacca, tahiṃ jeva Pāḍaliütte paḍi|vasadi.⌟

RĀKṢASAḤ: *(s'|āvegam)* kiṃ tatr' âiva prativasati? na tapo|vanaṃ gataḥ, pratijñāṃ vā na punaḥ samārūḍhavān?

KARABHAKAḤ: ⌜amacca, «tavo|vaṇaṃ gamissadi» tti suṇīadi.⌟

4.85 RĀKṢASAḤ: *(s'|āvegam)* sakhe Śakaṭadāsa, n' êdam upapadyate. paśya:

devasya yena pṛthivī|tala|vāsavasya
  s'|âgr'|āsan'|âpanaya|jā nikṛtir na soḍhā
so 'yaṃ svayaṃ|kṛta|nar'|âdhipater manasvī
  Mauryāt kathaṃ nu paribhūtim imāṃ saheta?

MALAYAKETUḤ: sakhe Bhāgurāyaṇa, Cāṇakyasya tapo|vana|gamane punaḥ|pratijñ"|ārohaṇe vā k" âsya sv'|ârtha|siddhiḥ?

BHĀGURĀYAṆAḤ: kumāra, n' âyam atyanta|durbodho 'rthaḥ. yāvad yāvac Cāṇakyo nirapekṣaś Candraguptād dūrī|bhavati tāvat tāvad asya sv'|ârtha|siddhiḥ.

ŚAKAṬADĀSAḤ: amātya, alam anyathā|saṃbhāvitena. upapadyata ev' âitat. paśyatv amātyaḥ:

4.90 rājñāṃ cūḍāmaṇ'|îndu|dyuti|khacita|śikhe
    mūrdhni vinyasta|pādaḥ
  svair' êv' ôtpādyamānaṃ kim iti viṣahate
    Maurya ājñā|vighātam
Kauṭilyaḥ kopito 'pi svayam abhicaraṇe
    jñāta|duḥkha|pratijñāṃ
  daivāt pūrṇa|pratijñaḥ punar api na karoty
    āyati|jyāni|bhītaḥ.

KÁRABHAKA: He is still living in Pátali·putra, sir.

RÁKSHASA: *(in disquiet)* Still living there? Hasn't he retired to a hermitage, or sworn a second oath?

KÁRABHAKA: It's said, sir, that he is going to retire to a hermitage.

RÁKSHASA: *(still disquieted)* Shákata·dasa, this doesn't make sense: 4.85

> How can he, who could not endure the insult of dismissal
> By His Majesty the Emperor Nanda, god on earth,
> Possibly in his arrogance endure this slight
> From the Mauryan, the king that he himself has made?

MÁLAYA·KETU: Bhagurâyana, how will it help him if Kautílya retires to a hermitage or enters on a second vow?

BHAGURÁYANA: Simple enough, Your Highness. Anything will help him that keeps Kautílya away from Chandra·gupta.

SHÁKATA·DASA: Do not trouble yourself, Minister: it does make sense. Consider—

> Now that the Mauryan has set his foot upon the gleaming crowns of princes, 4.90
> He will never let one of his own people flout his rule,
> And Kautílya, even in his anger recalling the painful discipline of a vow,
> Having been lucky once, will not risk a future failure.

RĀKṢASAḤ: Śakaṭadāsa, evam etat. tad gaccha viśrāmaya Karabhakam.

ŚAKAṬADĀSAḤ: yad ājñāpayaty amātyaḥ.

iti KARABHAKEṆA *saha niṣkrāntaḥ.*

RĀKṢASAḤ: aham api kumāraṃ draṣṭum icchāmi.

4.95 MALAYAKETUḤ: aham ev' āryaṃ draṣṭum āgataḥ.

RĀKṢASAḤ: *(nāṭyen' âvalokya)* aye kumāraḥ! *(āsanād utthāya)* idam āsanam. upaveṣṭum arhati kumāraḥ.

MALAYAKETUḤ: ayam upaviśāmi. upaviśatv āryaḥ.

iti yath"|āsanam upaviṣṭau.

MALAYAKETUḤ: ārya, api sahyā śiro|vedanā?

4.100 RĀKṢASAḤ: kumārasy' âdhirāja|śabden' ā|tiras|kṛte kumāra|śabde kutaḥ śiro|vedanāyāḥ sahyatā?

MALAYAKETUḤ: urī|kṛtam etad āryeṇa na duṣprāpaṃ bhaviṣyati. tat kiyantaṃ kālam asmābhir evaṃ saṃbhṛta|balair api śatru|vyasanam avekṣamāṇair udāsitavyam?

RĀKṢASAḤ: kumāra, kuto 'dy' âpi kāla|haraṇasy' âvakāśaḥ? pratiṣṭhasva vijayāya.

RÁKSHASA: Yes, you are right, Shákata·dasa. Go, then, and see that Kárabhaka is made comfortable.

SHÁKATA·DASA: Certainly, Minister.

He goes out with KÁRABHAKA.

RÁKSHASA: And I must go to see His Highness.

MÁLAYA·KETU: Here I am, sir, come to see you. 4.95

RÁKSHASA: *(seeing him)* Oh, Your Highness! *(rising from his seat)* Here, please be seated, Your Highness.

MÁLAYA·KETU: Thank you. Be seated yourself, sir.

They sit in their respective seats.

MÁLAYA·KETU: Is your headache better, my lord?

RÁKSHASA: How could it be so until Your Highness's title 4.100
of Prince is eclipsed by the title of Emperor?

MÁLAYA·KETU: Since you have engaged on the task, sir, that will not be difficult of fulfillment. How long must we sit passively with our forces massed in this way, watching for a deficiency in the enemy?

RÁKSHASA: Why delay a moment longer, Your Highness? Set out to victory.

MALAYAKETUḤ: ārya, api śatror vyasanam upalabdham?

RĀKṢASAḤ: kumāra, bāḍham upalabdham.

4.105 MALAYAKETUḤ: kīdṛśam?

RĀKṢASAḤ: saciva|vyasanam. kim anyat? apakṛṣṭaś Cāṇakyāc Candraguptaḥ.

MALAYAKETUḤ: ārya, saciva|vyasanam a|vyasanam eva.

RĀKṢASAḤ: kumāra, anyeṣāṃ bhūmi|pālānāṃ kadā cid amātya|vyasanam a|vyasanaṃ syāt, na punaś Candraguptasya.

MALAYAKETUḤ: nanu viśeṣataś Candraguptasya?

4.110 RĀKṢASAḤ: kiṃ kāraṇam?

MALAYAKETUḤ: Candragupta|prakṛtīnāṃ hi Cāṇakya|doṣā ev' âparāga|hetavaḥ. tasmiṃś ca nirākṛte prathamam api Candraguptam anuraktāḥ prakṛtayaḥ saṃprati sutarām eva tatr' ânurāgaṃ darśayiṣyanti.

RĀKṢASAḤ: kumāra, n' âitad evam. tāḥ khalu dvi|prakārāḥ prakṛtayaś Candragupta|sah'|ôtthāyinyo Nanda|kul'|ânuraktāś ca. tatra Candragupta|sah'|ôtthāyinīnāṃ Cāṇakya|doṣā eva virāga|hetavo na Nanda|kul'|ânuraktānām. tās tu khalu «Nanda|kulam anena pitṛ|kula|bhūtaṃ kṛtsnaṃ kṛta|ghnena ghātitam» ity aparāg'|âmarṣābhyāṃ viprakṛtāḥ satyaḥ sv'|āśrayam a|labhamānāś Candraguptam ev' ânuvartante. tvādṛśaṃ punaḥ pratipakṣ'|ôddharaṇe saṃbhāvya|śaktim abhiyoktāram āsādya kṣipram enaṃ parityajya tvām ev' āśrayanta iti. atra kumārasya vayam eva nidarśanam.

MÁLAYA·KETU: Have we found a deficiency in the enemy, sir?

RÁKSHASA: Most certainly we have, Your Highness.

MÁLAYA·KETU: What? 4.105

RÁKSHASA: No less than a deficiency in ministers! Chandra·gupta has fallen out with Kautílya.

MÁLAYA·KETU: A deficiency in ministers, sir, is no deficiency.

RÁKSHASA: In the case of other kings, Your Highness, that may be true, but not in Chandra·gupta's case.

MÁLAYA·KETU: Surely particularly in Chandra·gupta's case?

RÁKSHASA: Why so? 4.110

MÁLAYA·KETU: It is Kautílya's faults that have made Chandra·gupta's subjects disloyal. With Kautílya out of the way, his subjects, already loyal to him, will now display more loyalty than ever.

RÁKSHASA: That is not so, Your Highness. His subjects are of two kinds: those who helped him to power and those who are loyal to the Nandas. Kautílya's faults have been estranging his own supporters, not those who are loyal to the Nandas. The latter are bitterly hostile and resentful of Chandra·gupta's treachery in destroying the House of Nanda, his own father's family, and they have accepted him only because they have no one else to turn to. But with a champion like yourself whom they can rely on to defeat the enemy, they are rapidly leaving him and coming over to you—as Your Highness may judge from my own case.

MALAYAKETUḤ: amātya, kim etad ev' âikaṃ saciva|vyasanam abhiyoga|kāraṇaṃ Candraguptasya? āho svid anyad apy asti?

RĀKṢASAḤ: kumāra, kim anyair bahubhir api? etadd hi tatra pradhānatamam.

4.115 MALAYAKETUḤ: ārya, tat kathaṃ pradhānatamaṃ nāma? kim idānīṃ Candraguptaḥ sva|rājya|kārya|dhurām anyatra mantriṇy ātmani vā samāsajya svayaṃ pratividhātum a|samarthaḥ?

RĀKṢASAḤ: bāḍham a|samarthaḥ.

MALAYAKETUḤ: kiṃ kāraṇam?

RĀKṢASAḤ: sv'|āyatta|siddhiṣ' ûbhay'|āyatta|siddhiṣu vā bhū-mi|pāleṣv etat saṃbhavati. Candraguptas tu durātmā nityaṃ saciv'|āyatta|siddhāv ev' âvasthitaś cakṣur|vikala iv' â|pratyakṣa|sarva|loka|vyavahāraḥ katham iva svayaṃ pratividhātuṃ samarthaḥ syāt? kutaḥ:

nṛpo 'pakṛṣṭaḥ sacivād a|tantrakaḥ
stanaṃ|dhayo 'tyanta|śiśuḥ stanād iva
adṛṣṭa|loka|vyavahāra|mūḍha|dhīr
muhūrtam apy utsahate na vartitum.

4.120 MALAYAKETUḤ: *(ātma|gatam)* diṣṭyā na saciv'|āyatta|siddhir asmi! *(prakāśam)* ārya, yady evaṃ tath" âpi khalu bahuṣv abhiyoga|kāraṇeṣu satsu saciva|vyasanam abhiyuñjānasya śatrum abhiyoktur n' āikāntikī siddhir bhavati.

MÁLAYA·KETU: Is this deficiency in ministers the one and only reason for attack, or is there something else?

RÁKSHASA: It doesn't matter how many others there might be, Your Highness. This is the one that counts.

MÁLAYA·KETU: Why is it the one that counts, sir? Is Chandra·gupta incapable of entrusting the administration of his empire to another minister or of taking it on his own shoulders and meeting our challenge on its own? 4.115

RÁKSHASA: Quite incapable.

MÁLAYA·KETU: Why?

RÁKSHASA: Such a course is open to kings whose government is either monarchical or monarchical and ministerial. But the wretched Chandra·gupta has always depended on a totally ministerial government, and sees no further than a blind man into the workings of the administration: what resistance can he possibly offer us on his own?

> An inexperienced king torn from his minister
> Is like a babe in arms snatched from the breast.
> Confused and knowing nothing of the world around him,
> He cannot manage by himself for a single moment.

MÁLAYA·KETU: *(to himself)* How lucky that mine is not a ministerial government! *(aloud)* Even so, sir, the success of an attacker who is concentrating on the enemy's ministerial deficiency will obviously be more complete when there are a good many reasons for attacking. 4.120

RĀKṢASAḤ: aikāntikīm eva siddhim avagantum arhati kumāraḥ. kutaḥ:

tvayy utkṛṣṭa|bale 'bhiyoktari nṛpe
  Nand'|ânurakte pure
Cāṇakye calit'|âdhikāra|vimukhe
  Maurye nave rājani
sv'|âdhīne mayi—

ity ardh'|ôkte lajjāṃ nāṭayan

—mārga|mātra|kathana|
  vyāpāra|yog'|ôdyame
tvad|vāñch"|ântaritāni saṃprati vibho
  tiṣṭhanti sādhyāni naḥ.

4.125 MALAYAKETUḤ: amātya, yady evam abhiyoga|kālam āryaḥ paśyati tat kim āsyate. paśya:

uttuṅgās tuṅga|kūlaṃ sruta|mada|salilāḥ
  prasyandi|salilaṃ
śyāmāḥ śyām'|ôpakaṇṭha|drumam ali|mukharāḥ
  kallola|mukharam
śrotaḥ|khāt'|âvasīdat|taṭam uru|daśanair
  utsādita|taṭāḥ
Śoṇaṃ sindūra|śoṇā mama gaja|patayaḥ
  pāsyanti śataśaḥ.

api ca: gambhīra|garjita|ravāḥ sva|mad'|âmbu|miśram
  āsāra|varṣam iva śīkaram udgirantyaḥ
Vindhyaṃ vikīrṇa|salilā iva megha|mālā
  rotsyanti vāraṇa|ghaṭā nagaraṃ madīyāḥ.

iti BHĀGURĀYAṆENA *saha niṣkrānto* MALAYAKETUḤ.

RÁKSHASA: Your Highness may count on a truly complete success:

With yourself at the head of a mighty force and the city loyal to Nanda,
With Kautílya dismissed and estranged, and the Mauryan a fledgling king,
With myself free to act at last—

breaking off modestly

As your counselor, pointing out your path,
Our success waits now, sire, only on your word of command.

MÁLAYA·KETU: If you think it is the moment to attack, sir, let's not delay: 4.125

Lofty as its lofty sides, rut flowing down into its flowing stream,
Dark as its bordering woods, with bees to match the murmuring of its ripples,
Their tusks attacking from above the banks that the current strikes at from below,
My elephants, vermilion-red, shall churn the Red River's waters.*

With a deep roaring and a spewing forth
Of showers of water mixed with their own ichor,
Like thunderclouds beating upon the Vindhyas
My troops of elephants shall storm Pátali·putra.

He goes out with BHAGURÁYANA.

RĀKṢASAḤ: kaḥ ko 'tra bhoḥ!

4.130 *praviśya* PURUṢAḤ: ⌜āṇavedu amacco.⌟

RĀKṢASAḤ: Priyaṃvadaka, jñāyatāṃ sāṃvat|sarikāṇāṃ dvāri kas tiṣṭhati.

PRIYAṂVADAKAḤ: ⌜jaṃ amacco āṇavedi.⌟ *(iti niṣkramya punaḥ praviśya)* ⌜amacca, eso kkhu saṃvac|chario Khavaṇao—⌟

RĀKṢASAḤ: *(ātma|gatam a|nimittaṃ sūcayitvā)* katham, prathamam eva Kṣapaṇakaḥ!

PRIYAṂVADAKAḤ: ⌜—Jīvasiddhī.⌟

4.135 RĀKṢASAḤ: *(prakāśam)* bhadra, a|bībhatsa|darśanaṃ kṛtvā praveśaya.

PRIYAṂVADAKAḤ: ⌜jaṃ amacco āṇavedi.⌟ *(iti niṣkrāntaḥ)*

(tataḥ praviśati KṢAPAṆAKAḤ*)*

⌜śāśaṇam Alihantāṇaṃ
  paḍivayyadha moha|vādhi|veyyāṇaṃ
ye paḍhama|metta|kaḍuaṃ
  paścā patthaṃ uvadiśanti⌟

(upasṛtya) ⌜dhamma|lāhe śādhakāṇaṃ.⌟

RĀKṢASAḤ: bhadanta, nirūpyatāṃ tāvad asmākaṃ prasthāna|divasaḥ.

4.140 KṢAPAṆAKAḤ: *(nāṭyena cintayitvā)* ⌜śādhakā, ṇilūvide divaśe. ā mayyha|ṇṇādo ṇiutta|śaala|dośā śohaṇā tidhī bhodi śaṃpuṇṇa|candā puṇṇa|māśī. tumhāṇaṃ uttalāe diśāe daḥkiṇaṃ diśaṃ pastidāṇaṃ daḥkiṇa|duvālie ṇaḥkatte. avi a.⌟

RÁKSHASA: Hallo, hallo, there!

SERVANT *(entering)*: Command me, sir. 4.130

RÁKSHASA: Priyam·vádaka, find out what astrologers are available.

PRIYAM·VÁDAKA: Yes, sir. *(going out and returning)* I've found an astrologer, sir, the Jain monk—

RÁKSHASA: *(to himself, indicating an ill omen)* Oh, and the first thing is a Jain monk!

PRIYAM·VÁDAKA: —called Jiva·siddhi, sir.

RÁKSHASA: *(aloud)* Make him look respectable,* Priyam·vá- 4.135
daka, and bring him in.

PRIYAM·VÁDAKA: Yes, sir. *(He goes out.)*

(Enter the Jain monk JIVA·SIDDHI.*)*

Follow the teachings of the Sages,
Physicians that treat the sickness of illusion,
Whose medicine at first is bitter
But afterward will cure.

(going up to RÁKSHASA*)* The true faith be yours, brother.

RÁKSHASA: Reverend sir, would you please determine for me the auspicious day for setting forth?

JIVA·SIDDHI: *(after reflection)* It is determined, brother. The 4.140
day of the full moon is auspicious and will be wholly favorable to you in the afternoon. And the Lunar Mansion in the south will favor your march from the north.

⌜ast'|âhimuhe Śūle
udide śaṃpuṇṇa|maṇḍale Cande
gahavadi|Budhaśśa lagge
udid'|astamidammi Kedummi.⌟

RĀKṢASAḤ: bhadanta, tithir eva tāvan na śudhyati.

KṢAPAṆAKAḤ: ⌜śādhakā,⌟

⌜ekka|guṇā bhodi tidhī
cadug|guṇe bhodi ṇaḥkatte
cadu|śaṣṭi|guṇe lagge
eśe yodiśia|tanta|śiddhante.⌟

4.145 ⌜lagge hohi śulagge
śommaṃ pi gahaṃ yahāhi dullaggaṃ
pāvihiśi diggham āüṃ
candaśśa baleṇa gaścante.⌟

RĀKṢASAḤ: bhadanta, aparaiḥ sāṃvatsarikaiḥ saha saṃvādyatām.

KṢAPAṆAKAḤ: ⌜śaṃvādedu śādhake. hage kkhu gamiśśaṃ.⌟

RĀKṢASAḤ: na khalu kupito bhadantaḥ?

KṢAPAṆAKAḤ: ⌜kuvide tumhāṇaṃ ṇa bhadante.⌟

4.150 RĀKṢASAḤ: kas tarhi?

KṢAPAṆAKAḤ: ⌜bhaavaṃ kadante yeṇa attaṇo paḥkaṃ uyyhia pala|paḥkaṃ pamāṇī|kaleśi.⌟

iti niṣkrāntaḥ KṢAPAṆAKAḤ.

As the Sun sinks to its setting
And the full-orbed Moon rises,
Seize the moment of union with all-powerful
 Mercury,
When Ketu's brief hour is at an end.

RÁKSHASA: The very day is evil, sir!

JIVA·SIDDHI: Brother,

The day counts as one,
The mansion counts as four,
The juncture counts as sixty-four—
Such is the teaching of astrology.

The juncture with wise Mercury is auspicious. 4.145
Avoid the ill-omened Ketu.
Long life will be yours
If you go by the Moon.

RÁKSHASA: Sir, will you confirm this with other astrologers?

JIVA·SIDDHI: Confirm it yourself, brother. I am leaving.

RÁKSHASA: You are not angry with me, sir?

JIVA·SIDDHI: I am not, no.

RÁKSHASA: Who, then? 4.150

JIVA·SIDDHI: Destiny, because you shun what is meant for you, and look for good in the wrong place.

He goes out.

RĀKṢASAḤ: Priyaṃvadaka, jñāyatāṃ kā velā vartata iti.

PRIYAṂVADAKAḤ: ⌜jaṃ amacco āṇavedi.⌟ *(iti niṣkramya punaḥ praviśya ca)* ⌜amacca, atth'|âhilāsi bhaavaṃ sūro.⌟

4.155 RĀKṢASAḤ: *(āsanād utthāya vilokya ca)* aye ast'|âbhilāṣī bhagavān bhānuḥ. tathā hi:

āvir|bhūt'|ânurāgāḥ kṣaṇam udaya|girer
ujjihānasya bhānoḥ
pattra|cchāyaiḥ purastād upavana|taravo
dūram āśv eva gatvā
ete tasmin nivṛttāḥ punar apara|kakup|
prānta|paryasta|bimbe
prāyo bhṛtyās tyajanti pracalita|vibhavaṃ
svāminaṃ sevamānāḥ.

iti niṣkrāntāḥ sarve.

RÁKSHASA: Priyam·vádaka, find out what hour it is.

PRIYAM·VÁDAKA: Yes, sir. *(going out and returning)* The sun will soon be setting, sir.

RÁKSHASA: *(rising from his place and looking)* True, the sun 4.155
will soon be setting:

Struck by his radiance as he rose at dawn, the trees of the wood
Ran eagerly before him to offer him their shade.
But see how they all turn back as his orb sinks westward:
For a master is ever shunned in his decline by those who served him only with their shadow.

All go out.

PRELUDE TO ACT V

tataḥ praviśati lekham alaṃkāra|sthagikāṃ ca mudritām ādāya SIDDHĀRTHAKAḤ.

SIDDHĀRTHAKAḤ: ⌈hī mānahe!⌋

⌈buddhi|jala|ṇijjharehiṃ
siccantī desa|āla|kalasehiṃ
daṃsissadi kajja|phalaṃ
garuaṃ Cāṇakka|ṇīdi|ladā.⌋

⌈gahido mae ajja|Cāṇakkeṇa paḍhama|lehido leho amacca|Rakkhasassa muddā|laṃchido. tassa jjeva muddā|laṃchidā iaṃ pi āharaṇa|peḍiā. calido kila mhi Pāḍaliuttaṃ. tā jāva gacchāmi.⌋ *(parikramy' âvalokya ca)* ⌈kadhaṃ. khavaṇao āacchadi! tā jāva se a|saüṇa|bhūdaṃ daṃsaṇaṃ suddha|daṃsaṇeṇa paḍiharāmi.⌋

5.5 *tataḥ praviśati* KṢAPAṆAKAḤ.

KṢAPAṆAKAḤ:

⌈Alihantāṇa paṇamimo
ye de gambhīladāe buddhīe
lo|uttalehi loe
śiddhiṃ maggehi magganti.⌋

SIDDHĀRTHAKAḤ: ⌈bhadanta vandāmi.⌋

KṢAPAṆAKAḤ: ⌈śādhakā, dhamma|lāhe de bhodu.⌋ *(nirvarṇya)* ⌈śādhakā, a|stāṇa|śaṃtalaṇa|kada|vvavaśāaṃ via de peskāmi.⌋

5.10 SIDDHĀRTHAKAḤ: ⌈kadhaṃ bhadanto jāṇadi?⌋

Enter, carrying a letter and a jewel case, both sealed, SIDDHÁRTHAKA.

SIDDHÁRTHAKA: Oh, amazing!

> Nourished by the waters of his wisdom
> Streaming from watering cans of place and time,
> Kautílya's strategy is a fertile vine
> Yielding rich crops of Successes.

I have with me the letter originally commissioned by His Honor Kautílya but stamped with Minister Rákshasa's own seal—and this jewel case, also stamped with his own seal. And now I must look as if I'm making for Pátali·putra. Off I go, then. *(walking about and looking)* Oh, here comes a Jain monk! I must ward off the ill omen by looking at something pure.

Enter the Jain monk JIVA·SIDDHI. 5.5

JIVA·SIDDHI:

> My salutation to the Sages,
> Who by their profound wisdom
> Can find satisfaction in this life
> By transcendental paths.

SIDDHÁRTHAKA: Greetings, reverend sir!

JIVA·SIDDHI: The true faith be yours, my brother. *(scrutinizing him)* I notice, brother, that you seem to be planning some untimely journey.

SIDDHÁRTHAKA: How can you tell that, reverend sir? 5.10

KṢAPAṆAKAḤ: ⌜śādhakā, kiṃ ettha yāṇidavvaṃ? ṇaṃ eśe yyeva de magg'|ādeśa|kuśale śaüṇe kala|gade a lehe śūcedi.⌟

SIDDHĀRTHAKAḤ: ⌜āṃ jāṇidaṃ bhadanteṇa. des'|antaraṃ calido mhi. tā kadhedu bhadanto: kīdiso ajja divaso tti?⌟

KṢAPAṆAKAḤ: *(vihasya)* ⌜śādhakā, muṇḍaṃ muṇḍia ṇaḥkattāiṃ puśćaśi.⌟

SIDDHĀRTHAKAḤ: ⌜bhadanta, saṃpadaṃ pi kiṃ jādaṃ? tā kadhehi. jai aṇuūlaṃ bhavissadi tado gamissaṃ. aṇṇadhā ṇivattissaṃ.⌟

5.15 KṢAPAṆAKAḤ: ⌜śādhakā, ṇa śaṃpadaṃ edaśśiṃ Malaakedu|kaḍae aṇuūleṇa aṇ|aṇuūleṇa vā gaśćīadi.⌟

SIDDHĀRTHAKAḤ: ⌜bhadanta, tado kadhaṃ khu dāṇi?⌟

KṢAPAṆAKAḤ: ⌜śādhakā, ṇiśāmehi. paḍhamaṃ dāva ettha kaḍae loaśśa a|ṇivālide ṇikkamaṇa|ppaveśe āśi. idāṇiṃ ido paccāśaṇṇe Kuśumaüle ṇa ke vi a|muddā|laṃścide ṇikkamiduṃ paviśiduṃ vā aṇumodīadi. tā yaï Bhāgulāaṇaśśa muddā|laṃścide śi tado gaśca vīśaste. aññadhā ṇivattia ṇihude ciṣṭha. mā tumaṃ gumma|stāṇ'|āhiālie-hiṃ śaṃyamida|kala|calaṇe lāa|ülaṃ paveśīhiśi.⌟

SIDDHĀRTHAKAḤ: ⌜kiṃ ṇa jāṇadi bhadanto jadhā amacca|Rakkhasassa kerako Siddhatthao ahaṃ ti? tā a|muddā|laṃcchidaṃ pi maṃ ṇikkamantaṃ kassa sattī ṇivāriduṃ.⌟

KṢAPAṆAKAḤ: ⌜śādhakā, Laḥkaśaśśa piśāaśśa vā kelake hohi. ṇasti de a|muddā|laṃścidaśśa ṇikkamaṇ'|ôvāe.⌟

JIVA·SIDDHI: It doesn't need much fathoming, my brother. That bird to give you omens on the road and the letter in your hand, they give the game away.

SIDDHÁRTHAKA: Yes, you've guessed the truth, reverend sir. I'm off to foreign parts. So tell me: what kind of day have I got for it?

JIVA·SIDDHI: *(laughing)* What, brother, ask the omens when you've already shaved?

SIDDHÁRTHAKA: No harm in it even now, reverend sir. Come, tell me. If it's all right, I'll go. Otherwise I'll turn back.

JIVA·SIDDHI: You can't leave Málaya·ketu's camp nowadays, brother, whether the omens are all right or not. 5.15

SIDDHÁRTHAKA: Why not?

JIVA·SIDDHI: I'll tell you. At one time people could come and go at will in this camp. But now we're so near Pátali·putra, no one is allowed to go out or come in without a pass. So if you've got a pass stamped by Bhaguráyana, go with an easy mind. Otherwise turn back and keep quiet—or the guards will tie you hand and foot and march you to the Prince's headquarters.

SIDDHÁRTHAKA: Don't you know, then, reverend sir, that I'm Siddhárthaka, one of Minister Rákshasa's men? No one has the power to stop me leaving even if I don't have a pass.

JIVA·SIDDHI: Rákshasa, goblin or ghost,* it makes no difference. If you haven't got a stamped pass you can't leave.

5.20 SIDDHĀRTHAKAḤ: ⌜bhadanta, ṇa kuppa. kajja|siddhī me bhodu.⌟

KṢAPAṆAKAḤ: ⌜śādhakā, gaśca. bhodu de kayya|śiddhī. hage vi Bhāgulāaṇādo muddaṃ yācemi.⌟

iti niṣkrāntau.

SIDDHÁRTHAKA: Don't be angry with me, reverend sir. Give me good luck on my errand. 5.20

JIVA·SIDDHI: Go, my brother, and good luck be with you. But, speaking for myself, I'm going to ask Bhaguráyana for a pass.

They withdraw.

ACT V
THE FORGED LETTER

tataḥ praviśati PURUṢEṆ' *ânugamyamāno* BHĀGURĀYAṆAḤ.

BHĀGURĀYAṆAḤ: *(ātma|gatam)* aho vaicitryam ārya|Cāṇakya|nīteḥ. kutaḥ:

5.25 «muhur lakṣy'|ôdbhedā
muhur adhigam'|âbhāva|gahanā
muhuḥ saṃpūrṇ'|âṅgī
muhur atikṛśā kārya|vaśataḥ
muhur naśyad|bījā
muhur api bahu|prāpita|phal"
êty» aho citr'|ākārā
niyatir iva nītir naya|vidaḥ.

(prakāśam) bhadra Bhāsvaraka, na māṃ dūrī|bhavantam icchati kumāraḥ. ato 'sminn ev' āsthāna|maṇḍape vinyasyatām āsanam.

PURUṢAḤ: ⌜idaṃ āsaṇaṃ. uvavisadu ajjo.⌟

BHĀGURĀYAṆAḤ: *(upaviśya)* bhadra Bhāsvaraka, yaḥ kaś cin mudr"|ârthī māṃ draṣṭum icchati sa tvayā praveśayitavyaḥ.

PURUṢAḤ: ⌜jaṃ ajjo āṇavedi.⌟ *(iti niṣkrāntaḥ)*

5.30 BHĀGURĀYAṆAḤ: *(sva|gatam)* kaṣṭam. evam api nām' âyam asmāsu snehavān kumāro Malayaketur abhisaṃdhātavya ity aho duṣkaram. atha|vā

Enter BHAGURÁYANA, *attended by a* MANSERVANT.

BHAGURÁYANA: *(to himself)* The revered Kautílya's strategy is wonderfully various!

> Sometimes revealed, sometimes buried deep out of sight, 5.25
> Now complex, now simple, as the task requires,
> Now withering in the seed, now bearing rich fruit—
> His statecraft is as manifold as destiny.

(aloud) Bhásvaraka, His Highness wants me to keep near at hand. So put a seat right here in the audience hall.

MANSERVANT: Here is the seat, sir. Be seated.

BHAGURÁYANA: *(sitting down)* Show in anyone who wants to see me about a pass.

MANSERVANT: Yes, sir. *(He goes out.)*

BHAGURÁYANA: *(to himself)* Alas, this Prince Málaya·ketu is 5.30
so fond of me—it's hard that I have to deceive him! But then,

kule lajjāyāṃ ca
svalyaśasi ca māne ca vimukhaḥ
śarīraṃ vikrīya
kṣaṇika|dhana|lobhād dhanavati
tad|ājñāṃ kurvāṇo
«hitam ahitam» ity etad adhunā
vicār'|âtikrāntaḥ
kim iti para|tantro vimṛśati.

tataḥ praviśati PRATĪHĀRY/*anugamyamāno* MALAYAKETUḤ.

MALAYAKETUḤ: *(ātma/gatam)* aho Rākṣasaṃ prati me vitarka|bāhulyād ākulā buddhir na niścayam adhigacchati. kutaḥ:

«bhaktyā Nanda|kul'|ânurāga|dṛḍhayā
Nand'|ânvay'|ālambinā
kiṃ Cāṇakya|nirākṛtena kṛtinā
Mauryeṇa saṃdhāsyate?
sthairyaṃ bhakti|guṇasya vā vigaṇayan
kiṃ satya|sandho bhaved?»
ity ārūḍha|kulāla|cakram iva me
cetaś ciraṃ bhrāmyati.

5.35 *(prakāśam)* Vijaye, kva Bhāgurāyaṇaḥ?

PRATĪHĀRĪ: ⌜kumāra, eso kkhu kaḍaādo ṇikkamidu|kāmāṇaṃ muddā|saṃpadāṇaṃ aṇuciṭṭhadi.⌟

MALAYAKETUḤ: Vijaye, muhūrtaṃ nibhṛta|pada|saṃcārā bhava yāvad asya parāṅ|mukhasy' âiva pāṇibhyāṃ nayane niruṇadhmi.

PRATĪHĀRĪ: ⌜jaṃ kumāro āṇavedi.⌟

When someone has renounced family, shame, honor and reputation
To sell himself to a rich man, being greedy for a moment's wealth,
When he does that other's bidding, what has he, a mere hireling,
Who has passed beyond problems of right and wrong, to do with such reflections?

Enter MÁLAYA·KETU, *attended by a* FEMALE GUARD.

MÁLAYA·KETU: *(to himself)* Oh, my mind is in such a storm of conflicting thoughts about Rákshasa, I can decide nothing for certain—

His loyalty to the House of Nanda is strong, and the Mauryan is of Nanda's line:
Now that in victory he has rid himself of Kautílya, will Rákshasa treat with him?
Or put constancy first and keep his word to me?
My mind is on a potter's wheel, whirling and whirling around.

(aloud) Víjaya, where is Bhaguráyana? 5.35

FEMALE GUARD: There he is, Your Highness, seeing to passes for people who want to leave the camp.

MÁLAYA·KETU: Tread softly for a moment, Víjaya, and I'll put my hands over his eyes while he's not looking!

FEMALE GUARD: Yes, Your Highness.

(praviśya) PURUṢAḤ: ⌜ajja, eso kkhu khavaṇao muddā|ṇimittaṃ ajjaṃ pekkhiduṃ icchadi.⌟

5.40 BHĀGURĀYAṆAḤ: praveśaya.

PURUṢAḤ: ⌜jaṃ ajjo āṇavedi.⌟ *(iti niṣkrāntaḥ)*

(praviśya) KṢAPAṆAKAḤ. ⌜śādhakā, dhamma|lāhe de bhodu.⌟

BHĀGURĀYAṆAḤ: *(nāṭyen' âvalokya sva|gatam)* aye Rākṣasasya mitraṃ Jīvasiddhiḥ. *(prakāśam)* bhadanta, na khalu Rākṣasasya prayojanam eva kiṃ cid uddiśya gamyate?

KṢAPAṆAKAḤ: *(karṇau pidhāya)* ⌜śantaṃ pāvaṃ. śādhakā, tahiṃ gamiśśāmi yahiṃ Laḥkaśaśśa ṇāmaṃ pi ṇa śuṇīadi.⌟

5.45 BHĀGURĀYAṆAḤ: bhadanta, balīyān suhṛdi praṇaya|kopaḥ. tat kim aparāddhaṃ bhadantasya Rākṣasena?

KṢAPAṆAKAḤ: ⌜śādhakā, ṇa mama kiṃ|pi Laḥkaśeṇa avaladdhaṃ. śaaṃ yeva hage manda|bhagge attaṇo avalayyhāmi.⌟

BHĀGURĀYAṆAḤ: bhadanta, vardhayasi me kutūhalam.

MALAYAKETUḤ: *(sva|gatam)* mama ca.

BHĀGURĀYAṆAḤ: śrotum icchāmi.

5.50 MALAYAKETUḤ: *(sva|gatam)* aham api.

The MANSERVANT *enters.* Sir, there is a Jain monk who wants to see you about a pass.

BHAGURÁYANA: Show him in. 5.40

MANSERVANT: Yes, sir. *(He goes out.)*

Enter JIVA·SIDDHI. The true faith be yours, my brother.

BHAGURÁYANA: *(seeing him, to himself)* Why, it's Rákshasa's friend Jiva·siddhi. *(aloud)* Reverend sir, are you going on some business of Rákshasa's, then?

JIVA·SIDDHI: *(stopping his ears)* Perish the thought! I'm going, brother, where I shan't even have to hear his name.

BHAGURÁYANA: A quarrel with a friend is particularly bitter. 5.45
What has Rákshasa done to injure you, reverend sir?

JIVA·SIDDHI: Rákshasa's done nothing to injure me, brother. Wretch that I am, I am injuring myself.

BHAGURÁYANA: You rouse my curiosity, sir.

MÁLAYA·KETU: *(to himself)* And mine.

BHAGURÁYANA: I should like to hear more.

MÁLAYA·KETU: *(to himself)* So should I! 5.50

KṢAPAṆAKAḤ: ⌜śādhakā, kiṃ ediṇā a|śuṇidavveṇa śuṇideṇa?⌟

BHĀGURĀYAṆAḤ: bhadanta, yadi rahasyaṃ tadā tiṣṭhatu.

KṢAPAṆAKAḤ: ⌜śādhakā, ṇa lahaśśaṃ kiṃ tu adiṇiśaṃśaṃ.⌟

BHĀGURĀYAṆAḤ: yadi na rahasyaṃ tarhi kathyatām.

5.55 KṢAPAṆAKAḤ: ⌜śādhakā, tad" âvi ṇa kadhaïśśaṃ.⌟

BHĀGURĀYAṆAḤ: aham api mudrāṃ na prayacchāmi.

KṢAPAṆAKAḤ: *(sva/gatam)* ⌜yuktam idānīm arthine kathayitum.⌟ *(prakāśam)* ⌜kā gadī. śuṇādu śādhake. asti dāva hage manda|bhagge paḍhamaṃ Pāḍaliütte ṇivaśamāṇe Laḥkaśaśśa mittattaṇaṃ uvagade. tahiṃ ca antale Laḥkaśeṇa gūḍhaṃ viśa|kaññā|paoaṃ uppādia ghādide deve Pavvad'|îśale.⌟

MALAYAKETUḤ: *(sa/bāṣpam ātma/gatam)* katham! Rākṣasena ghātitas tāto na Cāṇakyena.

BHĀGURĀYAṆAḤ: bhadanta, tatas tataḥ.

5.60 KṢAPAṆAKAḤ: ⌜tado hage Laḥkaśaśśa mittaṃ ti kalia Cāṇakka|hadaeṇa śaṇiālaṃ ṇaalādo ṇivvāśide. idāṇiṃ pi Laḥkaśeṇa lāa|kayya|kuśaleṇa kiṃ|pi tādiśaṃ ālambhīadi yeṇa hage yīva|loādo vi ṇivvāśīāmi.⌟

BHĀGURĀYAṆAḤ: bhadanta, «pratiśruta|rājy'|ârdha|sampradānam anicchatā Cāṇakya|hataken' êdam akāryam anuṣṭhitaṃ na Rākṣasen' êti» śrutam asmābhiḥ.

KṢAPAṆAKAḤ: *(karṇau pidhāya)* ⌜śantaṃ pāvaṃ. śādhakā, Cāṇakke viśa|kaññāe ṇāmaṃ pi ṇa āṇadi.⌟

JIVA·SIDDHI: Why want to hear something so unspeakable?

BHAGURÁYANA: If it's a secret, sir, let it be.

JIVA·SIDDHI: No secret, brother, just very dreadful.

BHAGURÁYANA: If it's not a secret, tell me.

JIVA·SIDDHI: But no, I'll not tell you, brother. 5.55

BHAGURÁYANA: And I won't let you have a pass.

JIVA·SIDDHI: *(to himself)* It's all right to tell him now that he presses me. *(aloud)* You leave me no alternative, brother. Listen. Wretch that I am, when I was formerly living in Pátali·putra I became a friend of Rákshasa. And at that time he secretly arranged to employ a poison-girl to kill King Párvataka.

MÁLAYA·KETU: *(to himself, weeping)* What! Rákshasa, not Kautílya, killed my father?

BHAGURÁYANA: Go on, sir.

JIVA·SIDDHI: Then the accursed Kautílya had me banished 5.60
in disgrace from the city as a friend of Rákshasa. And now, with his political schemes, he's plotting something that will get me banished from the world of the living.

BHAGURÁYANA: We had heard, reverend sir, that it was Kautílya, not wanting to divide the empire as promised, who committed that crime, not Rákshasa.

JIVA·SIDDHI: Brother, Kautílya hadn't so much as heard of the poison-girl.

BHĀGURĀYAṆAḤ: bhadanta, iyaṃ mudrā. ehi. kumāraṃ śrāvaya.

MALAYAKETUḤ:

5.65 śrutaṃ sakhe śravaṇa|vidāraṇaṃ vacaḥ
suhṛn|mukhād ripum adhikṛtya bhāṣitam
pitur vadha|vyasanam idaṃ hi yena me
cirād api dvi|guṇam iv' âdya vardhate.

KṢAPAṆAKAḤ: *(sva|gatam)* aye śrutaṃ Malayaketu|hatakena. hanta kṛt'|ârthaḥ Kauṭilyaḥ. *(iti niṣkrāntaḥ* KṢAPAṆAKAḤ*)*

MALAYAKETUḤ: *(pratyakṣavad ākāśe lakṣyaṃ baddhvā)* Rākṣasa, yuktam idam?

«mitraṃ mam' âyam» iti nirvṛta|citta|vṛttiṃ
viśrambhatas tvayi niveśita|sarva|kāryam
tātaṃ nipātya saha bandhu|jan'|âkṣi|toyair
anvartha|saṃjña nanu Rākṣasa rākṣaso 'si.

BHĀGURĀYAṆAḤ: *(sva|gatam)* «rakṣaṇīyā Rākṣasasya prāṇā ity» āry'|ādeśaḥ. bhavatv evaṃ tāvat. *(prakāśam)* kumāra, alam āvegena. āsana|sthaṃ kumāraṃ kiṃ cid vijñāpayitum icchāmi.

5.70 MALAYAKETUḤ: *(upaviśya)* sakhe, kim asi vaktu|kāmaḥ?

BHĀGURĀYAṆAḤ: kumāra, iha khalv artha|śāstra|vyavahāriṇām artha|vaśād ari|mitr'|ôdāsīna|vyavasthā. na laukikānām iva sv'|êcchā|vaśāt. yatas tatra kāle Sarvārthasiddhiṃ rājānam icchato Rākṣasasya Candraguptād api

BHAGURÁYANA: Here, you can have your pass, reverend sir. Come and let His Highness hear this.

MÁLAYA·KETU:

> He has heard it, friend—a tale to split the ears, 5.65
> A tale of an enemy straight from the mouth of his friend,
> Which makes the evil of my father's murder,
> Though done long since, seem suddenly twice as great.

JIVA·SIDDHI: *(to himself)* Ah, the accursed Málaya·ketu has heard! My job is done. *(He goes out.)*

MÁLAYA·KETU: *(gazing into the air as if he could see him)* Rákshasa, was this well?

> When my father was happy in his mind because you were his friend
> And being confident entrusted everything to you,
> You killed him, bringing sorrow to his kin—
> Aptly named Rákshasa! You are in truth a devil.

BHAGURÁYANA: *(to himself)* His Honor Kautílya's instructions are to safeguard Rákshasa's life. So be it. *(aloud)* Do not overexcite yourself, Your Highness. If you will sit down, there is something I should like to say to you.

MÁLAYA·KETU: *(sitting down)* What is it, friend? 5.70

BHAGURÁYANA: In this life, Your Highness, those who practice politics choose enemies, allies and neutrals on political grounds, not on grounds of personal preference like ordinary people. At that particular time, when Rákshasa wanted Sarvártha·siddhi to be Emperor, it was His

balīyas tayā sugṛhīta|nāmā devaḥ Parvateśvara ev' âtyartha|paripanthī mahān arātir āsīt tasmiṃś ca Rākṣasen' êdam anuṣṭhitam iti na doṣam iv' âtra paśyāmi. paśyatu hi kumāraḥ:

mitrāṇi śatrutvam upānayantī
  mitratvam apy artha|vaśāc ca śatrūn
nītir nayaty a|smṛta|pūrva|vṛttaṃ
  janm'|ântaraṃ jīvata eva puṃsaḥ.

tad atra vastuny an|upālabhyo Rākṣasaḥ. ā Nanda|rājya|lābhād upagrāhyaś ca. paratas tasya parigrahe parityāge vā kumāraḥ pramāṇaṃ bhaviṣyati.

MALAYAKETUḤ: sakhe, samyag gṛhītavān asi. anyath" âsya vadhe prakṛti|kṣobhaḥ syād evaṃ ca saṃdigdho vijayaḥ syād asmākam.

5.75 *(praviśya)* PURUṢAḤ. ⌜jaadu jaadu kumāro. aaṃ khu ajjassa gumma|ṭṭhāṇ'|âdhikido Dīhacakkhū viṇṇavedi. eso kkhu amhehiṃ kaḍaādo ṇikkamanto a|gahida|muddo sa|leho puriso gahido. tā paccakkhī|karedu ṇaṃ ajjo tti.⌟

BHĀGURĀYAṆAḤ: bhadra, praveśaya.

PURUṢAḤ: ⌜jaṃ ajjo āṇavedi.⌟ *(iti niṣkrāntaḥ)*

tataḥ praviśati PURUṢEṆ' *ânugamyamānaḥ saṃyataḥ* SIDDHĀRTHAKAḤ.

SIDDHĀRTHAKAḤ: *(sva|gatam)*

Majesty King Párvataka of glorious memory who, being even more powerful than Chandra·gupta, was the most awkward obstacle in Rákshasa's path and his greatest enemy, and that is why he did this to him: in a sense I do not blame him. Consider, Your Highness—

Turning friend into foe, foe into friend,
On grounds of practical advantage,
Politics takes a man while he still lives
Into another birth where earlier memories are lost.

So don't take Rákshasa to task over this, but treat him well until you win the empire. Afterward Your Highness can please himself whether to keep him or drop him.

MÁLAYA·KETU: What you say, friend, is very sensible. And if he were executed it could cause popular unrest and jeopardize our chances of victory.

Enter the MANSERVANT. Victory to Your Highness. The Cap- 5.75
tain of the Guard begs to state that they have caught a man without a pass trying to leave the camp with a letter, and have brought him to be interviewed by His Honor.

BHAGURÁYANA: Bring him in, my good fellow.

MANSERVANT: Yes, sir. *(He goes out.)*

Enter, in the company of the MANSERVANT, SIDDHÁRTHAKA, *bound.*

SIDDHÁRTHAKA: *(to himself)*

5.80 ⌜āṇantīe guṇesu
dosesu paraṃ|muhaṃ karantīe
amhārisa|jaṇaṇīe
ṇamo|ṇamo sāmi|bhattīe.⌟

PURUṢAḤ: *(upasṛtya)* ⌜ajja, aaṃ so puriso.⌟

BHĀGURĀYAṆAḤ: *(nāṭyen' âvalokya)* bhadra, kim ayam āgantuka āho svid ih' âiva kasya cit parigrahaḥ?

SIDDHĀRTHAKAḤ: ⌜ajja, ahaṃ khu amacca|Rakkhasassa sevao kerako.⌟

BHĀGURĀYAṆAḤ: bhadra, tat kim|artham a|gṛhīta|mudraḥ kaṭakān niṣkrāmasi?

5.85 SIDDHĀRTHAKAḤ: ⌜ajja, kajja|goraveṇa tuvarido mhi.⌟

BHĀGURĀYAṆAḤ: kīdṛśaṃ tat kārya|gauravaṃ yad rāja|śāsanam ullaṅghayati?

MALAYAKETUḤ: sakhe Bhāgurāyaṇa, lekham apanaya.

BHĀGURĀYAṆAḤ: *(*SIDDHĀRTHAKA*/hastāl lekhaṃ gṛhītvā)* kumāra, ayaṃ lekhaḥ. *(mudrāṃ dṛṣṭvā)* Rākṣasa|nām'|âṅkit" êyaṃ mudrā.

MALAYAKETUḤ: mudrāṃ paripālayann udveṣṭya darśaya.

5.90 BHĀGURĀYAṆAḤ *(tathā kṛtvā darśayati)*

MALAYAKETUḤ: *(gṛhītvā vācayati)* «sv|asti. yathā|sthāne kuto 'pi ke 'pi kam api puruṣa|viśeṣam avagamayati. asmad|vipakṣaṃ nirākṛtya darśitā satyavatā satya|vāditā. sāmpratam eteṣām api prathamam upanyasta|sandhīnām asmat|suhṛdāṃ pūrva|pratijñāta|sandhi|paripaṇa|pratipādanena satya|sandhaḥ prītim utpādayitum arhati. ete

All homage to Loyalty, 5.80
Mother of such as me,
Who puts me in the path of right
And averts my gaze from wrong.

MANSERVANT: *(approaching)* Here is the man, Your Honor.

BHAGURÁYANA: *(looking at him)* Is he a stranger here, or in someone's service?

SIDDHÁRTHAKA: Sir, I am in Minister Rákshasa's service.

BHAGURÁYANA: Then why, my good man, were you leaving the camp without a pass?

SIDDHÁRTHAKA: It was an emergency, sir, and I was in a 5.85
hurry.

BHAGURÁYANA: What kind of emergency, to override a royal edict?

MÁLAYA·KETU: Bhaguráyana, take his letter.

BHAGURÁYANA: *(taking the letter from* SIDDHÁRTHAKA*'s hand)* Here it is, Your Highness. *(looking at the seal)* This seal bears Rákshasa's name.

MÁLAYA·KETU: Open it with the seal intact and show me.

BHAGURÁYANA *(does so.)* 5.90

MÁLAYA·KETU: *(takes it and reads out)* "Greetings. Someone somewhere sends the following message to a most distinguished person. In dismissing our rival, the Truthful One has shown himself to be as good as his word. He should now give pleasure by granting to our allies who have already entered into an agreement with him the price of the agreement as previously promised. They

hy evam upagṛhītāḥ santaḥ sv'|āśraya|vināśen' âiv' ôpakāriṇam ārādhayiṣyanti. a|vismṛtam apy etat satyavataḥ smārayāmi. eteṣāṃ madhye ke cid areḥ koṣa|daṇḍen' ârthinaḥ ke cid viṣayeṇ' êti. alaṃkāra|trayaṃ ca satyavatā yad anupreṣitaṃ tad upagatam. may" âpi lekhasy' â|śūny'|ârthaṃ kiṃ cid anupreṣitaṃ tad upagamanīyaṃ vācikaṃ c' āptamāt Siddhārthakāc chrotavyam iti.»

MALAYAKETUḤ: sakhe Bhāgurāyaṇa, kīdṛśo lekh'|ârthaḥ?

BHĀGURĀYAṆAḤ: bhadra Siddhārthaka, kasy' âyaṃ lekhaḥ?

SIDDHĀRTHAKAḤ: ⌜ajja, ṇa āṇāmi.⌟

5.95 BHĀGURĀYAṆAḤ: he dhūrta, lekho nīyate na ca jñāyate kasy' êti? sarvaṃ tāvat tiṣṭhatu. vācikaṃ tvattaḥ kena śrotavyam?

SIDDHĀRTHAKAḤ: ⌜tumhehiṃ.⌟

BHĀGURĀYAṆAḤ: kim asmābhiḥ?

SIDDHĀRTHAKAḤ: ⌜tumhehiṃ gahido ṇa āṇāmi kiṃ bhaṇāmi tti.⌟

BHĀGURĀYAṆAḤ: *(sa|krodham)* eṣa jñāsyasi. bhadra Bhāsvaraka, bahir nītvā tāvat tāḍyatāṃ yāvat kathyate 'nena.

5.100 PURUṢAḤ: ⌜jaṃ ajjo āṇavedi.⌟ *(iti* SIDDHĀRTHAKENA *saha niṣkrāntaḥ)*

(punaḥ praviśya) ⌜ajja, iaṃ tassa tāḍīamāṇassa mudda|laṃcchidā peḍiā kakkhādo ṇivaḍidā.⌟

will thus be encouraged to reward their benefactor by making an end of their present protector. We bring this to the Truthful One's attention, though he will not have forgotten it. Of the allies in question, some are seeking the enemy's treasury and armed forces, others his territory. The three ornaments sent by the Truthful One have been received. We in turn are sending something to support the present letter. This should be accepted and a verbal message received from our most trusted messenger Siddhárthaka."

MÁLAYA·KETU: Bhaguráyana, my friend, what does the letter mean?

BHAGURÁYANA: Who is this letter for, Siddhárthaka?

SIDDHÁRTHAKA: I don't know, sir.

BHAGURÁYANA: You're taking a letter, you scoundrel, and 5.95
you don't know whom to? All right, all right. Who is to hear your message?

SIDDHÁRTHAKA: You are.

BHAGURÁYANA: We are?

SIDDHÁRTHAKA: Now you've arrested me, I don't know what to say.

BHAGURÁYANA: *(angrily)* Then you soon shall. Bhásvaraka, take him outside and beat him till he talks.

MANSERVANT: Yes, sir. *(going out with* SIDDHÁRTHAKA*)* 5.100

(coming in again) Sir, as he was being beaten, this little box fell out of his pocket.

BHĀGURĀYAṆAḤ: *(vilokya)* kumāra, iyam api Rākṣasa|mudr"|âṅkit" âiva.

MALAYAKETUḤ: ayaṃ lekhasy' â|śūny'|ârtho bhaviśyati. imām api mudrāṃ paripālayann udveṣṭya darśaya.

BHĀGURĀYAṆAḤ *(tathā kṛtvā darśayati)*

5.105 MALAYAKETUḤ: *(vilokya)* aye tad idam ābharaṇaṃ yan mayā sva|śarīrād avatārya Rākṣasāya preṣitam. vyaktaṃ Candraguptasy' âyaṃ lekhaḥ.

BHĀGURĀYAṆAḤ: eṣa nirṇīyate saṃśayaḥ. bhadra, punar api tāḍyatām.

PURUṢAḤ: ⌜jaṃ ajjo āṇavedi.⌟ *(iti niṣkramya punaḥ praviśya ca)* ⌜ajja eso kkhu tāḍīamāṇo bhaṇādi. kumārassa jjeva ṇivedaïssaṃ ti.⌟

MALAYAKETUḤ: praveśaya.

PURUṢAḤ: ⌜jaṃ kumāro āṇavedi.⌟ *(iti niṣkramya* SIDDHĀRTHAKENA *saha praviṣṭaḥ)*

5.110 SIDDHĀRTHAKAḤ: *(pādayor nipatya)* ⌜abhaeṇa me kumāro pasādaṃ karedu.⌟

MALAYAKETUḤ: bhadra, paravato janasy' âbhayam eva. nivedyatām.

SIDDHĀRTHAKAḤ: ⌜suṇādu kumāro. ahaṃ khu amacca|Rakkhaseṇa imaṃ lehaṃ daïa Candaütta|saāsaṃ pesido.⌟

MALAYAKETUḤ: vācikam idānīṃ śrotum icchāmi.

BHAGURÁYANA: *(examining it)* Your Highness, this too is stamped with Rákshasa's seal.

MÁLAYA·KETU: It must be the thing that was to support the letter. Keep the seal intact again and open it and show me.

BHAGURÁYANA *(does so.)*

MÁLAYA·KETU: *(looking)* Oh, it is the jewelry I took from 5.105
myself and sent to Rákshasa. This must be a letter to Chandra·gupta.

BHAGURÁYANA: We'll soon clear up any doubts. Beat him again, Bhásvaraka.

MANSERVANT: Yes, Sir. *(going out and coming in again)* Sir, now he is beaten he says he wants to tell His Highness in person.

MÁLAYA·KETU: Bring him in.

MANSERVANT: Yes, Your Highness, *(He goes out and comes back with* SIDDHÁRTHAKA.*)*

SIDDHÁRTHAKA: *(falling at the* PRINCE*'s feet)* Grant me a 5.110
pardon, Your Highness, I beg you.

MÁLAYA·KETU: My good fellow, a servant who was merely obeying his master has nothing to fear. Speak out.

SIDDHÁRTHAKA: Hear me, Your Highness. Minister Rákshasa told me to take this letter to Chandra·gupta.

MÁLAYA·KETU: And now let me hear the message.

SIDDHĀRTHAKAḤ: ⌜kumāra, saṃdiṭṭho mhi amacca|Rakkhaseṇa jadhā «ede mama pia|vaassā pañca rāāṇo tae saha samuppaṇṇa|saṃdhāṇā jadhā Kulūd'|âdhivo Cittavammo Mala'|âdhivo Sīhaṇādo Kīra|desa|ṇādho Pukkharakkho Sindhu|rāo Sindhuṣeṇo Pārasī'|âhio* Mehaṇādo tti. ettha jjeva je ede paḍhama|bhaṇidā tiṇṇi rāāṇo te Malaakeduṇo visaaṃ ahilasanti. idare vi duve hatthi|balaṃ icchanti. tā jadhā Cāṇakkaṃ ṇirākaria mahā|bhāeṇa mama pīdī uppādidā tadhā edāṇaṃ pi paḍhama|bhaṇido attho paḍivādidavvo.» ettio vāā|saṃdeso tti.⌟

5.115 MALAYAKETUḤ: *(ātma/gatam)* katham, Citravarm'|ādayo 'pi mām abhidruhyanti? atha|vā. ata ev' âiteṣāṃ Rākṣase niratiśayā prītiḥ. *(prakāśam)* Vijaye, Rākṣasaṃ draṣṭum icchāmi.

PRATĪHĀRĪ: ⌜jaṃ kumāro āṇavedi.⌟ *(iti niṣkrāntā)*

tataḥ praveśaty āsana/sthaḥ sva/bhavana/gataḥ PURUṢEṆ' *ânugamyamānaḥ sa/cinto* RĀKṢASAḤ.

RĀKṢASAḤ: *(ātma/gatam)* «āpūrṇam asmad|balaṃ Candragupta|balair» iti yat satyaṃ na me manasaḥ śuddhir asti. kutaḥ:

sādhye niścitam anvayena ghaṭitaṃ
bibhrat sa|pakṣe sthitiṃ
vyāvṛttaṃ ca vipakṣato bhavati yat
tat sādhanaṃ siddhaye
yat sādhyaṃ svayam eva tulyam ubhayoḥ
pakṣe viruddhaṃ ca yat
tasy' âṅgī|karaṇena vādina iva
syāt svāmino nigrahaḥ.

SIDDHÁRTHAKA: Your Highness, Minister Rákshasa told me to say: "The following five princes, close friends of myself, have allied themselves with you: Chitra·varman, Prince of Kulúta; Simha·nada, Prince of Málaya; Pushkaráksha, Lord of Kashmir; Sindhu·shena, Prince of Sindh; Megha·nada, Ruler of the Persians. Of them, the first three seek Málaya·ketu's territory, the other two his troops of elephants. And so just as, noble sir, you have pleased me by dismissing Kautílya, so you should allow them too the abovementioned requests." Such was my message.

MÁLAYA·KETU: *(to himself)* What, Chitra·varman and the 5.115
others betraying me, too? But of course, that is why they have been so extremely friendly with Rákshasa. *(aloud)* Víjaya, I should like to speak to Rákshasa.

FEMALE GUARD: Yes, Your Highness. *(She goes out.)*

Enter, seated at home, attended by his MANSERVANT, RÁKSHASA *in anxious thought.*

RÁKSHASA: *(to himself)* Our army is full of Chandra·gupta's men, and truly I am not easy in my mind:

> If its aim is clear, its parts well knit, the whole securely based,
> An army like an argument wins every conflict.
> But when it is suspect, at war with itself, full of equivocation,
> The man that marshals it ensures his own defeat.

5.120 atha|vā: «tais tair vijñāt'|âparāga|hetubhiḥ prāk|parigṛhīt'|ôpajāpair āpūrṇam» iti na vikalpayitum arhāmi. *(prakāśam)* Priyaṃvadaka, ucyantām asmad|vacanāt kumār'|ânuyāyino rājānaḥ: «saṃprati dine|dine pratyāsīdati Kusumapuram. tataḥ parikalpita|pravibhāgair bhavadbhiḥ prayāṇe prayātavyam. katham iti:

prasthātavyaṃ purastāt Khasa|Magadha|gaṇair
 mām anu vyūḍha|sainyaiḥ
 Gāndhārair madhya|yāne Yavana|nṛpatibhiḥ
 saṃvidheyaḥ prayatnaḥ
paścād gacchantu vīrāḥ Śaka|narapatayaḥ
 saṃbhṛtāś Cedi|Hūṇaiḥ
 Kaulūt'|ādyo 'vaśiṣṭaḥ pathi parivṛṇuyād
 rāja|lokaḥ kumāram.»

PURUṢAḤ: ⌜jaṃ amacco āṇavedi.⌟ *(iti niṣkrāntaḥ)*

(praviśya) PRATĪHĀRĪ. ⌜jaadu jaadu amacco. icchadi de kumāro pekkhiduṃ.⌟

RĀKṢASAḤ: bhadre, muhūrtaṃ tiṣṭha. kaḥ ko 'tra bhoḥ!

5.125 *(praviśya)* PURUṢAḤ. ⌜āṇavedu amacco.⌟

RĀKṢASAḤ: bhadra, ucyatāṃ Śakaṭadāsaḥ: «yathā paridhāpitā vayam ābharaṇaṃ kumāreṇa. tan na yuktam asmābhir an|alaṃkṛtaiḥ kumāra|darśanam anubhavitum. ato yat tad alaṃkaraṇa|trayaṃ krītaṃ tan|madhyād ekaṃ dīyatām» iti.

And yet these people all had clear reasons for their defection 5.120
to us, and they had already accepted our overtures: there's no need for me to feel uneasy. *(aloud)* Priyam·vádaka, take this message in my name to the princes who attend His Highness: "We are now drawing nearer to Pátali·putra every day. Henceforth during our advance you should keep to your planned positions—namely,

In the van with me shall march the men of Khasa
and Mágadha;
The Greek kings of Gandhára shall form the core
of the advance;
In the rear will be the valiant Scythian princes,
supported by the Chedis and the Hunas;
The lord of Kulúta and the other princes shall
guard His Highness on the march!"

MANSERVANT: Yes, Your Honor. *(He goes out.)*

Enter the FEMALE GUARD. Victory to you, Minister. His Highness asks to speak with you.

RÁKSHASA: Then wait a moment. Hallo, hallo, there!

Enter another MANSERVANT. 5.125
Yes, Your Honor?

RÁKSHASA: Tell Shákata·dasa that since His Highness has presented me with decorations, I must not go into His Highness's presence undecorated, and that I should therefore like to have one of the three sets of ornaments we bought.

PURUṢAḤ: ⌜jaṃ amacco āṇavedi.⌟ *(iti niṣkramya punaḥ praviśya ca)* ⌜amacca, idaṃ taṃ alaṃkaraṇaṃ.⌟

RĀKṢASAḤ: *(nāṭyen' âvaloky' ātmānam alaṃkṛty' ôtthāya ca)* bhadre, rāja|kula|gāminaṃ mārgam ādeśaya.

PRATĪHĀRĪ: ⌜edu edu amacco.⌟

5.130 RĀKṢASAḤ: *(ātma|gatam)* adhikāra|padaṃ nāma nirdoṣasy' âpi puruṣasya mahad āśaṅkā|sthānam. kutaḥ:

bhayaṃ tāvat sevyād
abhiniviśate sevaka|janaṃ
tataḥ pratyāsannād
bhavati hṛdayeṣv eva nihitam
tato 'dhyārūḍhānāṃ
padam a|su|jana|dveṣa|jananaṃ
gatiḥ s'|ôcchrāyāṇāṃ
patanam anurūpaṃ kalayati.

PRATĪHĀRĪ: *(parikramya)* ⌜amacca, aaṃ kumāro ciṭṭhadi. uvasappadu ṇaṃ amacco.⌟

RĀKṢASAḤ: *(nāṭyen' âvalokya)* aye ayaṃ kumāras tiṣṭhati. eṣaḥ,

pād'|âgre dṛśam avadhāya niścalantīṃ
śūnyatvād a|parigṛhīta|tad|viśeṣām
vaktr'|ênduṃ vahati kareṇa durvahāṇāṃ
kāryāṇāṃ kṛtam iva gauraveṇa namram.

5.135 *(upasṛtya)* vijayatāṃ kumāraḥ.

MALAYAKETUḤ: ārya, abhivādaye. idam āsanam. āsyatām.

RĀKṢASAḤ: *(upaviśati)* kumāra, kim|arthaṃ vayam āhūtāḥ?

MALAYAKETUḤ: ciram adarśanen' āryasya vayam udvignāḥ.

MANSERVANT: Yes, Your Honor. *(going out and coming in again)* Here are the ornaments, Your Honor.

RÁKSHASA: *(inspecting the jewelry, decorating himself and getting up)* Conduct me to headquarters.

FEMALE GUARD: This way, Minister.

RÁKSHASA: *(to himself)* A post of authority causes even the 5.130
most blameless man much anxiety.

> Fear of his master may possess a servant,
> Or fear of the people about him may grip his heart;
> An exalted post earns the envy of the wicked,
> And in his thoughts one who has climbed high can
> foresee a fall as great.

FEMALE GUARD: *(walking about)* There is His Highness, Minister, approach him.

RÁKSHASA: *(looking)* So, there is His Highness,

> Gazing fixedly at his feet,
> But with thoughts elsewhere, not seeing them,
> His face supported by his hand,
> As if bowed down by the weight of all his problems.

(approaching) Victory to Your Highness. 5.135

MÁLAYA·KETU: Greetings, sir. Here, be seated.

RÁKSHASA: *(sitting)* Why did you summon me, Your Highness?

MÁLAYA·KETU: I was worried, sir, at not seeing you for so long.

RĀKṢASAḤ: kumāra, prayāṇa|pratividhānam anutiṣṭhatā mayā kumārād ayam upālambho 'dhigataḥ.

5.140 MALAYAKETUḤ: ārya, «prayāṇe kathaṃ prativihitam» iti śrotum icchāmi.

RĀKṢASAḤ: kumāra, evam ādiṣṭāḥ kumār'|ânuyāyino rājānaḥ.

(«prasthātavyam» ity|ādi punaḥ paṭhati:)

«prasthātavyaṃ purastāt Khasa|Magadha|gaṇair
māṃ anu vyūḍha|sainyaiḥ
Gāndhārair madhya|yāne Yavana|nṛpatibhiḥ
saṃvidheyaḥ prayatnaḥ
paścād gacchantu vīrāḥ Śaka|narapatayaḥ
saṃbhṛtāś Cedi|Hūṇaiḥ
Kaulūt'|ādyo 'vaśiṣṭaḥ pathi parivṛṇuyād
rāja|lokaḥ kumāram.»

MALAYAKETUḤ: *(ātma|gatam)* katham, ya eva mad|vināśena Candraguptam ārādhayitum udyatās ta eva māṃ parivṛṇvanti? *(prakāśam)* ārya, asti kaś cid yaḥ Kusumapuraṃ gacchati tata āgacchati vā?

RĀKṢASAḤ: kumāra, avasitam idānīṃ gat'|āgata|prayojanam. nanu pañcabhir ahobhir vayam eva tatra gantāraḥ.

5.145 MALAYAKETUḤ: *(ātma|gatam)* vijñāyate. *(prakāśam)* ārya, yady evaṃ tat kim ayam āryeṇa sa|lekhaḥ puruṣaḥ Kusumapuraṃ prasthāpitaḥ?

RĀKṢASAḤ: *(vilokya)* aye Siddhārthakaḥ! bhadra, kim idam?

RÁKSHASA: Your Highness, it is my preoccupation with arrangements for the march that has earned me this rebuke.

MÁLAYA·KETU: I should be glad to hear what your arrange- 5.140
ments for the march are.

RÁKSHASA: I will repeat to Your Highness the orders that I gave Your Highness's vassal princes—

"In the van with me shall march the men of Khasa and Mágadha;
The Greek kings of Gandhára shall form the core of the advance;
In the rear will be the valiant Scythian princes, supported by the Chedis and the Hunas;
The lord of Kulúta and the other princes shall guard His Highness on the march!"

MÁLAYA·KETU: *(to himself)* Am I to be surrounded, then, by the very men who want to endear themselves to Chandra·gupta by killing me? *(aloud)* Sir, have you anyone visiting Pátali·putra or coming here from there?

RÁKSHASA: Any need for such comings and goings is past, Your Highness. After all, we shall be there ourselves in five days' time.

MÁLAYA·KETU: *(to himself)* That settles it. *(aloud)* In that 5.145
case, sir, why did you send this man with a letter to Pátali·putra?

RÁKSHASA: *(seeing him)* Why, Siddhárthaka! What is all this?

SIDDHĀRTHAKAḤ: *(sa|bāṣpaṃ lajjāṃ nāṭayan)* ⌜pasīdadu pasīdadu amacco. amacca, tāḍīanteṇa mae ṇa pāridaṃ amacca|rahassaṃ dhāriduṃ.⌟

RĀKṢASAḤ: bhadra, kīdṛśaṃ rahasyam iti na khalv avagacchāmi.

SIDDHĀRTHAKAḤ: ⌜ṇaṃ viṇṇavemi. tāḍīanteṇa mae ṇa pāridaṃ amacca|rahassaṃ dhāriduṃ ti.⌟

5.150 MALAYAKETUḤ: Bhāgurāyaṇa, svāminaḥ purastād bhīta|lajjito n' âiṣa kathayiṣyati. tat svayam ev' āryāya kathaya.

BHĀGURĀYAṆAḤ: yad ājñāpayati kumāraḥ. amātya, eṣa kathayati: «yath" âham amātya|Rākṣasena lekhaṃ dattvā vācikaṃ ca saṃdiśya Candragupta|sakāśaṃ prasthāpita iti.»

RĀKṢASAḤ: bhadra Siddhārthaka, api satyam?

SIDDHĀRTHAKAḤ: *(lajjāṃ nāṭayan)* ⌜imaṃ rahassaṃ tāḍīanteṇa mae ṇivedidaṃ.⌟

RĀKṢASAḤ: kumāra, anṛtam etat. tāḍyamānaḥ kiṃ na brūyāt?

5.155 MALAYAKETUḤ: Bhāgurāyaṇa, darśaya lekham. vācikam apy asya sva|bhṛtyaḥ kathayiṣyati.

BHĀGURĀYAṆAḤ: amātya, ayaṃ lekhaḥ. *(ity arpayati)*

RĀKṢASAḤ: *(vācayitvā)* kumāra, śatroḥ prayoga eṣaḥ.

MALAYAKETUḤ: lekhasy' â|śūny'|ârtham āryeṇ' êdam ābharaṇam anupreṣitam. tat kathaṃ śatroḥ prayoga eṣa syāt?

SIDDHÁRTHAKA: *(weeping and looking ashamed)* I'm sorry, sir, I'm sorry. I couldn't keep it secret when they beat me.

RÁKSHASA: Keep what secret? What do you mean?

SIDDHÁRTHAKA: I mean I just couldn't keep it secret when they beat me.

MÁLAYA·KETU: Bhaguráyana, he is too afraid and embar- 5.150
rassed in front of his master to speak out. Tell His Honor yourself.

BHAGURÁYANA: As you wish, Your Highness. He tells us, Minister, that you gave him a letter and a verbal message and sent him to Chandra·gupta.

RÁKSHASA: Siddhárthaka, my good man, is this true?

SIDDHÁRTHAKA: *(looking ashamed)* I let it out when they beat me.

RÁKSHASA: It is false, Your Highness. A man who is beaten will say anything.

MÁLAYA·KETU: Show him the letter, Bhaguráyana. His own 5.155
servant can tell him the verbal message.

BHAGURÁYANA: Here is the letter, Minister. *(He hands it over.)*

RÁKSHASA: *(reading it)* This is a trick by the enemy, Your Highness.

MÁLAYA·KETU: You sent that jewelry to support the letter, sir. How might that be a trick by the enemy?

RĀKṢASAḤ: *(ābharaṇaṃ nirvarṇya)* kumāra, n' âitan mayā preṣitam. kumāreṇa me dattam etadd hi kasmiṃś cit paritoṣa|sthāne Siddhārthakāya dattam.

5.160 BHĀGURĀYAṆAḤ: amātya, īdṛśasy' ābharaṇa|viśeṣasya viśeṣataḥ kumāreṇa sva|gātrād avatārya prasādī|kṛtasya kim ayaṃ parityāga|bhūmiḥ?

MALAYAKETUḤ: «vācikam apy āptamāt Siddhārthakāc chrotavyam iti» likhitam.

RĀKṢASAḤ: kumāra, kuto vācikam? lekha ev' âsmadīyo na bhavati.

MALAYAKETUḤ: iyaṃ tarhi kasya mudrā?

RĀKṢASAḤ: kumāra, kapaṭa|mudrām apy utpādayituṃ śaknuvanti dhūrtāḥ.

5.165 BHĀGURĀYAṆAḤ: kumāra, samyag amātyo vijñāpayati. bhadra Siddhārthaka, ken' âyaṃ likhito lekhaḥ?

SIDDHĀRTHAKAḤ: (RĀKṢASA/*mukham avalokya tuṣṇīm adho/mukhas tiṣṭhati)*

BHĀGURĀYAṆAḤ: alaṃ punar ātmānaṃ tāḍayitum. kathaya.

SIDDHĀRTHAKAḤ: ⌜ajja, Saaḍadāseṇa.⌟

RĀKṢASAḤ: kumāra, yadi Śakaṭadāsena likhitas tadā may" âiva likhitaḥ.

5.170 MALAYAKETUḤ: Vijaye, Śakaṭadāsaṃ draṣṭum icchāmi.

RÁKSHASA: *(examining the jewelry)* I didn't send this, Your Highness. This was given me by Your Highness, and I gave it to Siddhárthaka to reward him for a service he had rendered me.

BHAGURÁYANA: Is this a suitable person, Minister, to be 5.160
given jewels of such value, particularly when they had been presented to you by His Highness from his own person?

MÁLAYA·KETU: It says in the letter: "And a verbal message should be received from our most trusted messenger Siddhárthaka."

RÁKSHASA: Verbal message, Your Highness? The letter itself is none of mine.

MÁLAYA·KETU: Then whose is this seal on it?

RÁKSHASA: Wicked men are quite capable of appending a false seal.

BHAGURÁYANA: Minister Rákshasa is right, Your Highness. 5.165
Siddhárthaka, my man, who wrote this letter?

SIDDHÁRTHAKA: *(Glances at* RÁKSHASA*'s face, then stays silent, staring down.)*

BHAGURÁYANA: Don't get yourself beaten again. Speak up.

SIDDHÁRTHAKA: It was Shákata·dasa, sir.

RÁKSHASA: Your Highness, if Shákata·dasa wrote it, then I wrote it myself.

MÁLAYA·KETU: Víjaya, I want to see Shákata·dasa. 5.170

PRATĪHĀRĪ: ⌜jaṃ kumāro āṇavedi.⌟ *(iti prasthitā)*

BHĀGURĀYAṆAḤ: *(ātma/gatam)* na khalv a|niścit'|ârtham ārya|Cāṇakya|praṇidhayo 'bhidhāsyanti. *(prakāśam)* kumāra, na kadā cid api Śakaṭadāso 'mātya|Rākṣasasy' âgrato «mayā likhitam» iti pratipatsyate. ato likhit'|ântaram asy' ānīyatām. varṇa|saṃvāda ev' âinaṃ bhāvayiṣyati.

MALAYAKETUḤ: Vijaye, evaṃ kriyatām.

PRATĪHĀRĪ: ⌜kumāra, muddaṃ pi jācemi?⌟

5.175 MALAYAKETUḤ: ubhayam api kriyatām.

PRATĪHĀRĪ: ⌜jaṃ kumāro āṇavedi.⌟ *(iti niṣkramya punaḥ praviśya)* ⌜kumāra, edaṃ khu pattaṃ ajja|Saaḍadāseṇa sa|hattha|lihidaṃ muddā a.⌟

MALAYAKETUḤ: *(ubhayam api nāṭyen' âvalokya)* ārya, saṃvadanty akṣarāṇi.

RĀKṢASAḤ: *(ātma/gatam)* saṃvadanty akṣarāṇi! «Śakaṭadāsas tu mama mitram» iti visaṃvadanty akṣarāṇi. tat kiṃ nu khalu Śakaṭadāsena,

smṛtaṃ syāt putra|dārasya
  vismṛta|svāmi|bhaktinā
caleṣv artheṣu lubdhena
  na yaśaḥsv anapāyiṣu.

FEMALE GUARD: Yes, Your Highness. *(She moves off.)*

BHAGURÁYANA: *(to himself)* No agent of the revered Kautílya would take an unnecessary risk. *(aloud)* Your Highness, Shákata·dasa will never admit in front of Minister Rákshasa that he wrote the letter. So let us get something else written by him, and a comparison of the handwriting will settle the matter.

MÁLAYA·KETU: Yes, see to that, Víjaya.

FEMALE GUARD: Shall I ask for the seal as well, Your Highness?

MÁLAYA·KETU: Yes, both. 5.175

FEMALE GUARD: Yes, Your Highness. *(going out and coming in again)* Your Highness, here is a letter just written by Shákata·dasa in his own hand, together with the seal.

MÁLAYA·KETU: *(comparing them both)* Minister, the characters agree.

RÁKSHASA: *(to himself)* The characters agree! But Shákata·dasa is my friend, and there's one character at odds. Is it conceivable that Shákata·dasa,

Remembered his wife and children
And forgot his loyalty to our Lord,
Eager for transient advantage
Instead of imperishable glory?

5.180 atha|vā kaḥ saṃdehaḥ?

mudrā tasya kar'|âṅguli|praṇayinī
  Siddhārthakas tat|suhṛt
tasy' âiv' âpara|lekha|sūcitam idaṃ
  pattraṃ prayog'|āśrayam
su|vyaktaṃ Śakaṭena bheda|paṭubhiḥ
  saṃdhāya sārdhaṃ paraiḥ
bhartuḥ sneha|parāṅ|mukhena kṛpaṇaṃ
  prāṇ'|ârthinā ceṣṭitam.

MALAYAKETUḤ: ārya, «alaṃkāra|trayaṃ śrīmatā yad anupreṣitaṃ tad upagatam» iti yal likhitaṃ tan|madhyāt kim idam ekam? *(nirvarṇy' ātma|gatam)* katham, tātena dhṛta|pūrvam idam ābharaṇam! *(prakāśam)* ārya, kuto 'yam alaṃkāraḥ?

RĀKṢASAḤ: vaṇigbhyaḥ krayād adhigataḥ.

MALAYAKETUḤ: Vijaye, api pratyabhijānāti bhavatī bhūṣaṇam idam?

5.185 PRATĪHĀRĪ: *(nirvarṇya sa|bāṣpam)* ⌜kumāra, kadhaṃ ṇa paccabhiāṇissaṃ? imaṃ khu su|gihīda|ṇāma|dheeṇa Pavvadīsareṇa dhārida|puvvaṃ.⌟

MALAYAKETUḤ: *(sa|bāṣpam)* hā tāta!

etāni tāni guṇa|vallabha vallabhāni
  gātr'|ôcitāni kula|bhūṣaṇa bhūṣaṇāni
yaiḥ śobhito 'si mukha|candra|kṛt'|âvabhāso
  nakṣatravān iva śarat|samaye pradoṣaḥ.

But it must be so: 5.180

> The signet ring does not leave his finger,
> Siddhárthaka is his friend;
> The treacherous letter is his, as the other letter shows:
> Clearly he has been plotting with enemies who know how to sow dissension,
> Forgetting affection, saving his skin by treachery.

MÁLAYA·KETU: Is that, sir, one of the three ornaments whose receipt was acknowledged in the letter? *(examining them, to himself)* Why, it is jewelry my father used to wear! *(aloud)* Where did you get these jewels?

RÁKSHASA: They were bought from traders.

MÁLAYA·KETU: Víjaya, do you recognize them?

FEMALE GUARD: *(examining them and weeping)* How could I 5.185
fail to, Your Highness? They are what His Majesty King Párvataka of blessed memory used to wear.

MÁLAYA·KETU: *(weeping)* Oh, father!

> These were the jewels you loved, beloved hero;
> Ornament of our house, these were the jewels that adorned you,
> That shone on you, beneath the moon-radiance of your face,
> Like autumn stars against the evening sky.

RĀKṢASAḤ: *(ātma|gatam)* katham? «Parvateśvara|dhṛta|pūrvāṇ' îty» āha. vyaktam etāny api tena Cāṇakya|prayuktena vaṇij" âsmāsu vikrītāni.

MALAYAKETUḤ: ārya, tātena dhṛta|pūrvāṇām ābharaṇa|viśeṣāṇāṃ viśeṣataś Candragupta|hasta|gatānāṃ krayād adhigama iti na yujyata etat. atha|vā yujyata ev' âitat. kutaḥ:

5.190 Candraguptasya vikretur
  adhikaṃ lābham icchataḥ
kalpitaṃ mūlyam eteṣāṃ
  krūreṇa bhavatā vayam.

RĀKṢASAḤ: *(ātma|gatam)* aho su|śliṣṭo bhūṣaṇa|prayogaḥ. kutaḥ:

«lekho 'yaṃ na mam' êti» n' ôttaram idaṃ,
  mudrā madīyā yataḥ;
«sauhārdaṃ Śakaṭena khaṇḍitam iti»
  śraddheyam etat katham?
Maurye bhūṣaṇa|vikrayaṃ nara|patau
  ko nāma saṃbhāvayet?
tasmāt saṃpratipattir eva hi varaṃ
  na grāmyam atr' ôttaram.

MALAYAKETUḤ: etad āryaṃ pṛcchāmi.

RĀKṢASAḤ: kumāra, ya āryas taṃ pṛccha. vayam idānīm an|āryāḥ saṃvṛttāḥ.

RÁKSHASA: *(to himself)* Once worn by King Párvataka, she says? Then the traders who sold them to me must have been agents of Kautílya.

MÁLAYA·KETU: It is hardly likely, sir, that you could have bought valuable jewels once worn by my father, especially when they had fallen into Chandra·gupta's hands. Or, rather, it's all too likely:

The seller was Chandra·gupta 5.190
Looking for a handsome profit,
And the price that you fixed on for them,
Monster, was me.

RÁKSHASA: *(to himself)* Alas, the enemy's trap is carefully sprung!

No use to say it is not my letter, when the seal on
it is mine.
That Shákata·dasa has broken faith would never
be credited.
And who would believe that the Mauryan
Emperor could sell his jewels?—
Better admit the charge than vulgarly dispute.

MÁLAYA·KETU: Let me ask Your Honor this—

RÁKSHASA: Ask one that has honor, Your Highness. I have no honor left.

5.195 MALAYAKETUḤ:

Mauryo 'sau svāmi|putraḥ paricaraṇa|paro
    mitra|putras tav' âhaṃ
dātā so 'rthasya tubhyaṃ satatam anugatas
    tvaṃ tu mahyaṃ dadāsi
dāsyaṃ sat|kāra|pūrvaṃ nanu saciva|padaṃ
    tatra te svāmyam atra
sv'|ârthe kasmin samīhā punar adhikatare
    tvām an|āryī|karoti?

RĀKṢASAḤ: evam abhiyukta|vyavahāriṇā kumāreṇ' âiva me nirṇayo dattaḥ.

Mauryo 'sau svāmi|putraḥ paricaraṇa|paras
    tvaṃ tu mitrasya putro
dātā so 'rthasya mahyaṃ satatam anugataṃ
    tv atra tubhyaṃ dadāmi
deyaṃ sat|kāra|pūrvaṃ nanu saciva|padaṃ
    tatra me svāmyam atra
sv'|ârthe kasmin samīhā punar adhikatare
    mām an|āryī|karoti?

MALAYAKETUḤ: *(lekham alaṃkaraṇaṃ ca vinirdiśya)* idam idānīṃ kim?

5.200 RĀKṢASAḤ: *(sa|bāṣpam)* Vidher vilasitam idaṃ na Cāṇakyasya. kutaḥ:

MÁLAYA·KETU: 5.195

The Mauryan is your master's son, I am your
friend's son eager in your service.
He would be your benefactor: here you are mine,
and always listened to.
There minister means politely treated slave, here
it means master.
What gain can you long for, to make you so
dishonored?

RÁKSHASA: Your Highness, you have answered yourself—

The Mauryan is my master's son, you my friend's
son, eager in my service.
He would be my benefactor: here I am yours, and
always listened to.
There minister means politely treated slave, here
it means master.
What gain can I long for, to make me so dishonored?

MÁLAYA·KETU: *(indicating the letter and the jewelry)* And what of these?

RÁKSHASA: *(weeping)* It is the hand of Destiny: 5.200

bhṛtyatve paribhāva|dhāmani sati
snehāt prabhūṇāṃ satāṃ
putrebhyaḥ kṛta|vedināṃ kṛta|dhiyāṃ
yeṣāṃ na bhinnā vayam
te lokasya parīkṣakāḥ kṣiti|bhujaḥ
pāpena yena kṣatāḥ
tasy' êdaṃ vipulaṃ Vidher vilasitaṃ
puṃsāṃ prayatna|cchidaḥ.

MALAYAKETUḤ: *(sa|krodham)* katham? ady' âpi nihnūyata eva? Vidher vilasitam idaṃ na lobhasya? an|ārya,

kanyāṃ tīvra|viṣa|prayoga|viṣamāṃ
kṛtvā kṛta|ghn'|ātmanā
viśrambha|pravaṇas tadā mama pitā
nītaḥ kathā|śeṣatām
saṃpraty āhita|gauraveṇa bhavatā
mantr'|âdhikāre ripoḥ
prārabdhāḥ punar āma|māṃsa|vad aho
vikretum ete vayam.

RĀKṢASAḤ: *(ātma|gatam)* ayam aparo gaṇḍasy' ôpari sphoṭaḥ. *(prakāśam, karṇau pidhāya)* śāntaṃ pāpam! a|pāpo 'haṃ Parvateśvare.

5.205 MALAYAKETUḤ: kena tarhi vyāpāditas tātaḥ?

RĀKṢASAḤ: daivam atra praṣṭavyam.

MALAYAKETUḤ: na Kṣapaṇako Jīvasiddhiḥ?

RĀKṢASAḤ: *(ātma|gatam)* katham? Jīvasiddhir api Cāṇakya|prayuktaḥ? hanta hṛdayam api me ripubhiḥ svī|kṛtam.

MALAYAKETUḤ: *(sa|krodham)* Bhāsvaraka, ājñāpyatāṃ Śikharasenaḥ senā|patiḥ. «ya ete Rākṣasena saha suhṛtt-

It is the hand of Destiny blighting man's efforts,
The same that has killed off the kings who could judge a man right;
Though servitude means contempt, yet those kings in their love
Being grateful and wise looked on me as their son.

MÁLAYA·KETU: *(angrily)* Do you still deny it? This is the hand of Destiny, is it, not your own greed? Dishonored one—

You have already treacherously primed a girl with deadly poison
And turned my too trusting father into a memory.
Now you are obsessed with becoming the enemy's minister
And try to sell me in turn like so much raw meat.

RÁKSHASA: *(to himself)* Here is a still unkinder thrust! *(aloud, stopping his ears)* Perish that thought! I am guiltless toward Párvataka.

MÁLAYA·KETU: Then who did kill my father? 5.205

RÁKSHASA: You must ask fate.

MÁLAYA·KETU: Ask fate? Not Jiva·siddhi the Jain?

RÁKSHASA: *(to himself)* What, is Jiva·siddhi, too, working for Kautílya? Alas, my enemies have made my very heart their own.

MÁLAYA·KETU: *(angrily)* Bhásvaraka, take the following order to General Shíkhara·sena: "The five princes who

vam utpādy' âsmac|charīr'|âbhidroheṇa Candraguptam ārādhayitu|kāmāḥ pañca rājānaḥ. tad yathā: Kaulūtaś Citravarmā Malaya|nara|patiḥ Siṃhanādaḥ Kāśmīraḥ Puṣkarākṣaḥ Sindhu|rājaḥ Sindhuṣeṇaḥ Pārasik'|âdhipo Meghanāda iti. atra ya eṣāṃ trayaḥ prathamā madīyāṃ bhūmiṃ kāmayante te gambhīra|śvabhram upanīya pāṃśubhiḥ pūryantām. itarau tu hasti|bala|kāmau hastin" âiva ghātyeyātām iti.»

5.210 PURUṢAḤ: ⌜jaṃ kumāro āṇavedi.⌟ *(iti niṣkrāntaḥ)*

MALAYAKETUḤ: Rākṣasa, n' âhaṃ viśrambha|ghātī Rākṣasaḥ. Malayaketuḥ khalv aham. tad gaccha. samāśrīyatāṃ sarv'|ātmanā Candraguptaḥ.

Viṣṇuguptaṃ ca Mauryaṃ ca
samam apy āgatau tvayā
unmūlayitum īśo 'haṃ
tri|vargam iva durṇayaḥ.

kṛtaṃ kāla|haraṇena. sāṃpratam eva Kusumapuram avarodhanāya pratiṣṭhantām asmad|balāni.

Gauḍīnāṃ lodhra|dhūlī|parimala|dhavalān
dhūmrayantaḥ kapolān
kliśnantaḥ kṛṣṇimānaṃ bhramara|kula|nibhaṃ
kuñcitasy' âlakasya
pāṃśu|stambhā balānāṃ turaga|khura|puṭa|
kṣoda|labdh'|ātma|lābhāḥ
śatrūṇām uttam'|âṅge gaja|mada|salila|
cchinna|mūlāḥ patantu.

have made a pact with Rákshasa and wish to do violence to my person to please Chandra·gupta—namely, Chitra·varman of Kulúta, Simha·nada of Málaya, Pushkaráksha of Kashmir, Sindhu·shena of Sindh, Megha·nada of the Persians—shall be executed: the three first, who want my land, shall be put in a pit and covered with earth; the two last, who want my troops of elephants, shall be trampled to death by an elephant."

MANSERVANT: Yes, Your Highness. *(He goes out.)* 5.210

MÁLAYA·KETU: Rákshasa, I am not Rákshasa the traitor: I am Málaya·ketu. Go, seek out Chandra·gupta with all your heart—

> Kautílya, yes, and the Mauryan,
> Though they unite with you,
> I can destroy as surely
> As evil drives out good.

We shall delay no longer. Let our troops march forth this very minute to take Pátali·putra.

> Graying the Eastern women's cheeks that were
> fragrant with *lodhra* pollen
> And spoiling the bee-dark blackness of their
> curling locks,
> Columns of dust from our troops, born of the
> horses' galloping, then cut down
> By the stream of our elephants' ichor, shall fall on
> the heads of our enemies.

5.215 *iti sa|parijano niṣkrānto* MALAYAKETUḤ.

RĀKṢASAḤ: *(s'|āvegam)* hā dhik ghātitās tapasvinaś Citra-varm'|ādayaḥ. tat kathaṃ suhṛd|vināśāya Rākṣasaś ceṣṭate na ripu|vināśāya? tat kim idānīṃ karavāṇi manda|bhāgyaḥ?

kiṃ gacchāmi tapo|vanaṃ? na tapasā
  śāmyet sa|vairaṃ manaḥ;
kiṃ bhartṝn anuyāmi? jīvati ripau
  strīṇām iyaṃ yogyatā;
kiṃ vā khaḍga|sakhaḥ patāmy ari|bale?
  n' âitan na yuktaṃ bhavet
cetaś Candanadāsa|mokṣa|rabhasaṃ
  rundhyāt kṛta|jñaṃ na cet.

iti niṣkrāntāḥ sarve.

MÁLAYA·KETU *and his retinue go out.* 5.215

RÁKSHASA: *(in distress)* Alas, poor Chitra·varman and the rest all killed! Does Rákshasa work to kill his friends and not his enemies? Miserable wretch that I am, what shall I do?

Shall I go to a hermitage? Austerities will not calm
my embittered heart.
Follow my lord? While the enemy lives, that is a
woman's way.
Fall with my sword on the foe? That would not be
ill
Did gratitude not prevent it, and tell me that
Chándana·dasa must be freed.

He goes out.

PRELUDE TO ACT VI

tatah praviśaty alamkrtah sa|harṣaḥ SIDDHĀRTHAKAḤ.

SIDDHĀRTHAKAH:

⌜jaadi jalada|ṇīlo Kesavo Kesi|ghādī
jaadi su|aṇa|diṭṭhī|candimā Candaütto
jaadi jaaṇa|sajjaṃ jāva kāūṇa seṇṇaṃ
paḍihada|paḍivakkhā ajja|Cāṇakka|ṇīdī.⌟

⌜tā jāva cirassa kālassa pia|vaassaṃ Samiddhatthaaṃ aṇṇesemi.⌟ *(parikramy' âvalokya ca)* ⌜aaṃ uṇa pia|vaasso Samiddhatthao ido jjeva āacchadi. tā jāva uvasappāmi.⌟

6.5 *(tataḥ praviśati* SAMIDDHĀRTHAKAḤ*)*

⌜saṃbhāvantā āvāṇaesu
geh'|ūsave ruāventā
hiaa|ṭṭhidā vi virahe
mittaṃ mittāï dūmenti.⌟

⌜sudaṃ ca mae jadhā Malaakedu|kaḍaādo pia|vaasso Siddhatthao āado tti. tā jāva ṇaṃ aṇṇesemi.⌟ *(parikramy' âvalokya)* ⌜eso Siddhatthao.⌟ *(upasṛtya)* ⌜avi suhaṃ pia|vaassassa?⌟

SIDDHĀRTHAKAH: *(vilokya)* ⌜kadhaṃ pia|vaasso Samiddhatthao!⌟ *(upagamya)* ⌜Samiddhatthaa avi suhaṃ pia|vaassassa?⌟

ubhāv anyonyam āliṅgataḥ.

Enter SIDDHÁRTHAKA, *decorated and in high spirits.*

SIDDHÁRTHAKA:

> Glory to Krishna, dark as a cloud, slayer of the demon,*
> Glory to Chandra·gupta, a full moon to the eyes of all good people,
> Glory to that which has prepared our forces for victory,
> The revered Kautílya's strategy that vanquishes our foes.

Now at long last I may seek out my good friend Samiddhárthaka. *(walking about and looking)* But there is good Samiddhárthaka coming this way. I'll go and meet him.

(Enter SAMIDDHÁRTHAKA.*)* 6.5

> The friends we embrace in our drinking-bouts
> Who bring joy to our festivities,
> When they are gone, though they stay in our hearts,
> They grieve us by their absence.

Now I have heard that my dear good friend Siddhárthaka is back from Málaya·ketu's camp. So I'm off to find him. *(walking about and seeing him)* There he is! *(going up to him)* How are you, my dear friend?

SIDDHÁRTHAKA: *(seeing him)* Hallo—it's my good friend Samiddhárthaka! *(coming up to him)* Samiddhárthaka! Are you well, my dear friend?

They embrace each other.

SAMIDDHĀRTHAKAḤ: ⌜kudo me suhaṃ jeṇa tumaṃ cira|ppavāsa|ppaccāado ajja vi ṇa me gehaṃ āacchasi?⌟

6.10 SIDDHĀRTHAKAH: ⌜pasīdadu pasīdadu pia|vaasso. diṭṭha|metto jjeva ajja|Cāṇakkeṇa āṇatto mhi jadhā Siddhatthaa gaccha. edaṃ vuttantaṃ pia|daṃsaṇassa Candasiriṇo ṇivedehi tti. tado tassa ṇivedia evaṃ aṇubhūda|patthiva|ppasādo ahaṃ pia|vaassaṃ pekkhiduṃ tava jjeva gehaṃ calido mhi.⌟

SAMIDDHĀRTHAKAḤ: ⌜vaassa, jaï mae suṇidavvaṃ tado kadhehi: kiṃ taṃ piaṃ pia|daṃsaṇassa Candasiriṇo ṇivedidaṃ ti?⌟

SIDDHĀRTHAKAH: ⌜vaassa, kiṃ tav' âvi a|kadhidavvaṃ atthi. tā ṇisāmehi. atthi dāva ajja|Cāṇakka|ṇīdi|mohida|madiṇā Malaakedu|hadaeṇa ṇirākaria Rakkhasaṃ hadā Cittavamma|ppamuhā pahāṇā pañca patthivā. tado a|samikkhida|kārī esa durāāro tti ujjhia Malaakedu|kaḍaa|bhūmiṃ kusakadāe bhaa|vilola|sesa|saiṇika|parivārā sakaṃsakaṃ visaaṃ ahippatthidā patthivā. tado Bhaddabhaḍa|Purisadatta|Hiṅgurāda|Valaütta|Rāaseṇa|Bhāürāaṇa|Rohidakkha|Vijaavamma|ppamuhehiṃ ṇigihido Malaakedū.⌟

SAMIDDHĀRTHAKAḤ: ⌜vaassa, Bhaddabhaḍa|ppamuhā kila devassa Candasiriṇo avarattā Malaakeduṃ samassida tti loe mantīadi. tā kiṃ ṇimittaṃ ku|kavi|ṇāḍaassa via aṇṇaṃ muhe aṇṇaṃ ṇivvahaṇe tti?⌟

SIDDHĀRTHAKAH: ⌜vaassa, deva|ṇadīe via a|suṇida|gadīe ṇamo ṇamo ajja|Cāṇakka|ṇīdīe.⌟

SAMIDDHÁRTHAKA: How can I be well, when you come back after such a long time and still haven't been to my house?

SIDDHÁRTHAKA: I'm sorry, my friend, I'm sorry. The moment he saw me, His Honor Kautílya told me to go and tell my news to His Glorious Majesty the Emperor. I told His Majesty and received marks of his royal favor, and I was just on my way to your house to see you, dear friend. 6.10

SAMIDDHÁRTHAKA: If I'm allowed to hear it, tell me what was the good news you told His Majesty?

SIDDHÁRTHAKA: There's nothing I'd keep from you, friend. Listen. The accursed Málaya·ketu's mind was so deluded by the strategy of His Honor Kautílya that he dismissed Rákshasa and executed Chitra·varman and four other leading princes. At which the remaining princes, thinking him reckless and wicked, left Málaya·ketu's camp for their own good, and attended by the rest of the soldiery in a state of fear and trembling set off for their respective domains. Then Málaya·ketu was arrested by Bhadra·bhata, Púrusha·datta, Hingu·rata, Bala·gupta, Raja·sena, Bhaguráyana, Rohitáksha, Víjaya·varman and others.

SAMIDDHÁRTHAKA: Friend, everyone said Bhadra·bhata and the others had defected from His Majesty the Emperor and gone over to Málaya·ketu. So why do they start one way and end another like a bad play?

SIDDHÁRTHAKA: Do homage, friend, to the noble Kautílya's strategy, that flows as silently as the heavenly Ganges.

6.15 SAMIDDHĀRTHAKAḤ: ⌜vaassa, tado tado.⌟

SIDDHĀRTHAKAH: ⌜vaassa, tado pahūda|sāra|sāhaṇa|samaṇṇideṇa ido ṇikkamia ajja|Cāṇakkeṇa paḍivaṇṇaṃ sa|rāakaṃ rāa|balaṃ.⌟

SAMIDDHĀRTHAKAḤ: ⌜vaassa, kahiṃ?⌟

SIDDHĀRTHAKAH: ⌜vaassa, jahiṃ ede:⌟

⌜Adisaa|garueṇaṃ dāṇa|dappeṇa dantī
sajala|jalada|ṇīlā ubbhamantā ṇadanti
kasa|pahara|bhaeṇaṃ jāda|kamp'|uttaraṅgā
gahida|jaaṇa|saddā saṃpavante turangā.⌟

6.20 SAMIDDHĀRTHAKAḤ: ⌜vaassa, savvaṃ dāva ciṭṭhadu. tadhā savva|loassa paccakkhaṃ ujjhid'|âhiāro ciraṃ ciṭṭhia ajja|Cāṇakko puṇo vi taṃ jeva manti|padaṃ ārūḍho?⌟

SIDDHĀRTHAKAH: ⌜vaassa, adi|muddho dāṇi si tumaṃ jo amacca|Rakkhaseṇa vi aṇ|avagāhida|puvvaṃ ajja|Cāṇakka|buddhiṃ avagāhiduṃ icchasi.⌟

SAMIDDHĀRTHAKAḤ: ⌜vaassa, adha amacca|Rakkhaso idāṇiṃ kahiṃ?⌟

SIDDHĀRTHAKAH: ⌜vaassa, so vi tahiṃ bhaa|vilole vattamāṇe Malaakedu|kaḍaādo ṇikkamia Undura|ṇāma|dheeṇa careṇa aṇusarīanto imaṃ jeva Kusumaüraṃ āado tti ajja|Cāṇakkassa ṇivedidaṃ.⌟

SAMIDDHĀRTHAKAḤ: ⌜vaassa, tadhā ṇāma amacca|Rakkhaso Nanda|rajja|paccāṇaaṇe kada|vvavasāo ṇikkamia saṃpadaṃ a|kad'|attho puṇo vi imaṃ jeva Kusumaüraṃ āado?⌟

SAMIDDHÁRTHAKA: Go on, friend. 6.15

SIDDHÁRTHAKA: Thereupon Kautílya marched out with large picked forces and overcame the princes and their soldiers.

SAMIDDHÁRTHAKA: Where, friend?

SIDDHÁRTHAKA: Over there, friend, where

> Elephants rear up and trumpet,
> Dark as swollen clouds in their high rutting frenzy,
> And horses, trembling in fear of the whip,
> Surge forward in a flood as they hear the victory
> cry.

SAMIDDHÁRTHAKA: But never mind that—why has the noble Kautílya resumed his post of minister after publicly renouncing it and standing aside for so long? 6.20

SIDDHÁRTHAKA: You're a fool, my friend, if you think you can fathom Kautílya's mind when even Minister Rákshasa couldn't, up till now.

SAMIDDHÁRTHAKA: And where is Minister Rákshasa at the present moment?

SIDDHÁRTHAKA: His Honor Kautílya has had a report that he escaped from Málaya·ketu's camp in the confusion, and has arrived here in Pátali·putra, shadowed by a spy they call the Rat.

SAMIDDHÁRTHAKA: You mean that, after leaving here resolved to restore the Nanda Empire, Minister Rákshasa has come back again without achieving his aim?

6.25 SIDDHĀRTHAKAH: ⌜vaassa, takkemi Candaṇadāsassa siṇeheṇa tti.⌟

SAMIDDHĀRTHAKAḤ: ⌜vaassa, adha Candaṇadāsassa mokkhaṃ pekkhasi?⌟

SIDDHĀRTHAKAH: ⌜kudo se adhaṇṇassa mokkho? so kkhu saṃpadaṃ ajja|Cāṇakkassa āṇattīe duvehiṃ pi amhehiṃ vajjha|ṭṭhāṇaṃ pavesia vāvādidavvo.⌟

SAMIDDHĀRTHAKAḤ: *(sa|krodham)* ⌜kiṃ ajja|Cāṇakkassa ghādaa|aṇo ṇ' atthi jeṇa amhe idisesuṃ ṇisaṃsesuṃ ṇioedi?⌟

SIDDHĀRTHAKAH: ⌜vaassa, ko jīva|loe jīvidu|kāmo ajja|Cāṇakkassa āṇattiṃ paḍiūledi. tā ehi. caṇḍāla|vesa|dhāriṇo bhavia Candaṇadāsaṃ vajjha|ṭṭhāṇaṃ ṇemha.⌟

6.30 *ity ubhau niṣkrāntau.*

SIDDHÁRTHAKA: I think it's out of his love for Chándana· 6.25
dasa, friend.

SAMIDDHÁRTHAKA: Do you think Chándana·dasa will be freed, then?

SIDDHÁRTHAKA: Freed, that unlucky man? On Kautílya's orders you and I, my friend, have got to take him right away to the Execution Ground and kill him.

SAMIDDHÁRTHAKA: *(angrily)* Does His Honor Kautílya have no executioners, employing us on such a loathsome errand?

SIDDHÁRTHAKA: My friend, no one questions Kautílya's orders if they want to stay in this world. So come on. Let's dress ourselves as outcastes and take Chándana·dasa to the Execution Ground.

Both go out. 6.30

ACT VI
THE EXECUTION

tataḥ praviśati rajju/hastaḥ PURUṢAḤ.

PURUṢAḤ:

⌜chag|guṇa|saṃjoa|daḍhā
uvāa|parivāḍi|ghaḍida|pāsa|muhī
Cāṇakka|ṇīdi|rajjū
riu|saṃjamaṇ'|ujjuā jaadi.⌟

⌜eso so ajja|Cāṇakkassa Unduraeṇa kaghido padeso jahiṃ mae ajja|Cāṇakk'|āṇattīe amacca|Rakkhaso pekkhidavvo.⌟ *(vilokya)* ⌜kadhaṃ, eso kkhu amacca|Rakkhaso kad'|âvaguṇṭhaṇo ido jjeva āacchadi. jāva imehiṃ jiṇṇ'|ujjāṇa|pādavehiṃ antarida|sarīro pekkhāmi kahiṃ āsaṇa|pariggahaṃ karedi.⌟ *(iti parikramya tathā sthitaḥ.)*

6.35 *tataḥ praviśati yathā/nirdiṣṭaḥ sa/śastro* RĀKṢASAḤ.

RĀKṢASAḤ: *(sa/bāṣpam)* kaṣṭaṃ bhoḥ kaṣṭam!

utsann'|āśraya|kātar" êva kulaṭā
gotr'|ântaraṃ Śrīr gatā
tām ev' ânugatā gat'|ânugatikās
tyakt'|ânurāgāḥ prajāḥ
āptair apy an|avāpta|pauruṣa|phalaiḥ
kāryasya dhūr ujjhitā
kiṃ kurvantv? atha|v" ôttam'|âṅga|rahitair
n' âṅgaiś ciraṃ sthīyate.

Enter a MAN *carrying a rope.*

MAN:

> Firmly twisted from the Six Strands
> And with a noose fashioned from the Chain of
> Tactics,
> Victory to the rope of Kautílya's strategy
> Waiting to bind the enemy.

Here is the place His Honor Kautílya heard about from the Rat, where His Honor has instructed me to meet with Rákshasa. *(looking)* Ah, there is Minister Rákshasa, coming this way with his face covered. I'll hide among the trees of this overgrown park and watch where he seats himself. *(He walks about and then stays still.)*

Enter RÁKSHASA *as described, carrying a sword.* 6.35

RÁKSHASA: *(weeping)* Alas, alas!

> Like a whore frightened by losing her man,
> Fortune has gone to another's house,
> And the people have followed after her like sheep,
> their loyalty forgotten.
> And even the best, finding courage unrewarded,
> have given up the task.
> But what could they do? Limbs do not last when
> the head is lopped.

api ca: patiṃ tyaktvā devaṃ
bhuvana|patim uccair abhijanaṃ
gatā khidreṇa Śrīr Vṛṣalam avinīt" êva vṛṣalī
sthirī|bhūtā c' âsmin
kim iha karavāma sthiram api
prayatnaṃ no yeṣāṃ
viphalayati Daivaṃ dviṣad iva?

mayā hi:

6.40 deve gate divam a|tad|vidha|mṛtyu|yogye
Śaileśvaraṃ tam adhikṛtya kṛtaḥ prayatnaḥ
tasmin hate tanayam asya tath" âpy a|siddhiḥ
Daivaṃ hi Nanda|kula|śatrur asau na vipraḥ.

aho viveka|śūnyatā mlecchasya! kutaḥ:

yo naṣṭān api jīva|nāśam adhunā
śuśrūṣate svāminaḥ
teṣāṃ vairibhir akṣataḥ katham asau
saṃdhāsyate Rākṣasaḥ?
itthaṃ vastu|viveka|mūḍha|manasā
mlecchena n' ālocitaṃ
daiven' ôpahatasya buddhir atha|vā
sarvaṃ viparyasyati.

tad idānīm api tāvad arāti|hasta|gato nāśaṃ gacchan na Rākṣasaś Candraguptena saha sandhiṃ kuryād iti. atha|vā «kāmam a|satya|sandha iti» param a|yaśo na punaḥ śatru|vañcanā|paribhūtiḥ. *(samantād avalokya s'|âsram)*

Leaving her husband, a great emperor of noble birth,
Fortune has eloped to the Mauryan, lowborn harlot to lowborn man,
And sticks to him. What can I do, I whose hardest struggles
Are frustrated by Fate, which seems to side against me?

For,

When my king went to heaven, never deserving such a death, 6.40
I centered all my efforts on Párvataka.
When he was killed, I turned to his son—but all without success.
Truly Fate is the Nanda's enemy, not the brahmin.

How poor an understanding the barbarian has!

A man who still serves his masters though they are dead and gone,
How could that same man while he has strength conspire with their bitterest enemies?
The barbarian in his blind folly could not see that—
But the mind that fate has smitten turns everything upside down.

Why, even now if Rákshasa falls into his enemy's hands, he shall die rather than bargain with Chandra·gupta. To be willfully false to one's word is a greater disgrace than to be worsted by the enemy's tricks. *(looking all about him and weeping)* Is this, then, the parkland about

etās tāvad devasya pāda|caṅkramaṇa|pavitrī|kṛta|talāḥ Kusumapur'|ôpakaṇṭha|bhūmayaḥ?

iha hi, śārṅga|jyā|kṛṣṭi|mukta|praśithila|kavikā|
pragraheṇ' âtra deśe
deven' âkāri citraṃ prajavita|turagaṃ
bāṇa|mokṣaś caleṣu
asyām udyāna|rājau sthitam iha kathitaṃ
rājabhis tair vin" êtthaṃ
saṃpraty ālokyamānāḥ Kusumapura|bhuvo
bhūyasā duḥkhayanti.

6.45 tat kva nu khalu gacchāmi manda|bhāgyaḥ? *(vilokya)* bhavatu. dṛṣṭam etaj jīrṇ'|ôdyānam. tad atra praviśya kutaś cic Candanadāsa|vṛttāntam upalapsye. *(parikramya)* aho, a|lakṣit'|ôpanipātāḥ puruṣāṇāṃ sama|viṣama|daśā|vibhāga|pariṇatayo bhavanti. kutaḥ:

paurair aṅgulibhir nav'|ênduvad ahaṃ
nirdiśyamānaḥ śanaiḥ
yo rāj" êva purā purān niragamaṃ
rājñāṃ sahasrair vṛttaḥ
bhūyaḥ saṃprati so 'ham eva nagare
tatr' âiva vadhyaiḥ samo
jīrṇ'|ôdyānakam eṣa taskara iva
trāsād gviśāmi drutam.

atha|vā yeṣāṃ prasādād idam āsīt ta eva na santi. *(nāṭyena praviśya vilokya ca)* aho, jīrṇ'|ôdyānasya nir|abhiramyatā!

Pátali·putra whose ground was once hallowed by my Emperor's tread?

In these parts, with slackened reins as he drew the bow,
His Majesty at full gallop would shoot at moving targets.
In this avenue he stayed, here gave audience—lacking such kings
The lands of the city are a most melancholy sight.

Where shall I go in my wretchedness? *(looking)* Ah, I see an overgrown park. I will go in and try to get news of Chándana·dasa from someone. *(walking about)* Alas, the good and evil turns of man's condition creep up on him all unnoticed! 6.45

Once, with the townsfolk pointing at me, as at the rising moon,
I went forth from the city like a prince, attended by a thousand princes.
Now here I am again, returning to the same city in despair,
And darting, fearful as a thief, into an overgrown garden.

But then the very ones whose favor made it possible are themselves no more. *(entering and looking)* How dreary the park is!

atra hi, viparyastaṃ saudhaṃ
kulam iva mah"|ārambha|racanaṃ
saraḥ śuṣkaṃ sādhor
hṛdayam iva nāśena suhṛdaḥ
phalair hīnā vṛkṣā
viguṇa|vidhi|yogād iva nayāḥ
tṛṇaiś channā bhūmir
matir iva kinītair a|viduṣaḥ.

api ca,

6.50 kṣat'|âṅgīnāṃ tīkṣṇaiḥ
paraśubhir udagra|klama|bhṛtāṃ
rujā kūjantīnām
avirata|kapot'|ôparuditaiḥ
sva|ni|cchedaiḥ
paricita|parikleśa|kṛpayā
śvasantaḥ śākhānāṃ
vraṇam iva nibadhnanti phaṇinaḥ.

ete tapasvinaḥ!

antaḥ|śarīra|pariśoṣam udīrayantaḥ
kīṭa|kṣatiṃ śucam iv' âti|guruṃ vahantaḥ
chāyā|viyoga|malinā vyasane nimagnā
vṛkṣāḥ śmaśānam upagantum iva pravṛttāḥ.

tad yāvad asmin viṣama|daśā|pariṇāma|sulabhe bhagna|śilā|tale muhūrtam upaviśāmi. *(upaviśy' ākarṇya ca)* aye tat kim ayam ākasmikaḥ śaṅkha|paṭaha|miśro nāndī|nādaḥ śrūyate?

The pavilion is in ruins, like a family that once did mighty things.
The lake is dried up, like a good man's heart when his friends all die.
The trees are barren of fruit, like schemes that are blighted by fate.
The ground is smothered with weeds, as the mind of a fool with error.

And,

Grievously wounded by the sharp axe 6.50
And moaning their pain through the pigeons' ceaseless cries,
The branches of trees are bandaged by sighing snakes
With strips of their slough, in pity for their friends.

Poor trees!

All withered up within,
Weeping their tears of woodworm dust,
Sunk in despair and mourning vanished shades,
They seem to be preparing for their funeral.

Here is a broken slab of stone that suits my degradation. I will sit down for a moment. *(sitting down and listening)* Oh, what is the sudden sound of cheering I can hear, mixed with the noise of conch and drum?

ya eṣaḥ, pramṛdnañ chrotṝṇāṃ
śruti|patham asāraṃ gurutayā
bahutvāt prāsādaiḥ
sapadi paripīt'|ôjjhita iva
asau nāndī|nādaḥ
paṭu|paṭaha|śaṅkha|dhvani|mahān
diśāṃ dairghyaṃ draṣṭuṃ
prasarati sa|kautūhala iva.

6.55 *(vicintya)* āḥ! bhavatu! jñātam. eṣa hi Malayaketu|saṃyamana|kṛtaṃ rāja|kulasya—*(ity ardh'|ôkte)* hā dhik Maurya|kulasya paritoṣaṃ piśunayati. *(sa|bāṣpam)* kaṣṭaṃ bhoḥ kaṣṭam!

śrāvito 'smi śriyaṃ śatror
abhinīya ca darśitaḥ
anubhāvayituṃ manye
yatnaḥ samprati māṃ Vidheḥ.

PURUṢAḤ: ⌜āsīṇo aaṃ jāva tāva ajja|Cāṇakk'|āṇattiṃ saṃpādemi.⌟ *(RĀKṢASAM a|paśyann iva tasy' âgrato rajju|pāśen' ātmānam anubadhnāti)*

RĀKṢASAḤ: *(vilokya)* aye katham! ātmānam anubadhnāti. nūnam aham iva duḥkhitas tapasvī. bhavatu. pṛcchāmy enam. *(upasṛtya)* bhadra, kim idam anuṣṭhīyate?

PURUṢAḤ: *(sa|bāṣpam)* ⌜jaṃ pia|vaassa|viṇāsa|dukkhido amhāriso manda|bhaggo aṇuciṭṭhadi.⌟

Bruising the fragile ear with its heavy din
So loud the houses spew it back again,
This cheering, swelled by the sounds of conch and
drum,
Leaps up to take the measurement of heaven.

(on reflection) Oh, of course! It means that Málaya·ketu's capture is being celebrated by the Emperor's—*(breaking off)* Alas, I mean the Mauryan's court. *(weeping)* Oh, wretchedness! 6.55

I have been made to hear the enemy's triumph,
I have been made to come and see it:
Now it would seem that Fate is striving
To make me live* it, too.

MAN: He is sitting down. Now to put His Honor Kautílya's plan into operation. *(Pretending not to notice* RÁKSHASA, *he stands in front of him, fastening the noose on himself.)*

RÁKSHASA: *(seeing him)* What's this, he's using a rope on himself! Why, the poor fellow must be as unhappy as I am. I must ask him. *(going up to him)* My dear man, what are you doing?

MAN: *(weeping)* I'm doing what any unlucky man like me would do when he grieves the loss of a dear friend.

6.60 RĀKṢASAḤ: *(ātma|gatam)* prathamam eva mayā jñātaṃ «nūnam aham iv' ārtas tapasv" îti.» bhavatu. pṛcchāmy enam. *(prakāśam)* he vyasana|sabrahmacārin yadi na guhyaṃ n' âtibhārikaṃ vā tataḥ śrotum icchāmi te prāṇa|parityāga|kāraṇam.

PURUṢAḤ: ⌜ajja, ṇa rahassaṃ ṇa vā adi|garuaṃ. kiṃ tu ṇa sakkaṇomi pia|vaassa|viṇāsa|dukkhida|hiao ettia|ṃettaṃ pi maraṇassa kāla|haraṇaṃ kāduṃ.⌟

RĀKṢASAḤ: *(niḥśvasy' ātma|gatam)* kaṣṭam! ete suhṛd|vyasaneṣu para|vad udāsīnāḥ pratyādiśyāmahe vayam anena. *(prakāśam)* bhadra, yadi na rahasyaṃ n' âti|gurukaṃ vā tataḥ śrotum icchāmi.

PURUṢAḤ: ⌜aho ṇibbandho ajjassa! kā gadī. eso ṇivedemi. atthi ettha ṇaare maṇi|āra|seṭṭhī Jiṇhudāso ṇāma.⌟

RĀKṢASAḤ: *(ātma|gatam)* asti Jiṣṇudāsaś Candanadāsasya suhṛd bhavati.

6.65 PURUṢAḤ: ⌜so mama pia|vaasso.⌟

RĀKṢASAḤ: *(sa|harṣam ātma|gatam)* «priya|vayasya ity» āha. atyanta|saṃnikṛṣṭaḥ saṃbandhaḥ. jñāsyati Candanadāsasya vṛttāntam.

RÁKSHASA: *(to himself)* I could tell right away that he was in the same plight as myself. I'll certainly ask him. *(aloud)* Fellow student in misery, if it is not a secret or too painful to tell, I should be glad to hear why you are ending your life. 6.60

MAN: It's not a secret, sir, nor too painful to tell. But my heart is so heavy with grief at the loss of my friend that I cannot bear to delay my own death for even a single moment.

RÁKSHASA: *(to himself with a sigh)* Alas, this man is a lesson to me, when I sit here as indifferent as a stranger to the plight of my friend. *(aloud)* Since it's not a secret or painful, my dear man, I should be glad to hear.

MAN: Oh, how persistent you are, sir! Well, if you insist, I'll tell you. There is a master jeweler in this city called Jishnu·dasa.

RÁKSHASA: *(to himself)* So there is, and he is a great friend of Chándana·dasa.

MAN: And Jishnu·dasa is the dear friend I mentioned. 6.65

RÁKSHASA: *(to himself, in delight)* A dear friend, he says! The connection is very close: he is bound to have news of Chándana·dasa.

PURUṢAḤ: *(sa|bāṣpam)* ⌜so saṃpadaṃ di'|ādi|jaṇa|diṇṇa|vihavo jalaṇaṃ pavisidu|kāmo ṇaarādo ṇikkanto. ahaṃ pi jāva tassa a|suṇidavvaṃ ṇa suṇāmi tāva attāṇaaṃ vāvādemi tti imaṃ jiṇṇ'|ujjāṇaṃ āado.⌟

RĀKṢASAḤ: bhadra, ath' âgni|praveśe suhṛdas te ko hetuḥ?

kim auṣadha|path'|âtigair
upahato mahā|vyādhibhiḥ?—

6.70 PURUṢAḤ: ⌜ajja, ṇa|hi ṇa|hi.⌟

RĀKṢASAḤ:

kim agni|viṣa|kalpayā
nara|pater nirastaḥ krudhā?

PURUṢAḤ: ⌜ajja, jaṃ saccaṃ ṇa. Candaüttassa jaṇa|vade aṇisaṃsā paḍivattī.⌟

RĀKṢASAḤ:

6.75 a|labhyam anuraktavān
kim uta cāru|nārī|janam?

PURUṢAḤ: *(karṇau pidhāya)* ⌜ajja, santaṃ pāvaṃ. a|bhūmi kkhu eso a|viṇaasya.⌟

RĀKṢASAḤ:

kim asti bhavato yathā
suhṛda eva nāśo 'vaśaḥ?

MAN: *(weeping)* He has now given away his wealth to brahmins and other deserving people, and left the city to enter fire. And I have come to this old park to kill myself before I could hear what I dreaded to hear about him.

RÁKSHASA: My dear man, why did your friend want to kill himself?—

> Was he afflicted with a fearful disease beyond the
> aid of medicine?

MAN: No, no, sir! 6.70

RÁKSHASA:

> Was he ruined by the King's wrath, deadly as fire
> or poison?

MAN: Assuredly not, sir. In Chandra·gupta's realm, we are not treated so harshly.

RÁKSHASA:

> Did he fall in love with some lovely woman 6.75
> forbidden to him?

MAN: *(stopping his ears)* Perish the thought, sir! He is incapable of such indecency.

RÁKSHASA:

> Then did he, like you, have a friend who was
> doomed to die?

PURUṢAḤ: ⌜ajja, adha iṃ.⌟

6.80 RĀKṢASAḤ: *(s'|āvegam ātma|gatam)* Candanadāso 'sya priya|suhṛt tad|vināśa ev' âsya hutavaha|praveśa|hetur iti? yat satyam. samākulita ev' âsmi suhṛt|pakṣa|pātinā hṛdayena. *(prakāśam)* bhadra, tasy' âpi tava suhṛdaḥ suhṛd|vatsalatayā śrotavyaṃ sucaritaṃ vistareṇa śrotum icchāmi.

PURUṢAḤ: ⌜ajja, ado avaraṃ ṇa sakkaṇomi manda|bhāggo maraṇassa vigghaṃ uppādiduṃ.⌟

RĀKṢASAḤ: śravaṇīyāṃ kathāṃ kathayatu bhadra|mukhaḥ.

PURUṢAḤ: ⌜kā gadī. eso ṇivedemi. ṇisāmedu ajjo.⌟

RĀKṢASAḤ: bhadra, datt'|âvadhāno 'smi.

6.85 PURUṢAḤ: ⌜atthi ettha ṇaare Pupphacattara|ṇivāsī maṇi|āra|seṭṭhī Candaṇadāso ṇāma.⌟

RĀKṢASAḤ: *(sa|viṣādam ātma|gatam)* etat tad apāvṛtaṃ mad|vināśa|dīkṣā|praveśa|dvāraṃ Daivena. hṛdaya, sthirī|bhava. kim api te kaṣṭataram ākarṇanīyam. *(prakāśam)* bhadra, śrūyate sa sādhur mitra|vatsalaḥ. kiṃ tasya?

PURUṢAḤ: ⌜so vi tassa Jiṇhudāsassa pia|vaasso bhodi.⌟

RĀKṢASAḤ: *(ātma|gatam)* ayam abhyarṇaḥ śoka|vajra|pāto hṛdayasya.

PURUṢAḤ: ⌜tado Jiṇhudāseṇa pia|vaassassa siṇeha|sarisaṃ ajja viṇṇavido Candaüttо.⌟

6.90 RĀKṢASAḤ: kim iti?

MAN: Exactly, sir.

RÁKSHASA: *(to himself, in alarm)* Chándana·dasa is his friend, 6.80
and the loss of a friend is his reason for suicide? I am shaken with fear for Chándana·dasa. *(aloud)* Your friend, too, in his devotion to a friend, has done a deed worth telling. I should like to hear of it in detail.

MAN: No sir, I can delay my death no longer, unhappy wretch that I am!

RÁKSHASA: It is a noble story: you must tell it, my dear man.

MAN: Well, if you insist, sir. Listen.

RÁKSHASA: I am listening.

MAN: There is living in this city, in the Square of Flowers, 6.85
a master jeweler called Chándana·dasa.

RÁKSHASA: *(to himself, in despair)* Now Fate opens the door that consecrates me to death. Be firm, my heart. You have worse to hear. *(aloud)* Yes, he is reputed to be a good man, devoted to his friends. What of him?

MAN: He, too, is a close friend of Jishnu·dasa.

RÁKSHASA: *(to himself)* The thunderbolt is near.

MAN: And today Jishnu·dasa, out of the love he bears his friend, petitioned Chandra·gupta.

RÁKSHASA: What was the petition? 6.90

PURUṢAḤ: ⌜deva, atthi me gehe kuḍumba|bharaṇa|pajjattā atthavattā. tā ediṇā viṇimaeṇa muñcīadu me pia|vaasso tti.⌟

RĀKṢASAḤ: *(ātma|gatam)* sādhu bho Jiṣṇudāsa, sādhu! aho darśito mitra|snehaḥ! kutaḥ?

pitṝn putrāḥ putrān
    paravad abhihiṃsanti pitaro
  yad|arthaṃ sauhārdaṃ
    suhṛdi ca samujjhanti suhṛdaḥ
priyasy' ârthe yo 'sau
    vyasana|sahitasya vyavasitaḥ
  kṛt'|ârtho 'yaṃ so 'rthas
    tava sati vaṇiktve 'pi vaṇijaḥ.

(prakāśam) bhadra, tatas tath" âbhihitena satā kiṃ pratipannaṃ Mauryeṇa?

6.95 PURUṢAḤ: ⌜ajja, tado evaṃ bhaṇideṇa Candaütteṇa paḍibhaṇido seṭṭhī Jiṇhudāso. ṇa mae atthassa kāraṇeṇa seṭṭhī saṃjamido. kiṃ tu pacchādido aṇeṇa bahuso jācīanteṇ' âvi amacca|Rakkhasassa ghara|aṇo ṇa samappido. tā jaï amacca|Rakkhasassa ghara|aṇaṃ samappedi tado atthi se mokkho. aṇṇadhā pāṇa|haro daṇḍo amhakovaṃ paḍimāṇedu tti bhaṇia vajjha|ṭṭhāṇaṃ āṇatto Candaṇadāso. tado jāva vaassassa Candaṇadāsassa a|suṇidavvaṃ ṇa suṇāmi tāva jalaṇaṃ pavisāmi tti seṭṭhī Jiṇhudāso ṇaarādo ṇikkanto. ahaṃ pi jāva pia|vaassassa Jiṇhudāsassa a|suṇidavvaṃ ṇa suṇāmi tāva attāṇaaṃ vāvādemi tti imaṃ jiṇṇ'|ujjāṇaṃ āado mhi.⌟

RĀKṢASAḤ: bhadra, na khalu vyāpāditaś Candanadāsaḥ?

MAN: That he had adequate resources for the support of his family, which he was offering in exchange for the release of his dear friend Chándana·dasa.

RÁKSHASA: *(to himself)* Bravo, Jishnu·dasa! What love you have shown for your friend!

> The wealth sons coldly kill their fathers for, and fathers their sons,
> For which friends withdraw their friendship from a friend,
> You wanted to give up for a loved one in distress.
> You are a merchant, but you use your money well.

(aloud) How did the Mauryan receive this petition?

MAN: Chandra·gupta replied that he hadn't imprisoned Chándana·dasa to get money but because he had sheltered Minister Rákshasa's family and wouldn't hand them over despite repeated demands. And so he would be released if he handed them over, and if he didn't he would be condemned to death. After which the Emperor ordered Chándana·dasa to be taken to the Execution Ground. Then Jishnu·dasa decided to enter the fire before he could hear such dreadful news of his friend, and left the city. And I have decided to kill myself before I can hear such dreadful news of Jishnu·dasa, and that is why I came to this old park. 6.95

RÁKSHASA: Has Chándana·dasa been executed, my good man?

PURUṢAḤ: ⌜ajja, ṇa dāva vāvādīadi. so kkhu sampadaṃ puṇopuṇo amacca|Rakkhasassa ghara|aṇaṃ jācīadi. ṇa eso mitta|vacchaladāe taṃ samappedi. tā ediṇā kāraṇeṇa bhodi se maraṇassa kāla|haraṇaṃ.⌟

RĀKṢASAḤ: *(sa|harṣam ātma|gatam)* sādhu, vayasya Candanadāsa, sādhu!

Śiber iva samudbhūtaṃ
  śaraṇ'|āgata|rakṣayā
nicīyate tvayā sādho
  yaśo 'pi suhṛdā vinā.

6.100 *(prakāśam)* bhadra, gaccha! śīghram idānīṃ Jiṣṇudāsaṃ jvalana|praveśān nivāraya. aham api Candanadāsaṃ maraṇān mocayāmi.

PURUṢAḤ: ⌜adha keṇa uvāeṇa ajjo Candaṇadāsaṃ maraṇādo moedi?⌟

RĀKṢASAḤ: *(khaḍgam ākṛṣya)* nanv anena vyasana|sahāyena nistriṃśena!

paśya: nistriṃśo 'yaṃ vigata|jalada|
  vyoma|saṃkāśa|mūrtir
yuddha|śraddhā|pulakita iva
  prāpta|sakhyaḥ karaṇe
sattv'|ôtkarṣāt samara|nikaṣe
  dṛṣṭa|sāraḥ parair me
mitra|sneho vivaśam atha|vā
  sāhase māṃ niyuṅkte.

MAN: They aren't actually executing him yet. At the moment they are asking him over and over again for Rákshasa's family, but he goes on refusing them out of love for his friend. And all that is delaying the execution.

RÁKSHASA: *(to himself, joyfully)* Bravo, my dearest Chándana·dasa!

The fame that Shibi won
By protecting the helpless
You now win for yourself
Though the friend you protect has deserted you.

(aloud) Go, my dear man. Hurry to stop Jishnu·dasa from entering the fire. I shall go and rescue Chándana·dasa. 6.100

MAN: How can you rescue Chándana·dasa, sir?

RÁKSHASA: *(drawing his sword)* Why, with this sword, my comrade in misfortune! Look!

This sword, the color of the cloudless sky,
Which seems to sparkle with lust to fight as it feels
the grasp of my hand,
Whose fine-tempered strength my enemies have
tried on the touchstone of war,
Calls me to adventure for love of my friend, all
powerless though I now am.

PURUṢAḤ: ⌜ajja, evaṃ seṭṭhi|Candaṇadāsa|jīvida|'bbhuvavattiṃ suṇia visama|dasā|vipāa|paḍido? ṇa sakkaṇomi ṇicchida|padaṃ bhaṇiduṃ sugihīda|ṇāma|dheā amacca|Rakkhasa|pādā tumhe tti? tā karedha me pasādaṃ saṃdeha|ṇiṇṇaeṇa.⌟

6.105 RĀKṢASAḤ: bhadra so 'ham anubhūta|bhartṛ|vaṃśa|vināśaḥ suhṛd|vipatti|hetur anāryo dur|gṛhīta|nāmā yath"|ârtho Rākṣasaḥ.

PURUṢAḤ: *(sa|harṣaṃ pādayor nipatya)* ⌜hī māṇahe! diṭṭhiā kadattho mhi.⌟

RĀKṢASAḤ: bhadra, uttiṣṭh' ôttiṣṭha. kṛtam idānīṃ kāla|haraṇena. nivedyatāṃ Jiṣṇudāsāya: «eṣa Rākṣasaś Candanadāsaṃ maraṇān mocayiṣyat' îti.» *(«nistriṃśo 'yaṃ... mūrtir» iti ślokam anubhāvayan khaḍgam ākṛṣya parikrāmati)*

nistriṃśo 'yaṃ vigata|jalada|
vyoma|saṃkāśa|mūrtir
yuddha|śraddhā|pulakita iva
prāpta|sakhyaḥ karaṇe
sattv'|ôtkarṣāt samara|nikaṣe
dṛṣṭa|sāraḥ parair me
mitra|sneho vivaśam atha|vā
sāhase māṃ niyuṅkte.

PURUṢAḤ: *(pādayor nipatya)* ⌜pasīdadu pasīdadu amacca|Rakkhasa|pādā! atthi dāva ettha paḍhamaṃ Candaütta|hadaeṇa ajja|Saaḍadāso vajjha|ṭṭhāṇaṃ āṇatto. so a keṇ'|âvi vajjha|ṭṭhāṇādo avaharia des'|antaraṃ avavāhido. tado

MAN: You want to save Master Chándana·dasa, and you have known better times? I cannot clearly tell, sir, but are you His Honor Minister Rákshasa of glorious name?

RÁKSHASA: I am that one who has seen his master's house destroyed and brought ruin on his friends, a man dishonored and of most inglorious name, and truly called Rákshasa. 6.105

MAN: *(falling joyfully at his feet)* Oh wonder! Thank god I have found you.

RÁKSHASA: Get up, get up, my dear man. There's not a moment to lose. Tell Jishnu·dasa that Rákshasa is going to save Chándana·dasa. *(He draws his sword and strides forth, again reciting:)*

This sword, the color of the cloudless sky,
Which seems to sparkle with lust to fight as it feels the grasp of my hand,
Whose fine-tempered strength my enemies have tried on the touchstone of war,
Calls me to adventure for love of my friend, all powerless though I now am.

MAN: *(falling at his feet)* Listen to me, Your Honor, please! The accursed Chandra·gupta once ordered the Honorable Shákata·dasa to be taken to the Execution Ground and someone came and rescued him. Chandra·gupta was enraged by the negligence that had cheated him of Shákata·dasa's death, and quenched his anger by having the executioners put to death. And ever since then if the

Candaütta|hadaeṇa kīsa pamādo kado tti ajja|Saaḍadāsa|vaha|vañcaṇāe samujjalido ros'|aggī ghādaa|aṇa|vaha|jaleṇa ṇivvāvido. tado|pahudi ghādaā jaṃ kaṃ|pi gahida|satthaṃ apuvvaṃ purisaṃ pacchādo aggado vā pekkhanti tado attaṇo jīvidaṃ parirakkhantā appattā jeva vajjha|ṭṭhāṇaṃ vajjhaṃ vāvādenti. tā evaṃ gahida|satthehiṃ amacca|pādehiṃ gacchantehiṃ seṭṭhi|Candaṇadāsassa vaho tuvarāvido bhodi.⌟ *(niṣkrāntaḥ)*

6.110 RĀKṢASAḤ: *(ātma/gatam)* aho durbodhaś Cāṇakya|baṭor nīti|mārgaḥ. kutaḥ:

«yadi sa Śakaṭo nītaḥ śatror matena mam' ântikaṃ
kim iti nihatas tena krodhād vadh'|âdhikṛto janaḥ?
atha na kṛtakaṃ tādṛg|lekhaṃ kathaṃ nu vibhāvayet?»
iti mama matis tark'|ārūḍhā na paśyati niścayam.

vicintya.

n' âyaṃ nistriṃśa|kālaḥ prathamam iha kṛte
ghātakānāṃ vighāte
nītiḥ kāl'|ântareṇa prakaṭayati phalaṃ
kiṃ tayā kāryam atra
audāsīnyaṃ na yuktaṃ priya|suhṛdi gate
mat|kṛtām eva ghorāṃ
vyāpattim jñātam asya sva|tanum aham imāṃ
niṣkrayaṃ kalpayāmi.

iti niṣkrāntāḥ sarve.

executioners see anyone they don't know anywhere near them, then to protect their own lives they kill their prisoner without waiting to get to the proper spot. So if Your Honor goes there carrying a sword, it will only hasten Chándana·dasa's death. *(He goes out.)*

RÁKSHASA: *(to himself)* I can't see what that fellow Kautílya is up to. 6.110

If I was deliberately sent Shákata·dasa by the enemy,
Why should he grow angry and kill the executioners?
But if it wasn't a trick, how explain the letter?
My mind fills with doubts, I can see nothing for certain.

(After reflection.)

This is no time for the sword—the executioners have learned their lesson.
Plots take their time to mature—no use for them here.
I cannot sit idle, when a friend is going to a hideous death for me.
Ah, but I have the answer—to trade my life for his.

He goes out.

ACT VII
MINISTER TO THE EMPEROR

tataḥ praviśati CĀṆḌĀLAḤ.

CĀṆḌĀLAḤ: ⌜ośaladha, ayyā, ośaladha. avedha māṇahe avedha.⌟

⌜yaï ichadha laḥkiduṃ śe
    pāṇe vihave kulaṃ kalattaṃ ca
tā palihaladha viśaṃ via
    lā'|âvaścaṃ paatteṇa.⌟

⌜bhodi puliśaśśa vādhī
    malaṇaṃ vā śevide avaścammi
lā'|âvaśce uṇa
    śevidammi śaalaṃ kulaṃ maladi.⌟

7.5 ⌜tā yaï ṇa pattiāadha tado peskadha edaṃ lā'|âvaśca|kāliṇaṃ śeṣṭi|Candaṇadāśaṃ vayyha|stāṇaṃ ṇīamāṇaṃ śa|putta|kalattaṃ.⌟ *(śrutvā ākāśe)* ⌜ayyā kiṃ bhaṇādha? asti śe ke|vi moḥk'|ôvāe tti? evaṃ uṇa asti yaï amacca|Laḥkaśaśśa ghala|aṇaṃ śamappedi. kiṃ bhaṇādha? eśe śalaṇ'|āgada|vaścale attaṇo yīvida|mettaśśa kālaṇeṇa imaṃ akayyaṃ ṇa kaliśśadi tti? ayyā yaï evaṃ teṇa hi avadhāledha śe śuha|gadiṃ. kiṃ dāṇīṃ tuṃhāṇaṃ ettha paḍiāra|viāreṇa?⌟

tataḥ praviśati dvitīya/CĀṆḌĀL'/*ânugato vadhya/veṣa/dhārī śūlaṃ skandhen' ādāya* KUṬUMBINYĀ PUTREṆA *c' ânugamyamānaś* CANDANADĀSAḤ.

CANDANADĀSAḤ: ⌜haddhī haddhī.⌟

⌜amhārisāṇa vi jado
    ṇiccaṃ cāritta|bhaṅga|bhīrūṇaṃ
cora|jaṇ'|ôida|maraṇaṃ
    pattaṃ ti ṇamo Kadantassa.⌟

Enter an EXECUTIONER.*

EXECUTIONER: Away, sirs, away! Be off!

> If you want to keep safe
> Your wealth and your life, your wife and your family,
> Be sure you shun like the plague
> All acts of treason to the Emperor.

> A man can grow sick or die
> If he does things that don't agree with him.
> But if he does what doesn't agree with the king,
> The disease is fatal to the whole of his family.

If you have any doubt, just look at the traitor Master Chándana·dasa here, being led to execution with his wife and son. *(listening, and then addressing the air)* What's that you say? Has he no way out? Yes, if he surrenders Minister Rákshasa's family. What? He tenderly protects the helpless, he would never consider such wickedness just to save his own skin? Well, in that case he's quite happy, isn't he? Why bother with trying to save him? 7.5

Enter, attended by another EXECUTIONER,* CHÁNDANA·DASA, *dressed as a condemned man and carrying the stake on his shoulder. His* WIFE *and* SON *accompany him.*

CHÁNDANA·DASA: Alas!

> If even men like me
> That dread the thought of sin
> Can die the death of thieves,
> Then I bow to the God of Death.

⌜adha|vā ṇisaṃsāṇaṃ udāsīṇesuṃ idaresuṃ vā viseso ṇ' atthi. tadhā hi.⌟

7.10 ⌜mottūṇa āmisāīṃ
  maraṇa|bhaeṇaṃ taṇehi jīvante
vāhāṇa muddha|hariṇe
  hantuṃ ko ṇāma ṇibbandho.⌟

(samantād avalokya) ⌜bhāva pia|vaassa Jiṇhudāsa kadhaṃ paḍivaaṇaṃ pi me ṇa paḍivajjasi? adha|vā dullahā khu te purisā je edassiṃ kāle diṭṭhi|vadhe vi ciṭṭhanti.⌟ *(sa|bāṣpam)* ⌜ede amha|pia|vaassā assu|vāda|mettakeṇa kada|padīārā sarīrehiṃ ṇivattamāṇā parivattida|soa|dīṇa|vaaṇā vāha|garuāe diṭṭhīe maṃ aṇugacchanti.⌟

CĀṆḌĀLAU: *(parikramya)* ⌜ayya Candaṇadāśa, palāgade śi vayyha|stāṇaṃ. tā viśayyehi ghala|aṇaṃ.⌟

CANDANADĀSAḤ: ⌜ajje kuḍumbiṇi, ṇivattasu saṃpadaṃ sa|puttā. ado avaraṃ a|bhūmi aṇugacchiduṃ.⌟

KUṬUMBINĪ: *(sa|bāṣpam)* ⌜para|loaṃ patthido ajjo. ṇa des'|antaraṃ. tā aṇ|ucidaṃ khu kula|vahū|aṇassa ṇivattiduṃ.⌟

7.15 CANDANADĀSAḤ: ⌜ahaha! kiṃ vavasidaṃ ajjāe?⌟

KUṬUMBINĪ: ⌜bhattuṇo calaṇe aṇugacchantīe appāṇuggaho.⌟

CANDANADĀSAḤ: ⌜ajje, du|vvavasidaṃ edaṃ de. idāṇiṃ ajjāe aaṃ kumāro a|suṇida|loa|saṃvavahāro aṇugeṇhidavvo.⌟

But a cruel man can never distinguish between those who don't wish him harm and those who do.

> When the innocent deer, renouncing flesh, 7.10
> Live only on grass for fear of taking life,
> Why is it that the huntsman
> Is so stubbornly bent on their destruction?

(looking about him) Oh, my dear friend Jishnu·dasa, do you make me no reply? But few are the men who will so much as show themselves at such a time. *(weeping)* There I see my friends, with nothing but their tears to help me, retreating with sad faces still turned toward me, following me only with their weeping eyes.

THE TWO EXECUTIONERS: Master Chándana·dasa, you have come to the Execution Ground. Say goodbye to your family.

CHÁNDANA·DASA: Dear wife, you must go back now with our son. This is as far as you can come.

WIFE: *(weeping)* You are off to another world, sir, not a foreign country. It would not be right for a true wife to leave you now.

CHÁNDANA·DASA: Ah! What are you planning? 7.15

WIFE: To bless myself by following in my husband's footsteps.

CHÁNDANA·DASA: An ill resolve, my wife. Keep your blessings for our son here, who knows nothing yet of the world.

KUṬUMBINĪ: ⌜aṇugeṇhantu ṇaṃ pasaṇṇāo bhaavadīo kula|devadāo. jāda puttaa, paḍasu avacchimaṃ piduṇo pāesuṃ.⌟

PUTRA: *(pādayor nipatya)* ⌜tāda, mae tāda|virahideṇa kiṃ aṇuciṭṭhidavvaṃ?⌟

7.20 CANDANADĀSAḤ: ⌜puttaa, Cāṇakka|virahide dese vasidavvaṃ.⌟

CĀṆḌĀLAḤ: ⌜ayya Candaṇadāśa, eśe ṇikhāde śūle. tā śayye dāṇi hohi.⌟

KUṬUMBINĪ: ⌜ajjā parittāadha parittāadha.⌟

CANDANADĀSAḤ: ⌜aï jīvida|vacchale kiṃ ettha akkandasi? saggaṃ gadā khu te devā Ṇandā je dukkhidaṃ jaṇaṃ aṇukampanti.⌟

PRATHAMAŚ CĀṆḌĀLAḤ: ⌜ale Billavattaā, geṇha Candaṇadāśaṃ.⌟

7.25 DVITĪYAŚ CĀṆḌĀLAḤ: ⌜ale Vayyalomaā, eśe geṇhāmi.⌟

CANDANADĀSAḤ: ⌜bhadda|muha, ciṭṭha muhuttaaṃ jāva puttaaṃ parissaāmi.⌟ *(iti putraṃ mūrdhni samāghrāya)* ⌜jāda puttaa, avassaṃ bhavidavve vi vināse mitta|kajjaṃ uvvahamāṇo vināsaṃ aṇuhohi.⌟

PUTRA: ⌜tāda, kiṃ edaṃ pi bhaṇidavvaṃ? kula|kkamo kkhu eso amhāṇaṃ.⌟ *(iti pādayoḥ patati)*

CĀṆḌĀLAḤ: ⌜geṇha le. śaaṃ yeva śe ghala|aṇe gamiśśadi.⌟

KUṬUMBINĪ: ⌜ajjā, parittāadha parittāadha!⌟

WIFE: Let the blessings of our family gods fall kindly upon him. My son, kneel to your father for the last time.

SON: *(falling at his feet)* Father, what should I do without you?

CHÁNDANA·DASA: My son, you must live somewhere beyond 7.20
Kautílya's reach.

EXECUTIONERS: Master Chándana·dasa, the stake is now fixed. Prepare yourself.

WIFE: Save him, sirs, save him!

CHÁNDANA·DASA: What love of life is this? Why are you calling? The Nanda kings who pitied the distressed are all gone to heaven.

FIRST EXECUTIONER: Hey, Bilva·páttraka, take hold of Chándana·dasa!

SECOND EXECUTIONER: Right you are, Vajra·lómaka! 7.25

CHÁNDANA·DASA: One moment, sir, while I embrace my son. *(putting his lips to his son's head)* My son, even though death should be certain, you must die still doing your duty to your friends.

SON: Need you say it, father? That is the tradition in our family. *(He falls again at his feet.)*

EXECUTIONERS: Take hold of him. His family will leave by themselves.

WIFE: Help, sirs, help!

7.30 *pravíśya a|paṭīkṣepeṇa* RĀKṢASAḤ. bhavati, na bhetavyaṃ na bhetavyam. bho bhoḥ senā|pate, na khalu vyāpādanīyo 'yaṃ sādhuḥ. kutaḥ:

yena svāmi|kulaṃ ripor iva kulaṃ
  dṛṣṭaṃ vinaśyat purā
 mitrāṇāṃ vyasane mah"|ôtsava iva
  svasthena yena sthitam
ātmā yasya ca vañcanā|paribhava|
  kṣetrī|kṛto 'pi priyaḥ
 tasy' êyaṃ mama mṛtyu|loka|padavī
  vadhya|srag ābadhyatām.

CANDANADĀSAḤ: *(vilokya sa / bāṣpam)* ⌜amacca, kiṃ kiṃ edaṃ?⌟

RĀKṢASAḤ: tvadīya|sucarit'|âika|deśasy' ânukaraṇaṃ kila.

CANDANADĀSAḤ: ⌜amacca, savvaṃ pi me ṇipphalaṃ edaṃ paāsaṃ karanteṇa ṇa me piaṃ aṇuciṭṭhidaṃ amacceṇa.⌟

7.35 RĀKṢASAḤ: sakhe Candanadāsa, sv'|ârtha|pradhāno hi jīva|lokaḥ. kṛtam upālambhena. bhadra|mukha, nivedyatāṃ tāvad durātmane Cāṇakyāya.

CĀṆḌĀLAU: ⌜kiṃ ti?⌟

Enter, without ceremony, RÁKSHASA. Have no fear, lady, have no fear! Ho there, officer, you need not kill this good man: 7.30

The man who once watched his lord's family being
killed like the family of an enemy,
And in the plight of his friends stayed at his ease
as if it were a holiday,
Who loved his own life though it held nothing but
trickery and humiliation,
That is the man, and I am he, who must wear this
garland leading to the world of death.

CHÁNDANA·DASA: *(looking at him and weeping)* What is this, Minister?

RÁKSHASA: An imitation, as you see, of a part of your goodness.

CHÁNDANA·DASA: You have done me no service, sir, to make all my efforts useless.

RÁKSHASA: Well, dear Chándana·dasa, everyone thinks of 7.35
himself first in this world. Don't blame me. Tell the accursed Kautílya, my good man.

EXECUTIONERS: What?

RĀKṢASAḤ:

«duṣkāle 'pi Kalāv asajjana|rucau
prāṇaiḥ paraṃ rakṣatā
nītaṃ yena yaśasvinā pralaghutām
Auśīnarīyaṃ yaśaḥ
Buddhānām api ceṣṭitaṃ sucaritaiḥ
kliṣṭaṃ viśuddh'|ātmanā
pūj"|ârho 'pi sa yat|kṛte tava gataḥ
śatrutvam eṣo 'smi saḥ.»

PRATHAMAḤ: ⌜ale Billavattaā, tumaṃ tāva śeṣṭi|Candaṇadāśaṃ geṇhia imaśśa maśāṇa|pādavaśśa chāāe muhuttaaṃ ciṣṭha yāva hage ayya|Cāṇakkāha ṇivedemi. gahide amacca|Laḥkaśe tti.⌟

7.40 DVITĪYAḤ: ⌜ale Vayyalomaā, evaṃ bhodu.⌟

*iti sa/*PUTRA/DĀREṆA CANDANADĀSENA *saha niṣkrāntaḥ.*

PRATHAMAḤ: (RĀKṢASENA *saha parikramya)* ⌜ke ke ettha duvāliāṇaṃ! ṇivededha dāva Ṇanda|kula|śela|śaṃcaa|śaṃcūṇa|ṇakuliśāha Molia|kula|paḍiṣṭāvakāha pola|dhamma|śaṃcaāha ayya|Cāṇakkāha—⌟

RĀKṢASAḤ: *(ātma/gatam)* etad api nāma Rākṣasena śrotavyam.

CĀṆḌĀLAḤ: ⌜eśe kkhu ayya|ṇīdi|ṇiala|śaṃyamida|buddhi|puliśaāle gahide amacca|Laḥkaśe tti.⌟

7.45 *tataḥ praviśati yamanik"/āvṛtta/śarīro mukha/mātra/dṛśyaś* CĀṆAKYAḤ.

RÁKSHASA:

> "Here I am, for whose sake this worthy man made himself your enemy,
> Sacrificing himself for another, in this evil Kali age which loves the wicked:
> By his side the glory of Shibi pales to nothing,
> And his saintly heroism eclipses the deeds of the Buddhas."

FIRST EXECUTIONER: Well, Bilva·páttraka, you'd better take Master Chándana·dasa and wait over there in the shade of the tree in the Burning Ground while I go and tell His Honor Kautílya that we've caught Minister Rákshasa.

SECOND EXECUTIONER: Right you are, Vajra·lómaka. 7.40

He goes out with CHÁNDANA·DASA *and the* WIFE *and* SON.

FIRST EXECUTIONER: *(walking about with* RÁKSHASA*)* Hey, there at the gate! Report to His Honor Kautílya, the thunderbolt that pulverized the Nanda Mountain, establisher of the House of Maurya and light of truth to the citizens—

RÁKSHASA: *(to himself)* Must Rákshasa hear even this?

EXECUTIONER: —that here, with his cleverness and bravery trapped in the noose of His Honor Kautílya's skill, stands Minister Rákshasa, a prisoner.

Enter, but with the curtain concealing his body and only his face visible, KAUTÍLYA. 7.45

CĀṆAKYAḤ: bhadra, kathaya kathaya:

ken' ôttuṅga|śikhā|kalāpa|kapilo
baddhaḥ paṭānte śikhī?
pāśaiḥ kena sadāgater a|gatitā
sadyaḥ samāsāditā?
ken' ânekapa|dāna|vāsita|saṭaḥ
siṃho 'rpitaḥ pañjare?
bhīmaḥ kena ca naika|nakra|makaro
dorbhyāṃ pratīrṇo 'rṇavaḥ?

CĀṆḌĀLAḤ: ⌜ṇaṃ ṇīdi|ṇiuṇa|buddhiṇā ayyeṇa yyeva.⌟

CĀṆAKYAḤ: bhadra, mā m" âivam. «Nanda|kula|dveṣiṇā Daiven' êti» brūhi. (RĀKṢASAṂ *dṛṣṭvā)* aye ayam amātya|Rākṣasaḥ. yena mah"|ātmanā,

7.50 gurubhiḥ kalpanā|kleśair
dīrgha|jāgara|hetubhiḥ
ciram āyāsitā senā
Vṛṣalasya matiś ca me.

(yamanikām apanīy' ôpasṛtya ca) bho amātya|Rākṣasa Viṣṇugupto 'bhivādayate.

RĀKṢASAḤ: *(viloky' ātma|gatam)* «amātya iti» lajjā|karam idānīṃ viśeṣaṇa|padam. aye ayaṃ durātmā, atha|vā mah"|ātm" âiva Kauṭilyaḥ.

ākaraḥ sarva|śāstrāṇāṃ
ratnānām iva sāgaraḥ
guṇair na parituṣyāmo
yasya matsariṇo vayam.

KAUTÍLYA: Tell me, good fellow, tell me—

> Who caught the fire with its leaping flames and
> put it in his pocket?
> Who roped the restless wind and kept it still?
> Who trapped the lion that reeked of elephant rut
> and caged him?
> Who swam the ocean, with its sharks and
> crocodiles?

EXECUTIONER: Why, you, Your Honor, with your strategic brilliance.

KAUTÍLYA: No, my man, no! It was Destiny, hating the race of Nanda. *(seeing* RÁKSHASA, *to himself in joy)* Ah, here is Minister Rákshasa, that great and noble man, who—

> Long exercised my mind 7.50
> And Vríshala's army
> With that wearying need for alertness
> Which caused many sleepless hours.

(putting off the curtain and approaching him) Minister Rákshasa, I, Vishnu·gupta, salute you.

RÁKSHASA: *(seeing him, to himself)* "Minister"? That is a title that shames me now. So here is the accursed—no, here is the great Kautílya!

> Mine of all learning
> As the ocean is of gems,
> Whose worth we take no pleasure in
> Because of our own envy.

(prakāśam) bho Viṣṇugupta, na māṃ śvapāka|sparśa|dūṣitaṃ sprastum arhasi.

7.55 CĀṆAKYAḤ: amātya|Rākṣasa, n' âyaṃ śvapākaḥ. ayaṃ khalu dṛṣṭa|pūrva eva bhavatā Siddhārthaka|nāmā rāja|puruṣo yena vyāja|sauhṛdam utpādya Śakaṭadāso 'pi tapasvī tādṛśaṃ kapaṭa|lekham a|jānann eva may" âiva lekhitaḥ. yo 'py asau dvitīyaḥ so 'pi Samṛddhārthako nāmā rāja|puruṣa eva.

RĀKṢASAḤ: *(ātma/gatam)* diṣṭyā Śakaṭadāsaṃ pratyapanīto me vikalpaḥ!

CĀṆAKYAḤ: kiṃ bahunā? eṣa saṃkṣepaḥ—

ete Bhadrabhaṭ'|ādayaḥ sa ca tathā
lekhaḥ sa Siddhārthakaḥ
tac c' âlaṃkaraṇa|trayaṃ sa bhavato
mitraṃ bhadantaḥ kila
jīrṇ'|ôdyāna|gataḥ sa c' ārta|puruṣaḥ
kleśaḥ sa ca śreṣṭhinaḥ
sarvo 'sau mama—*(ity ardh'/ôkte lajjāṃ nāṭayati)* Vṛṣalasya dhīra bhavatā
saṃyogam icchor nayaḥ.

tad eṣa Vṛṣalas tvāṃ draṣṭum āgacchati. paśy' âinam.

7.60 RĀKṢASAḤ: *(ātma/gatam)* kā gatiḥ? eṣa paśyāmi.

tataḥ praviśati RĀJĀ *vibhavataś ca parivāraḥ.*

RĀJĀ: *(ātma/gatam)* «vin" âiva yuddhād āryeṇa parājitaṃ dur|jayaṃ ripu|balam» iti yat satyaṃ lajjita iv' âsmi. mama hi:

(aloud) Vishnu·gupta, don't touch me—I am defiled by the touch of an outcaste.

KAUTÍLYA: He is no outcaste, Minister Rákshasa. He is someone you know already—Siddhárthaka, a servant of the Emperor, who pretended to be friends with Shákata·dasa and got the poor fellow at my instigation to write that false letter all unwittingly. And the other executioner was another of the Emperor's servants, called Samiddhárthaka.* 7.55

RÁKSHASA: *(to himself)* Thank god my doubts about Shákata·dasa are set at rest!

KAUTÍLYA: In fact, to tell you briefly—

> Bhadra·bhata and his friends, the letter,
> Siddhárthaka,
> Those jewels you bought, your friend the supposed
> monk,
> The poor wretch in the park and the plight of his
> friend the merchant
> Were all schemes of mine—
> *(he breaks off modestly)* Of Vríshala's, to gain,
> noble sir, your allegiance.

And here comes Vríshala to see you. Look.

RÁKSHASA: *(to himself)* What can I do? I must see him. 7.60

Enter the EMPEROR *with his retinue in order of rank.*

EMPEROR: *(to himself)* I feel almost ashamed to think that my preceptor has beaten the enemy's formidable forces without even a fight.

phala|yogam avāpya sāyakānām
a|niyogena vilakṣatāṃ gatānām
sva|śuc" êva bhavaty adho|mukhānāṃ
nija|tūṇī|śayana|vratasya niṣṭhā.

atha|vā:

7.65 viguṇī|kṛta|kārmuko 'pi jetuṃ
bhuvi jetavyam asau samartha eva
svapato 'pi mam' êva yasya tantre
guravo jāgrati kārya|jāgarūkāḥ.

(CĀṆAKYAM upasṛtya) ārya, Candraguptaḥ praṇamati.

CĀṆAKYAḤ: Vṛṣala, saṃpannās te sarv'|āśiṣaḥ. tad abhivādayasva tāvad atra|bhavantam amātya|Rākṣasam. ayaṃ te paitṛko 'mātya|mukhyaḥ.

RĀKṢASAḤ: *(ātma|gatam)* yojito 'nena saṃbandhaḥ.

RĀJĀ: *(RĀKṢASAM upasṛtya)* ārya, Candragupto 'bhivādayate.

7.70 RĀKṢASAḤ: *(viloky' ātma|gatam)* aye ayaṃ Candraguptaḥ, ya eṣa,

bāla eva hi lokena
saṃbhāvita|mah"|ônnatiḥ
krameṇ' ārūḍhavān rājyaṃ
yūth'|āiśvaryam iva dvipaḥ

(prakāśam) rājan, vijayasva!

Though their aim is achieved, my arrows lie
Ashamed that they have not been called upon,
Hanging their heads as if in grief
Observing a vow of lying in their quiver.

But no—

Though his bow stays unstrung, 7.65
That man has won all that on earth may be won,
In whose realm even while he sleeps
There are guardians like mine to watch over his affairs.

(approaching KAUTÍLYA*)* Chandra·gupta bows to you, sir.

KAUTÍLYA: Vríshala, all your hopes are fulfilled. Salute Minister Rákshasa here—your hereditary Chief Minister.

RÁKSHASA: *(to himself)* He has made the connection.

EMPEROR: *(approaching* RÁKSHASA*)* Sir, Chandra·gupta salutes you.

RÁKSHASA: *(looking at him, to himself)* Here is Chandra·gupta, who, 7.70

Even as a child was known to the world
As one of extraordinary promise,
And by degrees has grown to Emperor
As an elephant grows to be lord of the herd.

(aloud) Victory, sire!

RĀJĀ: ārya,

«jagataḥ kiṃ na vijitaṃ
  may" êti» pravicintyatām
gurau ṣāḍ|guṇya|cintāyām
  ārye kārye ca jāgrati.

7.75 RĀKṢASAḤ: *(ātma|gatam)* spṛśati māṃ bhṛtya|bhāvena Kauṭilya|śiṣyaḥ. atha|vā vinaya eṣa Candraguptasya. matsaras tu me 'bhiprāyo viparītaṃ kalpayati. sarvathā sthāne yaśasvī Cāṇakyaḥ. kutaḥ:

dravyaṃ jigīṣum adhigamya jaḍ'|ātmano 'pi
  netur yaśasvini pade niyataṃ pratiṣṭhā
a|dravyam etya tu vivikta|nayo 'pi mantrī
  śīrṇ'|āśrayaḥ patati kūla|ja|vṛkṣa|vṛttyā.

CĀṆAKYAḤ: amātya|Rākṣasa, ap' îṣyate Candanadāsasya jīvitam?

RĀKṢASAḤ: bho Viṣṇugupta, kutaḥ saṃdehaḥ?

CĀṆAKYAḤ: amātya|Rākṣasa, a|gṛhīta|śastreṇa bhavatā n' ânugṛhyate Vṛṣala ity ataḥ saṃdehaḥ. tad yadi satyam eva Candanadāsasya jīvitam iṣyate tato gṛhyatām idaṃ śastram.

7.80 RĀKṢASAḤ: bho Viṣṇugupta, mā m" âivam! a|yogyā vayam asya śastrasya grahaṇe viśeṣatas tvayā gṛhītasya.

CĀṆAKYAḤ: amātya|Rākṣasa, yogyam a|yogyaṃ vā kim anena?

EMPEROR: Sir,

> What victory is left me
> To win, pray, in this world
> When I have Your Honor as my guardian
> Vigilant instructor in the Six Strands of
> government.

RÁKSHASA: *(to himself)* This pupil of Kautílya is making me 7.75
his servant. But no, this is courtesy on Chandra·gupta's part: my jealousy makes me misinterpret it. No wonder Kautílya has won such glory:

> If he finds a worthy and ambitious man,
> The dullest-witted counselor is sure of renown,
> While the cleverest minister, relying on a fool,
> Is undermined, like a tree on the bank of a river.

KAUTÍLYA: Minister Rákshasa, do you want Chándana·dasa to live?

RÁKSHASA: How can you ask, Vishnu·gupta?

KAUTÍLYA: I ask because you have not granted Vríshala the favor of accepting the sword of office. If you really want Chándana·dasa to live, accept it.

RÁKSHASA: Impossible, Vishnu·gupta, I am not worthy to 7.80
accept it, particularly when it has been yours.

KAUTÍLYA: Do not talk of worthy and unworthy, sir.

aśvaiḥ sārdham ajasra|datta|kavikā|
    kṣāmair a|śūny'|āsanaiḥ
snān'|āhāra|vihāra|pāna|śayana|
    sv'|êcchā|sukhair varjitān
māhātmyāt tava pauruṣasya matiman
    dṛpt'|âri|darpa|cchidaḥ
paśy' âitān parikalpanā|vyatikara|
    procchūna|vaṃśān gajān.

atha|vā kim anena? na khalu bhavataḥ śastra|grahaṇam antareṇa Candanadāsasya jīvitam asti.

RĀKṢASAḤ: *(ātma|gatam)*

7.85 Nanda|sneha|guṇāḥ spṛśanti hṛdayaṃ
    bhṛtyo 'smi tad|vidviṣāṃ
ye siktāḥ kara|pallav'|âñjali|puṭaiś
    chedyās ta eva drumāḥ
śastraṃ mitra|śarīrakeṣu sa|ruṣā
    vyāpāraṇīyaṃ mayā
kāryāṇāṃ gatayo Vidher api nayanty
    ālocanā|gocaram

bho Viṣṇugupta, namaḥ sarva|kārya|pratipatti|hetave suhṛt|snehāya. kā gatiḥ? eṣa grahvo 'smi.

CĀṆAKYAḤ: *(sa|harṣaṃ śastram arpayitvā)* Vṛṣala Vṛṣala, amātya|Rākṣasen' êdānīṃ gṛhīt'|âdhikāreṇ' ânugṛhīto 'si. diṣṭyā vardhate bhavān.

RĀJĀ: ārya|prasāda eṣa Candragupten' ânubhūyate.

Look at our elephants, backs swollen with the
rubbing of their accoutrements,
Robbed of the joys of bathing, feeding, roaming,
drinking, sleeping when they would,
And the horses, too, exhausted with endless
bridling, their saddles never empty—
All due, wise counselor, to that brave resolution
which has humbled your enemy's pride.

But that is all beside the point: if you won't accept office, Chándana·dasa's life is forfeit.

RÁKSHASA: *(to himself)*

Love for the Nandas fills my heart, yet I must serve 7.85
their enemies.
The trees I watered and made tall are all cut down.
To protect a friend I must bear the sword of office.
The things that happen make us all Fate's servants
in the end.

(aloud) Then Vishnu·gupta, I bow to that love of friends which may lead one anywhere. I have no choice, I am ready.

KAUTÍLYA: *(joyfully handing over the sword of office)* Vríshala, Vríshala, Minister Rákshasa has now graciously consented to accept office under you. My congratulations to you.

EMPEROR: Chandra·gupta acknowledges this great blessing from Your Honor.*

pravíśya PURUṢAḤ. ⌈jaadu jaadu ajjo. ajja eso kkhu Bhadda-bhaḍa|Bhāürāaṇa|ppamuhehiṃ saṃjamida|kara|calaṇo Malaakedū paḍihāra|bhūmiṃ uvatthāvido. evaṃ suṇia ajjo pamāṇaṃ.⌋

7.90 CĀṆAKYAḤ: bhadra, nivedyatām amātya|Rākṣasāya. ayam idānīṃ jānīte.

RĀKṢASAḤ: *(ātma/gatam)* katham, vaśī|kṛtya mām idānīṃ vijñāpanāyāṃ mukharī|karoti Kautilyaḥ? kā gatiḥ? *(pra-kāśam)* rājan, Candragupta, viditam eva te yathā vayaṃ Malayaketau kiṃ|cit|kāl'|ântaram uṣitāḥ. tat parirakṣya-ntām asya prāṇāḥ.

RĀJĀ: *(*CĀṆAKYA*/mukham avalokayati)*

CĀṆAKYAḤ: Vṛṣala, pratimānayitavyo 'yam amātya|Rākṣasasya prathamaḥ praṇayaḥ. *(*PURUṢAM *avalokya)* bha-dra, mad|vacanād ucyantāṃ Bhadrabhaṭa|prabhṛtayaḥ: «amātya|Rākṣasa|vijñāpito devaś Candraguptaḥ prayac-chati Malayaketave pitryam eva viṣayam. ato gacchantu bhavantaḥ sah' ânena pratiṣṭhite c' âsmin punar āganta-vyam» iti.

PURUṢAḤ: ⌈jaṃ ajjo āṇavedi.⌋ *(iti niṣkrāmati)*

7.95 CĀṆAKYAḤ: tiṣṭha tāvat. idaṃ c' âparaṃ vaktavyo Vijaya-pālo durga|pālaḥ: «amātya|Rākṣasasya prītyā devaś Ca-ndraguptaḥ samājñāpayati: ‹ya eṣa tāvac chreṣṭhī Can-danadāsaḥ sa pṛthivyāṃ sarva|nagareṣu śreṣṭhi|padam

Enter a MANSERVANT. Victory to Your Honor. Bhadra·bhata, Bhaguráyana and their companions have brought Málaya·ketu to the gate, bound hand and foot. What is Your Honor's desire in the matter?

KAUTÍLYA: Tell Minister Rákshasa, my dear man. He is the 7.90
judge now.

RÁKSHASA: *(to himself)* Does Kautílya first enslave me, then make me the Emperor's adviser? Well, what choice have I! *(aloud)* Your Majesty, as you well know, I was in Málaya·ketu's service for some time. For that reason I ask you to spare his life.

EMPEROR: *(Looks at* KAUTÍLYA.*)*

KAUTÍLYA: Vríshala, you must honor the first request that Minister Rákshasa makes of you. *(to the* MANSERVANT*)* Tell Bhadra·bhata and the others in my name that, in response to a request by Minister Rákshasa, His Majesty the Emperor grants Málaya·ketu those territories which are his by ancestral right. They are therefore to go back with him and return when they have seen him established.

MANSERVANT: Yes, sir. *(He moves off.)*

KAUTÍLYA: Wait a moment. Here is another message—for 7.95
the Governor of the Prison: "Out of the affection he bears Minister Rákshasa, His Majesty the Emperor commands that the master jeweler Chándana·dasa be granted the title of Chief Merchant in all cities throughout the world. And, furthermore, let all be freed from bondage save the horses and elephants. But no! With Minister Rákshasa

āropyatām› iti. anyac ca: ‹vinā hasty|aśvaṃ kriyatāṃ sarva|bandhana|mokṣa iti.› atha|vā amātya|Rākṣase netari kiṃ hasty|aśvena prayojanam? tad idānīm:

‹vinā vāhana|yugyebhyo mucyatāṃ sarva|bandhanam
pūrṇa|pratijñena mayā kevalaṃ badhyate śikhā.›»

PURUṢAḤ: ⌜jaṃ ajjo āṇavedi.⌟ *(iti niṣkrāntaḥ)*

CĀṆAKYAḤ: Candragupta, kiṃ te bhūyaḥ priyam upakaromi?

RĀJĀ:

7.100 Rākṣasena samaṃ maitrī
rājye c' āropitā vayam
Nandāś c' ônmūlitāḥ sarve
kiṃ kartavyam ataḥ priyam?

RĀKṢASAḤ: tath" âp' îdam astu:

Vārāhīm Ātmayones tanum a|tanu|balām
āsthitasy' ânurūpāṃ
yasya prāk danta|koṭiṃ pralaya|parigatā
śiśriye bhūta|dhātrī
mlecchair udvejyamānā bhuja|yugam adhunā
pīvaraṃ rāja|mūrteḥ
sa śrīmad|bandhu|bhṛtyaś ciram avatu mahīṃ
pārthivaś Candraguptaḥ.

iti niṣkrāntāḥ sarve.

to guide us, what need of horses and elephants? Now therefore:

Save only for draft animals
Let every bond be loosed.
With the vow I swore fulfilled,
I will keep nothing bound except my hair."

MANSERVANT: As Your Honor commands. *(He goes out.)*

KAUTÍLYA: Chandra·gupta, what further service may I do you?

EMPEROR:

I have Rákshasa's friendship, 7.100
I am established on the throne,
The Nandas are all rooted out:
What further service could there be?

RÁKSHASA: Yet let this be—

Vishnu, who once, incarnate in the sturdy body of a boar,
Held the Earth safe amid chaos on the tip of his tusk,
And now, incarnate as a king shelters her in his strong arms from the barbarians' threats,
Long let him save the world, prospering his people and his house, our monarch Chandra·gupta.

All go out.

CHĀYĀ

The following is a Sanskrit paraphrase (chāyā) *of the Prakrit passages (marked with* ⌜corner brackets⌟) *in the play. References are to chapter and paragraph.*

1.8 ārya, iyam asmi. ājñā|niyogena mām āryo 'nugṛhṇātu.

1.10 ārya, āmantritā mayā bhagavanto brāhmaṇāḥ.

1.12 ārya, uparajyate kila bhagavāṃś candra iti.

1.14 evaṃ khalu nagara|nivāsī jano mantrayate.

1.21 ārya, kaḥ punar eṣa dharaṇī|gocaro bhūtvā candraṃ grah'|ôparāgād rakṣitum icchati?

1.59 praṇamata Yamasya caraṇau kiṃ kāryaṃ devair anyaiḥ? eṣa khalu anya|bhaktānāṃ harati jīvaṃ parisphurantam.

1.60 api ca, Puruṣasya jīvitavyaṃ viṣamād bhavati bhakti|gṛhītān mārayati sarva|lokaṃ yas tena Yamena jīvāmaḥ.

1.61 yāvad etad gṛhaṃ praviśya Yama|paṭaṃ darśayan gītāni gāyāmi.

1.63 aho brāhmaṇa, kasy' âitad gṛham?

1.65 aho brāhmaṇa, ātmīyasy' âiva dharma|bhrātur gṛhaṃ bhavati. tasmād dehi me praveśaṃ yāvat tav' ôpadhyāyāya dharmam upadiśāmi.

1.67 aho brāhmaṇa, mā kupya. na khalu sarvaḥ sarvaṃ jānāti. kim api tav' ôpādhyāyo jānāti kim apy asmādṛśā api jānanti.

1.69 aho brāhmaṇa, yadi tav' ôpādhyāyaḥ sarvaṃ jānāti tarhi jānātu tāvat keṣāṃ candro 'nabhipreta iti.

1.71 aho brāhmaṇa, tav' ôpādhyāya eva jñāsyati yad etena jñātena bhavati. tvaṃ punar etāvad eva jānāsi kamalānāṃ candro 'n|abhipreta iti.

1.72 kamalānāṃ mano|harāṇām api rūpād visaṃvadati śīlaṃ saṃpūrṇa|maṇḍale 'pi yāni candre viruddhāni.

1.75 aho brāhmaṇa, susaṃbaddham ev' âitad bhaved yadi—

1.77 yadi śrotuṃ jānantaṃ janaṃ labhe.

1.79 eṣa praviśāmi.

1.79 jayatu jayatv āryaḥ!

1.81 yad ārya ājñāpayati.

1.83 atha kim? āryena khalu teṣu teṣu virāga|kāraṇeṣu parihriyamāṇeṣu sugṛhīta|nāma|dheyaṃ devaṃ Candraguptaṃ dṛdhataraṃ anuraktāḥ prakṛtayaḥ. kiṃ punar idānīm asty atra nagare 'mātya|Rākṣasena saha prathamaṃ samutpanna|sneha|bahumānās trayaḥ puruṣā ye devasya Candraśriyaḥ śriyaṃ na sahante.

1.85 ārya, a|śruta|nāma|dheyā āryasya kathaṃ nivedyante?

1.87 śṛṇotv āryaḥ. prathamaṃ tāvad āryasya ripu|pakṣe baddha|pakṣa|pātaḥ Kṣapaṇako.

1.89 Jīvasiddhir nāma yena s" âmātya|Rākṣasa|prayuktā viṣa|kanyakā deve Parvateśvare samāveśitā.

1.91 ārya, aparo 'py amātya|Rākṣasasya priya|vayasya kāyasthaḥ Śakaṭadāso nāma.

1.93 tṛtīyo 'py amātya|Rākṣasasya dvitīyam iva hṛdayaṃ Puṣpapura|nivāsī maṇi|kāra|śreṣṭhī Candanadāso nāma yasya gṛhe kalatraṃ nyāsī|kṛty' âmātya|Rākṣaso nagarād apakrāntaḥ.

1.95 iyam aṅguli|mudr" āryam apy avagamayiṣyati.

1.97 śṛṇotv āryaḥ. asti tāvad aham āryeṇa paura|jana|carit'|ânveṣaṇe niyuktaḥ. tataḥ para|gṛha|praveśe parasy' âśaṅkanīyen' ânena

Yama|paṭena hiṇḍamāna ārya|maṇi|kāra|śreṣṭhi|Candanadāsasya gṛhaṃ praviṣṭo 'smi tatra ca Yama|paṭaṃ prasārya pravṛtto 'smi gātum.

1.99 tata ekasmād apavarakāt pañca|varṣa|deśīyaḥ priya|darśanīya|śarīr'|ākṛtiḥ kumārako bāla|jana|sulabha|kautūhal'|ôtphulla|nayana|yugalo niṣkramituṃ pravṛttaḥ. tato «hā nirgato hā nirgata iti» śaṅkā|parigraha|nibhṛta|gurukas tasy' âiv' âpavarakasy' ânte strī|janasy' ôtthito mahān kolāhalaḥ. tata īṣad|dvāra|deśa|dāpita|mukhy" âikayā striyā sa kumārako niṣkrāmann eva nirbhartsy' âvalambitaḥ komalayā bāhulatayā. tasyāḥ kumāra|saṃgrahaṇa|saṃbhrama|calit'|âṅguleḥ karāt puruṣ'|âṅguli|pariṇāha|pramāṇa|ghaṭitā vigalit" êyam aṅguli|mudrikā dehalī|pṛṣṭhe nipatitā. ucchalitā tay" ân|avabuddh" âiva mama caraṇa|pārśvaṃ samāgatya praṇāma|nibhṛtā kula|vadhūr iva niścalā saṃvṛttā. may" âpy amātya|Rākṣasasya nām'|âṅkit" êty āryasya pāda|mūlaṃ prāpitā. tad eṣo 'syā mudrikāyā āgama iti.

1.101 yad ārya ājñāpayati.

1.107 jayatu jayatv āryaḥ.

1.109 ārya, kamala|makul'|ākāram añjaliṃ śīrṣe niveśya devaś Candraśrīr āryaṃ vijñāpayati: «icchāmy aham āryeṇ' âbhyanujñāto devasya Parvateśvarasya pāralaukikaṃ kartuṃ tena ca dhārita|pūrvāṇi bhūṣaṇāni bhagavadbhyo brāhmaṇebhyaḥ pratipādayām' îti.»

1.111 yad ārya ājñāpayati.

1.124 jayatu jayatv āryaḥ. ārya, ayaṃ sa Śakaṭadāsena ālikhito lekhaḥ.

1.126 yad ārya ājñāpayati.

1.133 ārya, mudrito lekhaḥ. ājñāpayatv āryaḥ kim aparam anuṣṭhīyatām iti.

1.135 ārya, anugṛhīto 'smi. tad ājñāpayatv āryo yad anena dāsa|janen' āryasy' ânuṣṭhātavyam.

1.137 ārya, gṛhītaḥ!

1.139 gṛhīto may" āryasya saṃdeśaḥ. tad gamiṣyāmy ahaṃ kārya|siddhaye.

1.141 yad ārya ājñāpayati.

1.148 Cāṇakyen' â|karuṇena sahasā śabdāyitasya vartate nirdoṣasy' âpi śaṅkā kiṃ punaḥ saṃjāta|doṣasya.

1.149 tad bhaṇitā mayā Dhanasena|pramukhās trayo gṛha|jana|sevakāḥ. yathā: kad" âpi Cāṇakya|hatako gṛham api me vicāyayati. tasmād apavāhayata bhartur amātya|Rākṣasasya gṛha|janam. mam' êdānīṃ yad bhavatu tad bhavatv iti.

1.151 ārya, ayam āgacchāmi.

1.153 jayatu jayatv āryaḥ.

1.155 kiṃ na jānāty āryo yath"|ân|ucita upacāraḥ parijana|hṛdayasya paribhavād api mahad duḥkham utpādayati? tad ih' âiv' âham ucitāyāṃ bhūmāv upaviśāmi.

1.157 upalakṣitam anena kim api.

1.157 yad ārya ājñāpayati.

1.159 ārya, atha kim. āryasya prasāden' â|khaṇḍit" âiva vaṇijyā.

1.161 śāntaṃ pāpam!

1.162 uditena śārada|niśā vimal" êva pūrṇimā|mṛg'|âṅkeṇa devena Candraśriy" âdhikaṃ nandanti prakṛtayaḥ.

1.164 ājñāpayatv āryaḥ: kiṃ kiyad v" âsmāj janād artha|jātam iṣyata iti?

1.166 ārya, anugṛhīto 'smi.

1.168 ājñāpayatv āryaḥ.

1.170 ārya, ka eṣo ’|dhanyo yo rājñā saha viruddha ity āryeṇ’ âvagamyate?

1.172 śāntaṃ pāpam! kīdṛśas tṛṇānām agninā saha virodhaḥ?

1.174 ārya, alīkam etat ken’|âpy an|āryeṇ’ āryāya niveditam.

1.176 evaṃ nv idam. tasmin samaya āsīd asmad|gṛhe ’mātya|Rākṣasasya gṛha|janaḥ.

1.178 ārya, atr’|ântare ’sti me vāk|chalam.

1.180 ārya, nanu vijñāpayāmi tasmin samaya āsīd asmad|gṛhe ’mātya|Rākṣasasya gṛha|jana iti.

1.182 na jānāmi kva gata iti.

1.187 phalena saṃvāditaṃ śobhati te vikatthitam.

1.192 ārya, gṛhe ’|santaṃ kutaḥ samarpyate?

1.197 ārya, kiṃ me bhayaṃ darśayasi? santam apy ahaṃ gṛhe ’mātya|Rākṣasasya gṛha|janaṃ na samarpayāmi kiṃ punar a|santam.

1.199 bāḍham. eṣa me sthiro niścayaḥ.

1.203 bāḍham. eṣa sthiro me niścayaḥ.

1.205 sajjo ’smi. anutiṣṭhatv ārya ātmano ’dhikārasy’ ânurūpam.

1.208 ayam āgacchāmi.

1.208 diṣṭyā mitra|kāryeṇa me vināśo na punaḥ puruṣa|doṣeṇa.

2.2 jānanti tantra|yuktiṃ yathā|sthitaṃ maṇḍalam abhilikhanti/
ye mantra|rakṣaṇa|parās te sarpa|nar’|âdhipān upacaranti.

2.3 ārya, kiṃ bhaṇasi? kas tvam iti? ārya, ahaṃ khalv āhituṇḍiko Jīrṇaviṣo nāma. kiṃ bhaṇasi? aham apy ahinā khelitum icchām’ îti. atha katarāṃ punar āryo vṛttim upajīvati? kiṃ bhaṇasi? rāja|kula|sevako 'sm' îti. nanu khelaty ev' āryo 'hinā. katham iva,

2.4 vyāla|grāhy a|mantr'|âuṣadhi|kuśalo matta|gaja|var'|ārohaḥ/
rāja|kula|sevaka ity avaśyaṃ trayo 'pi vināśam anubhavanti.

2.5 katham? atikrānta eṣaḥ.

2.5 ārya, tvaṃ kiṃ bhaṇasi? kim eteṣu peṭaka|samudgakeṣv iti? ārya, jīvikā|saṃpādakāḥ sarpāḥ sa|daṃṣṭrāḥ. kiṃ bhaṇasi? prekṣitum icchām' îti. prasīdatu prasīdatv āryaḥ. a|sthānaṃ khalv etat. tasmād yadi kautūhalaṃ tad ehi. etasminn āvāse darśayāmi. kiṃ bhaṇasi? etat khalu bhartur amātya|Rākṣasasya gṛham. n' âsty asmādṛśānāṃ praveśa iti? tena hi gacchatv āryaḥ. jīvikāyāḥ prasāden' âsti ma iha praveśa iti. katham, eṣo 'py atikrāntaḥ!

2.28 idam āsanam. upaviśatv āryaḥ.

2.38 yad ārya ājñāpayati.

2.38 ārya, kas tvam?

2.39 bhadra, ahaṃ khalv āhituṇḍiko Jīrṇaviṣo nāma. icchāmy amātya|Rākṣasasya purataḥ sarpaiḥ khelitum.

2.40 tiṣṭha tāvad yāvad amātyāya nivedayāmi.

2.40 ārya, eṣa khalu sarpa|jīv" îcchaty amātyasya purataḥ sarpaiḥ khelitum.

2.42 yad ārya ājñāpayati.

2.42 ārya, a|darśanen' âpy āryaḥ prasādaṃ karoti na punar darśanena.

2.43 bhadra, vijñāpaya mama vacanen' âmātyam: Na kevalam ahaṃ sarpa|jīvī. prākṛta|kaviḥ khalv aham. tasmād yadi me darśanen' âmātyaḥ prasādaṃ na karoti tad etad api pattrakaṃ vācayituṃ prasīdatv iti.

2.44 amātya, eṣa khalu sarpa|jīvī vijñāpayati: na kevalam ahaṃ sarpa|jīvī. prākṛta|kaviḥ khalv aham. tasmād yadi me darśanen' âmātyaḥ prasādaṃ na karoti tad etad api pattrakaṃ vācayituṃ prasīdatv iti.

2.46 pītvā nir|avaśeṣaṃ kusuma|rasam ātmanaḥ kuśalatayā/ yad udgirati bhramaras tad anyeṣām karoti kāryam.

2.48 yad ārya ājñāpayati.

2.48 upasarpatv āryaḥ.

2.51 jayatu, jayatv āryaḥ.

2.53 yad amātya ājñāpayati.

2.130 jayatu jayatv āryaḥ. ārya, eṣa khalu Śakaṭadāsaḥ pratīhāra|bhūmyām upasthito.

2.132 kim alīkam amātya|pād'|ôpajīvino mantrayituṃ jānanti?

2.136 yad amātya ājñāpayati.

2.148 ayaṃ khalv āry'|ôpadeśaḥ. bhavatu. tathā kariṣyāmi.

2.148 amātya, atra me prathamaṃ praviṣṭasya n' âsti ko 'pi paricito yatr' âitam amātyasya prasādaṃ nikṣipya nirvṛto bhaviṣyāmi. tasmād icchāmy aham anayā mudrayā mudrayitv" âmātyasy' âiva bhāṇḍāgāre nikṣipitum. yadā ma etena prayojanaṃ bhaviṣyati tadā grahīṣyāmi.

2.152 amātya, asti Kusumapure maṇi|kāra|śreṣṭhī Candanadāso nāma. tasya gṛha|dvāre patitā mayā labdhā.

2.154 amātya, kim atra yujyate?

2.157 ārya, nanv eṣa eva me paritoṣo yad asyā mudrāyā amātyaḥ parigrahaṃ karoti.

2.160 amātya, vijñāpayāmi kim api.

2.162 jānāty ev' âmātyo yathā Cāṇakya|hatakasya vipriyaṃ kṛtvā n' âsti me Pāṭaliputre praveśa iti. tasmād icchāmy aham amātyasy' âiva suprasannasya caraṇeṣu sevitum.

2.164 anugṛhīto 'smi.

2.173 jayatu, jayatv amātyaḥ. amātya, Śakaṭadāso vijñāpayati: ete khalu trayo 'laṃkārā vikrīyante. tān pratyakṣīkarotv amātyaḥ.

2.175 yad amātya ājñāpayati.

3.8 ita ito devaḥ.

3.38 deva, idaṃ siṃh'|āsanam. upaviśatu devaḥ.

3.117 yad ārya ājñāpayati.

3.117 ārya, idaṃ pattram.

3.178 etu etu devaḥ.

4.2 āścaryam.

4.3 yojana|śataṃ samadhikaṃ ko nāma gat'|āgataṃ kuryāj janaḥ/
a|sthāna|gamana|gurvī prabhor ājñā yadi na bhaved.

4.4 tad yāvad amātya|Rākṣasasy' âiva gṛhaṃ praviśyāmi.

4.4 idaṃ bhartur amātya|Rākṣasya gṛham. ko 'tra dauvārikāṇām? nivedaya tāvad bhartre 'mātya|Rākṣāya: eṣa khalu Karabhakaḥ karabhaka iva tvarayan Pāṭaliputrād āgata iti.

4.5 bhadra bhadra, mā uccair mantrayasva. eṣa khalu bhart" âmātya|Rākṣasaḥ kārya|cintā|janitena samutpanna|śīrṣa|vedan" âdy' âpi na tāvac chayana|talaṃ muñcati. tasmād tiṣṭha muhūrtaṃ yāvat sa labdh'|âvasaro bhūtvā bhagavata āgamanaṃ nivedayāmi.

4.6 bhadra|mukha, yathā te rocate.

4.12 jayatu jayatu—

4.14 amātyaḥ.

4.16 amātya, eṣa khalu Karabhakaḥ Pāṭaliputrād āgata icchati amātyaṃ prekṣitum.

4.18 yad amātya ājñāpayati.

4.18 bhadra, eṣa amātyas tiṣṭhati. upasarp' âinam.

4.20 jayatu jayatv amātyaḥ.

4.22 yad amātya ājñāpayati.

4.25 apasarata, āryā, apasarata. apeta, mānavā, apeta. kiṃ na paśyatha—

4.26 dūre pratyāsattir darśanam api durlabham a|dhanyaiḥ / kalyāṇa|manoharāṇāṃ devānām iva bhūmi|devānām.

4.27 āryāḥ, kiṃ bhaṇatha? kiṃ nimittam avasāraṇā kriyata iti? āryāḥ, eṣa khalu kumāro Malayaketuḥ samutpanna|śīrṣa|vedanam amātya|Rākṣasaṃ prekṣitum ita ev' āgacchati. tasmād etena kāraṇena avasāraṇā kriyate.

4.49 amātya, atha kim.

4.54 amātyasya prasādena siddham.

4.58 śṛṇotv amātyaḥ. asti tāvad aham amātyen' ājñāpto yathā Karabhaka, Kusumapuraṃ gatvā mama vacanena bhaṇitavyas tvayā vaitālikaḥ Stanakalaśo yathā Cāṇakya|hatakena teṣu teṣv ājñā|bhaṅgeṣv anuṣṭhīyamāneṣu Candraguptas tvayā samuttejana|samarthaiḥ ślokair upaślokayitavya iti.

4.60 tato mayā Pāṭaliputraṃ gatvā śrāvito 'mātya|saṃdeśaṃ Stanakalaśaḥ.

4.62 atr'|āntare Nanda|kula|vināśa|dūṣitasya paura|janasya paritoṣam utpādayatā Candragupten' āghoṣitaḥ Kusumapure kaumudī|mah"|ôtsavaḥ. sa ca cira|kāla|pravartana|janita|paritoṣo 'bhimata|bandhu|jana|samāgama iva sa|snehaṃ bahu|mānito nagara|janena.

4.66 amātya, tataḥ sa locan|ānanda|bhūto 'n|icchata eva nāgara|janasya nivāritaś Cāṇakya|hatakena Kaumudī|mah"|ôtsavaḥ. atr'|āntare Stanakalaśena prayuktā Candragupta|samuttejana|samarthā śloka|paripāṭī.

4.71 tataś Candragupten' ājñā|bhaṅga|kaluṣita|hṛdayena su|ciram amātya|guṇaṃ praśasya nirbhraṃśito 'dhikārāc Cāṇakya|hatakaḥ.

4.77 amātya, santy anyāny api Candraguptasya kopa|kāraṇāni Cāṇakye. upekṣitāv anen' âpakrāmantau kumāro Malayaketur amātya|Rākṣasaś ca.

4.82 amātya, tasminn eva Pāṭaliputre prativasati.

4.84 amātya, «tapo|vanaṃ gamiṣyat' îti» śrūyate.

4.130 ājñāpayatv amātyaḥ.

4.132 yad amātya ājñāpayati.

4.132 amātya, eṣa khalu sāṃvatsarikaḥ Kṣapaṇakaḥ—

4.134 —Jīvasiddhiḥ.

4.136 yad amātya ājñāpayati.

4.137 śāsanam arhatāṃ pratipadyadhvaṃ moha|vyādhi|vaidyānām/
ye prathama|mātra|kaṭakaṃ paścāt pathyam upadiśanti.

4.138 dharma|lābhaḥ sādhakānām.

4.140 sādhaka, nirūpito divasaḥ. ā mādhyaṃ|dinān nivṛtta|sakala|doṣā śobhanā tithir bhavati saṃpūrṇa|candrā paurṇamāsī. yuṣmākam uttarasyā diśo dakṣiṇāṃ diśaṃ prasthitānāṃ dakṣiṇa|dvārikaṃ nakṣatram. api ca.

4.141 ast'|âbhimukhe Sūrya udite saṃpūrṇa|maṇḍale Candre/ grahapati|Budhasya lagna udit'|âstamite ca Ketau.

4.144 eka|guṇā bhavati tithiś catur|guṇaṃ bhavati nakṣatram/ catuḥ|ṣaṣṭi|guṇaṃ lagnam eṣa jyotiṣa|tantra|siddhāntaḥ.

4.145 lagnaṃ bhavati sulagnaṃ saumyam api grahaṃ jahīhi durlagnam/ prāpsyasi dīrgham āyuś candrasya balena gacchan.

4.147 saṃvādayatu sādhakaḥ. ahaṃ khalu gamiṣyāmi.

4.149 kupito yuṣmākaṃ na bhadantaḥ.

4.151 bhagavān kṛtānto yen' âtmanaḥ pakṣam ujjhitvā para|pakṣaṃ pramāṇī|karoṣi.

4.154 yad amātya ājñāpayati.

4.154 amātya, ast'|âbhilāṣī bhagavān sūryaḥ.

5.2 āścaryam!

5.3 buddhi|jala|nirjharaiḥ sicyamānā deśa|kāla|kalaśaiḥ/ darśayiṣyati kārya|phalaṃ gurukaṃ Cāṇakya|nīti|latā.

5.4 gṛhīto may" ārya|Cāṇakyena prathama|lekhito lekho 'mātya|Rākṣasasya mudrā|lāñchitaḥ. tasy' âiva mudrā|lāñchit" êyam ābharaṇa|peṭikā. calitaḥ kil' âsmi Pāṭaliputram. tad yāvad gacchāmi.

5.4 kathaṃ, kṣapaṇaka āgacchati. tad yāvad asy' â|śakuna|bhūtaṃ darśanaṃ śuddha|darśanena pratiharāmi.

5.7 Arhantānāṃ praṇamāmo ye te gambhīratayā buddheḥ/ lok'|ôttarair loke siddhiṃ mārgair mārgayanti.

5.8 bhadanta, vande.

5.9 sādhaka, dharma|lābhas te bhavatu.

5.9 sādhaka, a|sthāna|saṃtaraṇa|kṛta|vyavasāyam iva tvāṃ prekṣe.

5.10 kathaṃ bhadanto jānāti?

5.11 sādhaka, kim atra jñātavyam? eṣa te mārg'|ādeśa|kuśalaḥ śakunaḥ kara|gataś ca lekhaḥ sūcayati.

5.12 āṃ jñātaṃ bhadantena. deś'|ântaraṃ calito 'smi. tat kathayatu bhadantaḥ: kīdṛśo 'dya divasa iti?

5.13 sādhaka, muṇḍaṃ muṇḍito nakṣatrāṇi pṛcchasi?

5.14 bhadanta, sāmpratam api kiṃ jātam? tat kathaya. yady anukūlaṃ bhaviṣyati tadā gamiṣyāmi. anyathā nivartiṣye.

5.15 sādhaka, na sāṃpratam etasmin Malayaketu|kaṭake 'nukūlen' ân|anukūlena vā gamyate.

5.16 bhadanta, tataḥ kathaṃ khalv idānīm?

5.17 sādhaka, niśāmaya. prathamaṃ tāvad atra kaṭake lokasy' â|nivārito niṣkramaṇa|praveśa āsīt. idānīm itaḥ pratyāsanne Kusumapure na ko 'py a|mudrā|lāñchito niṣkrāntuṃ praveṣṭuṃ v" ânumodyate. tad yadi Bhāgurāyaṇasya mudrā|lāñchito 'si tado gaccha viśvastaḥ. anyathā tiṣṭha. mā tvaṃ gulma|sthān'|ādhikārikaiḥ saṃyamita|kara|caraṇo rāja|kulaṃ praveśyase.

5.18 kiṃ na jānāti bhadanto yath" âmātya|Rākṣasasya sevakaḥ Siddhārthako 'ham iti? tad a|mudrā|lāñchitam api māṃ niṣkrāmantaṃ kasya śaktir nivāritum.

5.19 sādhaka, Rākṣasasya piśācasya vā bhava. n' âsti te '|mudrā|lāñchitasya niṣkramaṇ'|ôpāyaḥ.

5.20 bhadanta, mā kupya. kārya|siddhir me bhavatu.

5.21 sādhaka, gaccha. bhavatu te kārya|siddhiḥ. aham api Bhāgurāyaṇān mudrāṃ yāce.

5.27 idam āsanam. upaviśatv āryaḥ.

5.29 yad ārya ājñāpayati.

5.36 kumāra, eṣa khalu kaṭakān niṣkramitu|kāmānāṃ mudrā|saṃpradānam anutiṣṭhati.

5.38 yat kumāra ājñāpayati.

5.39 ārya, eṣa khalu kṣapaṇako mudrā|nimittam āryaṃ prekṣitum icchati.

5.41 yad ārya ājñāpayati.

5.42 sādhaka, dharma|lābhas te bhavatu.

5.44 śāntaṃ pāpam. sādhaka, tatra gamiṣyāmi yatra Rākṣasasya nām' âpi na śrūyate.

5.46 sādhaka, na mama kim api Rākṣasen' âparāddham. svayam eva manda|bhāgya ātmano 'parādhyāmi.

5.51 sādhaka, kim anen' â|śrotavyena śrutena?

5.53 sādhaka, na rahasyaṃ kiṃ tv atinṛśaṃsam.

5.55 sādhaka, tath" âpi na kathayiṣyāmi.

5.57 kā gatiḥ. śṛṇotu sādhakaḥ. asti tāvad ahaṃ manda|bhāgyaḥ prathamaṃ Pāṭaliputre nivasan Rākṣasena mitratvam upagataḥ. tasmiṃś c' ântare Rākṣasena gūḍhaṃ viṣa|kanyā|prayogam utpādya ghātito devaḥ Parvateśvaraḥ.

5.60 tato 'haṃ Rākṣasasya mitram iti kṛtvā Cāṇakya|hatakena sanikāraṃ nagarān nirvāsitaḥ. idānīm api Rākṣasena rāja|kārya|kuśalena kim api tādṛśam ārabhyate yen' âhaṃ jīva|lokād api nirvāsiṣye.

5.62 śāntaṃ pāpam. sādhaka, Cāṇakyena viṣa|kanyāyā nām' âpi n' jānāti.

5.75 jayatu jayatu kumāraḥ. ayaṃ khalv āryasya gulma|sthān'|âdhikṛto Dīrghacakṣur vijñāpayati. eṣa khalv asmābhiḥ kaṭakān niṣkrāmann a|gṛhīta|mudraḥ sa|lekhaḥ puruṣo gṛhītaḥ. tat pratyakṣī|karotv enam ārya iti.

5.77 yad ārya ājñāpayati.

5.80 ānayantyai guṇeṣu doṣeṣu parāṅ|mukhaṃ kurvatyai/ asmādṛśa|jananyai praṇamā svāmi|bhaktyai.

5.81 ārya, ayaṃ sa puruṣaḥ.

5.83 ārya, ahaṃ khalv amātya|Rākṣasasya sevakaḥ.

5.85 ārya, kārya|gauraveṇa tvarito 'smi.

5.94 ārya, na jānāmi.

5.96 yuṣmābhiḥ.

5.98 yuṣmābhir gṛhīto na jānāmi kiṃ bhaṇām' îti.

5.100 yad ārya ājñāpayati.

5.101 ārya, iyaṃ mudrā|lāñchitā peṭikā kakṣāyā nipatitā.

5.107 yad ārya ājñāpayati.

5.107 ārya, eṣa khalu tāḍyamāno bhaṇati. kumārasy' âiva nivedayiṣyām' îti.

5.109 yat kumāra ājñāpayati.

5.110 abhayena me prasādaṃ karotu.

5.112 śṛṇotu kumāraḥ. ahaṃ khalv amātya|Rākṣasasen' êmaṃ lekhaṃ dattvā Candragupta|sakāśaṃ preṣitaḥ.

5.114 kumāra, saṃdiṣṭho 'smi amātya|Rākṣasena yath" «âite mama priya|vayasyāḥ pañca rājānas tvayā saha samutpanna|saṃdhānā yathā Kulūt'|âdhipaś Citravarmā Malay'|âdhipaḥ Siṃhanādaḥ Kāśmīra|deśa|nāthaḥ Puṣkarākṣaḥ Sindhu|rājaḥ Sindhuṣeṇaḥ Pārasīk'|âdhipo Meghanāda iti. atr' âiva ye ete prathama|bhaṇitās trayo rājānas te Malayaketor viṣayam abhilaṣanti. itare 'pi dve hasti|balam icchataḥ. tad yathā Cāṇakyaṃ nirākṛtya mahā|bhāgena mama prītir utpāditā tath" âiteṣām api prathama|bhaṇito 'rthaḥ pratipādayitavyaḥ.» etāvān vāk|saṃdeśa iti.

5.116 yat kumāra ājñāpayati.

5.122 yad amātya ājñāpayati.

5.123 jayatu jayatv amātyaḥ. icchati tvāṃ kumāraḥ prekṣitum.

5.125 ājñāpayatv amātyaḥ.

5.127 yad amātya ājñāpayati.

5.127 amātya, idaṃ tam alaṃkaraṇam.

5.129 etv etv amātyaḥ.

5.132 amātya, ayaṃ kumāras tiṣṭhati. upasarpatv enam amātyaḥ.

5.147 prasīdatv amātyaḥ. amātya, tāḍyamānena mayā na pāritam amātya|rahasyaṃ dhārayitum.

5.149 nūnaṃ vijñāpatāmi. tāḍyamānena mayā na pāritam amātya|rahasyaṃ dhārayitum iti.

5.153 idaṃ rahasyaṃ tāḍyamānena mayā niveditam.

5.168 ārya, Śakaṭadāsena.

5.171 yat kumāra ājñāpayati.

5.174 kumāra, mudrām api yāce?

5.176 yat kumāra ājñāpayati.

5.176 kumāra, idaṃ khalu pattram ārya|Śakaṭadāsena sva|hasta|likhitaṃ mudrā ca.

5.185 kumāra, kathaṃ na pratyabhijānāmi? idaṃ khalu su|gṛhīta|nāma|dheyana Parvateśvareṇa dhārita|pūrvam.

5.210 yat kumāra ājñāpayati.

6.3 jayati jalada|nīlaḥ Keśavaḥ Keśi|ghātī jayati su|jana|dṛṣṭi|candramāś Candraguptaḥ/ jayati jayana|sajjaṃ yāvat kṛtvā sainyaṃ pratihata|pratipakṣ" ārya|Cāṇakya|nītiḥ.

6.4 tat tāvac cirassa kālasya priya|vayasyaṃ Samiddhārthakam anveṣayāmi.

6.4 ayaṃ punar priya|vayasyaḥ Samiddhārthaka ita ev' āgacchati. tad yāvad upasarpāmi.

6.5 saṃbhāvayanta āpānakeṣu geh'|ôtsave rocayantaḥ/ hṛdaya|sthitāny api virahe mitraṃ mitrāṇi durmanāyante.

6.6 śrutaṃ ca mayā yathā Malayaketu|kaṭakāt priya|vayasyaḥ Siddhārthaka āgata iti. tad yāvad enam anveṣayāmi.

6.6 eṣa Siddhārthakaḥ.

6.6 api sukhaṃ priya|vayasyasya?

6.7 kathaṃ priya|vayasyaḥ Samiddhārthakaḥ!

6.7 Samiddhārthaka, api sukhaṃ priya|vayasyasya?

6.9 kuto me sukhaṃ yena tvaṃ cira|pravāsa|pratyāgato 'dy' âpi na me geham āgacchasi?

6.10 prasīdatu prasīdatu priya|vayasyaḥ. dṛṣṭa|mātra ev' ārya|Cāṇakyen' ājñapto 'smi yathā Siddhārthaka gaccha. idaṃ vṛttāntaṃ priya|darśanāya Candraśriye niveday' êti. tatas tasmai nivedy' âivam anubhūta|pārthiva|prasādo 'haṃ priya|vayasyaṃ prekṣituṃ tav' âiva gehaṃ calito 'smi.

6.11 vayasya, yadi mayā śrotavyaṃ tataḥ kathaya kiṃ tat priyaṃ priya|darśanāya Candraśriye niveditam iti?

6.12 vayasya, kiṃ tav' âpy a|kathayitavyam asti. tan niśāmaya. asti tāvad ārya|Cāṇakya|nīti|mohita|matinā Malayaketu|hatakena nirākṛtya Rākṣasaṃ hatāś Citravarma|pramukhāḥ pradhānāḥ pañca pārthivāḥ. tato '|samīkṣita|kāry eṣa durācāra ity ujjhitvā Malayaketu|kaṭaka|bhūmiṃ kuśalatāyai bhaya|vilola|sainika|parivārāḥ svakaṃ svakaṃ viṣayam abhiprasthitāḥ pārthivāḥ.

6.13 vayasya, Bhadrabhaṭa|pramukhāḥ kila devāc Candraśriya aparaktā Malayaketuṃ samāśritā iti loke mantryate. tat kiṃ nimittaṃ ku|kavi|nāṭakasy' êv' ânyan mukhe anyan nirvahaṇe?

6.14 vayasya, deva|nadyā iv' â|śruta|gatyai namo nama ārya|Cāṇakya|nītyai.

6.15 vayasya, tatas tataḥ.

6.16 vayasya, tataḥ prabhūta|sāra|sādhana|sameten' êto niṣkramy' ārya|Cāṇakyena pratipannaṃ sa|rājakaṃ rāja|balam.

6.17 vayasya, kutra?

6.18 vayasya, yatr' âite:

6.19 atiśaya|gurukeṇa dāna|darpeṇa dantinaḥ sajala|jalada|nīlā ud-dahanto nadanti/ kaśā|prahara|bhayena jāta|kamp'|ôttararaṅgā gṛhīta|jayana|śabdāḥ saṃplavante turaṅgāḥ

6.20 vayasya, sarvaṃ tāvat tiṣṭhatu. tathā sarva|lokasya pratyakṣam ujjhit'|âdhikāraś ciraṃ sthitv" ārya|Cāṇakyaḥ punar api tad eva mantri|padam ārūḍhaḥ?

6.21 vayasya, ati|mugdha idānīm asi tvaṃ yo 'mātya|Rākṣasen' âpy an|avagāhita|pūrvam ārya|Cāṇakya|buddhim avagāhitum icchasi.

6.22 vayasya, ath' âmātya|Rākṣasa idānīṃ kutra?

6.23 vayasya, so 'pi tasmin bhaya|vilole vartamāne Malayaketu|kaṭakān niṣkramy' Ôndura|nāma|dheyena careṇ' ânusriyamāna idaṃ Kusumapuram āgata ity ārya|Cāṇakyasya niveditam.

6.24 vayasya, tathā nām' âmātya|Rākṣaso Nanda|rājya|pratyānayane kṛta|vyavasāyo niṣkramya sāṃpratam a|kṛt'|ârthaḥ punar api idaṃ Kusumapuram āgataḥ?

6.25 vayasya, tarkayāmi Candanadāsasya snehen' êti.

6.26 vayasya, atha Candanadāsasya mokṣaṃ prekṣase?

6.27 kuto 'sy' âdhanyasya mokṣaḥ? sa khalu sāṃpratam ārya|Cāṇakyasy' ājñaptyā dvābhyām apy āvābhyāṃ vadhya|sthānaṃ praveśya vyāpādayitavyaḥ.

6.28 kim ārya|Cāṇakyasya ghātaka|jano n' âsti yen' āvām īdṛśeṣu nṛśaṃseṣu niyojayati?

6.29 vayasya, ko jiva|loke jīvitu|kāma ārya|Cāṇakyasy' ājñaptiṃ pratikūlayati? tad ehi. caṇḍāla|veśa|dhāriṇau bhūtvā Candanadāsaṃ vadhya|sthānam nayāvaḥ.

6.33 ṣaḍ|guṇa|saṃyoga|dṛḍhā upāya|paripāṭi|ghaṭita|pāśa|mukhī/
Cāṇakya|nīti|rajjū ripu|saṃyaman'|ôdyatā jayati.

6.34 eṣa sa pradeśa ārya|Cāṇakyāy' Ôndureṇa kathito yatra may" ārya|Cāṇaky'|ājñapty" âmātya|Rākṣasaḥ prekṣitavyaḥ.

6.34 katham, eṣa khalv amātya|Rākṣasaḥ kṛt'|âvaguṇṭhana ita ev' āgacchati. yāvad ebhir jīrṇ'|ôdyāna|pādapair antarita|śarīraḥ prekṣe kutr' āsana|parigrahaṃ karoti.

6.57 āsīno 'yaṃ yāvat tāvad ārya|Cāṇaky'|ājñaptiṃ saṃpādayāmi.

6.59 yat priya|vayasya|vināśa|duḥkhito 'smādṛśo manda|bhāgyo 'nutiṣṭhati.

6.61 ārya, na rahasyaṃ na v" âtigurukam. kiṃ tu na śaknomi priya|vayasya|vināśa|duḥkhita|hṛdaya etāvan|mātram api maraṇasya kāla|haraṇaṃ kartum.

6.63 aho nirbandha āryasya! kā gatiḥ. eṣa nivedayāmi. asty atra nagare maṇi|kāra|śreṣṭhī Jiṣṇudāso nāma.

6.65 sa mama priya|vayasyaḥ.

6.67 sa saṃprati dvij'|ādi|jana|datta|vibhavo jvalanaṃ praveṣṭu|kāmo nagarān niṣkrāntaḥ. aham api yāvat tasy' â|śrotavyaṃ na śṛṇomi tāvad ātmānaṃ vyāpādayām' ît' îdaṃ jīrṇ'|ôdyānam āgataḥ.

6.70 ārya, na|hi na|hi.

6.73 ārya, yat satyaṃ na. Candraguptasya jana|pade '|nṛśaṃsā pratipattiḥ.

6.76 ārya, śāntaṃ pāpam. a|bhūmiḥ khalv eṣo '|vinayasya.

6.79 ārya, atha kim.

6.81 ārya, ato 'paraṃ na śaknomi manda|bhāgyo maraṇasya vighnam utpādayitum.

6.83 kā gatiḥ. eṣa nivedayāmi. niśāmayatv āryaḥ.

6.85 ast' îha nagare Puṣpacatvara|nivāsī maṇi|kāra|śreṣṭhī Candanadāso nāma.

6.87 so 'pi tasya Jiṣṇudāsasya priya|vayasyo bhavati.

6.89 tato Jiṣṇudāsena priya|vayasyasya sneha|sadṛśam adya vijñaptaś Candraguptaḥ.

6.91 deva, asti me gehe kuṭumba|bharaṇa|paryāpt" ârthavattā. tad etena vinimayena mucyatāṃ me priya|vayasya iti.

6.95 ārya, tata evaṃ bhaṇitena Candraguptena pratibhaṇitaḥ śreṣṭhī Jiṣṇudāsaḥ. na may" ârthasya kāraṇena śreṣṭhī saṃyamitaḥ. kiṃ tu pracchādito 'nena bahuśo yāciten' âpy amātya|Rākṣasasya gṛha|jano na samarpita iti. tad yady amātya|Rākṣasasya gṛha|janaṃ samarpayati tad" âsty asya mokṣaḥ. anyathā prāṇa|harasya daṇḍo 'smat|kopaṃ pratimānayatv iti bhaṇitvā vadhya|sthānam ānayitaś Candanadāsaḥ. tato yāvad vayasyasya Candanadāsasy' â|śrotavyaṃ na śṛṇomi tāvaj jvalanaṃ praviśām' îti śreṣṭhī Jiṣṇudāso nagarān niṣkrāntaḥ. aham api yāvat priya|vayasyasya Jiṣṇudāsasy' â|śrotavyaṃ na śṛṇomi tāvad ātmānaṃ vyāpādayām' ît' îdaṃ jīrṇ'|ôdyānam āgato 'smi.

6.97 ārya, na tāvad vyāpādyate. sa khalu sāṃprataṃ punaḥ punar amātya|Rākṣasya gṛha|janaṃ yācyate. n' âiṣa mitra|vatsalatayā taṃ samarpayati. tad etena kāraṇena bhavaty asya maraṇasya kāla|haraṇam.

6.101 atha ken' ôpāyen' āryaś Candanadāsaṃ maraṇān mocayati?

6.104 ārya, evaṃ śreṣṭhi|Candanadāsa|jīvit'|âbhyupapattiṃ śrutvā viṣama|daśā|vipāka|patitaḥ? na śaknomi niścita|padaṃ bhaṇituṃ sugṛhīta|nāma|dhey" âmātya|Rākṣasa|pādā yūyam iti. tat kuru me prasādaṃ sandeha|nirṇayena.

6.106 āścaryam! dṛṣṭyā kṛt'|ârtho 'ham.

6.109 prasīdatu prasīdatv amātya|Rākṣasa|pādāḥ! asti tāvad atra prathamaṃ Candragupta|hataken' ārya|Śakaṭadāso vadhya|sthānam ājñaptaḥ. sa ca ken'|âpi vadhya|sthānād apahṛtya deś'|ântaraṃ apoḍhaḥ. tataś Candragupta|hatakena kasmāt pramādaḥ kṛta ity ārya|Śakaṭadāsa|vadha|vañcanayā samujjvalito roṣ'|âgnir ghātaka|jana|jvalena nirvāpitaḥ. tataḥ|prabhṛti ghātakā yaṃ kam api gṛhīta|śastram apūrvaṃ puruṣaṃ pṛṣṭhato v" âgrato vā prekṣante tad" ātmano jīvitaṃ parirakṣanto '|prāptā eva vadhya|sthānaṃ vadhyaṃ vyāpādayanti. tad evaṃ gṛhīta|śastrair amātya|pādair gacchadbhiḥ śreṣṭhi|Candanadāsasya vadhas tvarāyito bhavati.

7.2 apasarata, āryā, apasarata! apeta, manuṣā, apeta!

7.3 yad' îcchata rakṣituṃ svān prāṇān vibhavān kulaṃ kalatraṃ ca/ tat pariharata viṣam iva rāj'|âpathyaṃ prayatnena.

7.4 bhavati puruṣasya vyādhir maraṇaṃ vā sevite a|pathye/ rāj'|âpathye punaḥ sevite sakalaṃ kulaṃ mriyate.

7.5 tad yadi na pratītha tadā prekṣadhvam enaṃ rāj'|âpathya|kāriṇaṃ śreṣṭhi|Candanadāsaṃ vadhya|sthānaṃ nīyamānaṃ sa|putra|kalatraṃ.

7.5 āryāḥ, kiṃ bhaṇatha? asty asya ko|'pi mokṣ'|ôpāya iti? Evaṃ punar asti yady amātya|Rākṣasasya gṛha|janaṃ samarpayati. kiṃ bhaṇatha? eṣa śaraṇ'|āgata|vatsala ātmano jīvita|mātrasya kāraṇen' êdaṃ a|kāryaṃ na kariṣyat' îti? āryāḥ, yady evaṃ tena hy avadhārayat' âsya sukha|gatim. kim idānīṃ yuṣmākam atra pratīkāra|vicāreṇa?

7.7 hā dhik, hā dhik.

7.8 asmādṛśānām api yato nityaṃ cāritra|bhaṅga|bhīrūṇāṃ/ cora|jan'|ôcita|maraṇaṃ prāptam iti namaḥ Kṛtāntāya.

7.9 atha|vā nṛśaṃsānām udāsīneṣv itareṣu vā viśeṣo n' âsti. tathā hi.

7.10 muktv" āmiṣāṇi maraṇa|bhayena tṛṇair jīvantam vyādhānāṃ mugdha|hariṇaṃ hantuṃ ko nāma nirbandhaḥ.

7.11 bhō priya|vayasya Jiṣṇudāsa, kathaṃ prativacanam api me na pratipadyase? atha|vā durlabhāḥ khalu te puruṣā ya etasmin kāle dṛṣṭi|pathe 'pi tiṣṭhanti.

7.11 ete 'smat|priya|vayasyā aśru|pāta|mātreṇa kṛta|pratīkārāḥ śarīrair nivartamānāḥ parivartita|śoka|dīna|vadanā bāṣpa|garukayā dṛṣṭyā mām anugacchanti.

7.12 ārya Candanadāsa, parāgato 'si vadhya|sthānam. tad visarjaya gṛha|janam.

7.13 ārye kuṭumbini, nivartasva sāmpratam sa|putrā. ato 'param a|bhūmir anugantum.

7.14 para|lokam prasthita āryaḥ. na deś'|ântaram. tad an|ucitam khalu kula|vadhū|janasya nivartitum.

7.15 ahaha! kiṃ vyavasitam āryayā?

7.16 bhartuś caraṇāv anugacchanty" ātm'|ânugrahaḥ.

7.17 ārye, dur|vyavasitam idaṃ te. idānīm āryay" âyaṃ kumāro '|śruta|loka|saṃvyavahāro 'nugṛhītavyaḥ.

7.18 anugṛhṇantv enaṃ prasannā bhagavatyaḥ kula|devatāḥ. jāta putraka, pata 'paścimaṃ pituḥ pādayoḥ.

7.19 tāta, mayā tāta|virahitena kim anuṣṭhātavyam?

7.20 putraka, Cāṇakya|virahite deśe vastavyam.

7.21 ārya Candanadāsa, nikhātaḥ śūlaḥ. tat sajjo bhava.

7.22 āryāḥ, paritrāyadhvaṃ paritrāyadhvam!

7.23 ayi, jīvita|vatsalaḥ kim atr' ākrandasi? svargaṃ gatāḥ khalu te devā Nandā ye duḥkhitaṃ janam anukampante.

7.24 are Bilvapattraka, gṛhāṇa Candanadāsam.

7.25 are Vajralomaka, eṣa gṛhṇāmi.

7.26 bhadramukha, tiṣṭha muhūrtaṃ yāvat putrakaṃ pariṣvaje.

7.26 jāta putraka, avaśyaṃ bhavitavyo 'pi vināśo mitra|kāryam udvahamāno vināśam anubhava.

7.27 tāta, kim idam api bhaṇitavyam? kula|kramaḥ khalv eṣo 'smākam.

7.28 gṛhāṇa re. svayam eva sa gṛha|jano gamiṣyati.

7.29 āryāḥ, paritrāyadhvaṃ paritrāyadhvam!

7.32 amātya, kim idam?

7.34 amātya, sarvam api me niṣphalam imaṃ prayāsaṃ kurvatā na me priyam anuṣṭhitam.

7.36 kim iti?

7.39 are Bilvapattraka, tvaṃ tāvac chreṣṭhi|Candanadāsaṃ gṛhītv" âsya śmaśāna|pādapasya chāyāyāṃ muūrtaṃ tiṣṭha yāvad aham ārya|Cāṇakyāya nivedayāmi. gṛhīto 'mātya|Rākṣasa iti.

7.40 are Vajralomaka, evaṃ bhavatu.

7.42 kaḥ ko 'tra dvārikāṇām! nivedayata tāvan Nanda|kula|śaila|saṃcaya|saṃcūrṇana|kuliśasya Maurya|kula|pratiṣṭhāpakasya paura|dharma|samcayasy' ārya|Cāṇakyasya—

7.44 eṣa khalv ārya|nīti|nigaḍa|saṃyamita|buddhi|puruṣakāro gṛhīto 'mātya|Rākṣasa iti.

7.48 nanu nīti|nipuṇa|buddhin" āryeṇ' âiva.

7.89 jayatu jayatv āryaḥ. ady' âiṣa khalu Bhadrabhaṭa|Bhāgurāyaṇa|pramukhaiḥ saṃyamita|kara|caraṇo Malayaketuḥ pratihāra|bhūmim upasthāpitaḥ. evaṃ śrutv" āryaḥ pramāṇam.

7.94 yad ārya ājñāpayati.

7.97 yad ārya ājñāpayati.

NOTES

Bold *references are to the English text;* ***bold italic*** *references are to the Sanskrit text. An asterisk (*) in the body of the text marks the word or passage being annotated.*

1.30 He had once unbound his hair and vowed not to bind it up again until the Nandas were destroyed. That vow is over and done with; but here, as at the and of Act III, he unbinds his hair again and threatens to begin a new vow.

1.39 This name has the inauspicious literal meaning of "demon."

1.88 Jain monks were regarded as inauspicious.

1.183 Vishnu·gupta is Kautílya's own name.

1.201 A legendary king, renowned for generosity, who once offered his life to protect a dove.

2.2 Alludes also to mystical diagrams.

2.3 "Digester of Venom."

2.13 The Vrishni (or Yádava) clan, whose capital Dváraka is said to have been submerged by the sea within seven days of Krishna's death.

2.41 I.e., immediately after the ill omen of the twitching of the eye.

2.55 Now that he is Virádha·gupta and not Jirna·visha the snake charmer, he speaks again in educated tones—i.e., in Sanskrit (see Introduction).

2.70 In the "Maha·bhárata" it is recounted how Karna, the half brother but bitter enemy of the five Pándavas and especially of Árjuna, had been given by the god Indra a special weapon that would be fatal but could be used only once: he attempted to kill Árjuna with it, but instead it struck Ghatótkacha, the son of Árjuna's powerful brother Bhima and the demoness Hidímba. The god Krishna was Árjuna's protector, acting as his charioteer in the battle.

2.133 This is despite Rákshasa's elaborate efforts earlier to conceal Virádha·gupta's identity. In contrast to Kautílya, his emotions are stronger than his calculating mind.

3.72 Play upon Vríshala and *vrisha*, 'bull.'

4.4 His name, Kárabhaka, itself means 'camel.'

4.126 The Red River is a tributary that joins the Ganges from the southwest just above Pátali·putra. The bees as usual are depicted clustering around the elephants for the rut-fluid.

4.135 Jain monks went about naked, and were regarded as inauspicious.

5.19 Rákshasa means 'demon.'

5.114 ***Pārasī'/âhio***: HILLEBRANDT reads: *Pārasī'/âdhivadī Mehakkho*. The only manuscript which reads Meghanāda is N *(pārasiāhio)*. N.B. short *i* and not long *ī*, so the corresponding Sanskrit should actually be *Pārasika* rather than the standard *Pārasīka*. Elsewhere COULSON has the name Meghākṣa (§1.117) which he is rejecting here. [Ed.]

6.3 Keshin, who took the form of a horse and was slain by Krishna with his bare hands.

6.56 By thinking of the Mauryan as the Emperor.

7.1 In reality, Siddhárthaka.

7.6 Samiddhárthaka.

7.55 COULSON's translation closely follows B which here reads *Samṛddhārthako*. Among the manuscripts which read *Samiddhārthako*, K seems to be the only one which is close to COULSON's translation: *ayaṃ khalu pūrva/dṛṣṭa eva bhavatā Siddhārthaka/nāmā rāja/puruṣaḥ. yo 'py asau dvitīyo 'yam api Samiddhārthaka/nāmā rāja/puruṣa eva. anena Siddhārthakena saha sauhārdam utpādya Śakaṭadāso 'pi tapasvī tādṛśam ajānann eva kapaṭa/lekhaṃ may" âiva lekhitaḥ.* [Ed.]

7.88 This is addressed to Kautílya and is a normal response to the formula of congratulation.

INDEX

Sanskrit words are given in the English alphabetical order, according to the accented CSL pronunciation aid. They are followed by the conventional diacritics in brackets.

k	ṭ	t	p	ṅ	n	m	(Except āḥ/aḥ) ḥ/r	āḥ	aḥ	Initial letters:
k	ṭ	t	p	ṅ	n	ṃ	ḥ	āḥ	aḥ	k/kh
g	ḍ	d	b	ṅ	n	ṃ	r	ā	o	g/gh
k	ṭ	c	p	ṅ	ṃś	ṃ	ś	āś	aś	c/ch
g	ḍ	j	b	ṅ	ñ	ṃ	r	ā	o	j/jh
k	ṭ	ṭ	p	ṅ	ṃṣ	ṃ	ṣ	āṣ	aṣ	ṭ/ṭh
g	ḍ	ḍ	b	ṅ	ṇ	ṃ	r	ā	o	ḍ/ḍh
k	ṭ	t	p	ṅ	ṃs	ṃ	s	ās	as	t/th
g	ḍ	d	b	ṅ	n	ṃ	r	ā	o	d/dh
k	ṭ	t	p	ṅ	n	ṃ	ḥ	ā	aḥ	p/ph
g	ḍ	d	b	ṅ	n	ṃ	r	ā	o	b/bh
ṅ	ṇ	n	m	ṅ	n	ṃ	r	ā	o	*nasals* (n/m)
g	ḍ	d	b	ṅ	n	ṃ	r	ā	o	y/v
g	ḍ	d	b	ṅ	n	ṃ	*zero*[1]	ā	o	r
g	ḍ	l	b	ṅ	l̃[2]	ṃ	r	ā	o	l
k	ṭ	c ch	p	ṅ	ñ ś/ch	ṃ	ḥ	āḥ	aḥ	ś
k	ṭ	t	p	ṅ	n	ṃ	ḥ	āḥ	aḥ	ṣ/s
gg h	ḍḍ h	dd h	bb h	ṅ	n	ṃ	r	ā	o	h
g	ḍ	d	b	ṅ/ṅṅ[3]	n/nn[3]	m	r	ā	a[4]	*vowels*
k	ṭ	t	p	ṅ	n	m	ḥ	āḥ	āḥ	*zero*

Permitted finals: (columns k through aḥ)

[1]ḥ or r disappears, and if a/i/u precedes, this lengthens to ā/ī/ū. [2]e.g. tān+lokān=tāl̃ lokān.
[3]The doubling occurs if the preceding vowel is short. [4]Except: aḥ+a=o '.

Final vowels:

a	ā	i	ī	u	ū	ṛ	e	ai	o	au	*Initial vowels:*
' â	" â	y a	y a	v a	v a	r a	e '	ā a	o '	āv a	a
' ā	" ā	y ā	y ā	v ā	v ā	r ā	a ā	ā ā	a ā	āv ā	ā
' ê	" ê	' î	" î	v i	v i	r i	a i	ā i	a i	āv i	i
' ē	" ē	' ī	" ī	v ī	v ī	r ī	a ī	ā ī	a ī	āv ī	ī
' ô	" ô	y u	y u	' û	" û	r u	a u	ā u	a u	āv u	u
' ō	" ō	y ū	y ū	' ū	" ū	r ū	a ū	ā ū	a ū	āv ū	ū
a' r	a" r	y ṛ	y ṛ	v ṛ	v ṛ	' ṛ̂	a ṛ	ā ṛ	a ṛ	āv ṛ	ṛ
' âi	" âi	y e	y e	v e	v e	r e	a e	ā e	a e	āv e	e
' āi	" āi	y ai	y ai	v ai	v ai	r ai	a ai	ā ai	a ai	āv ai	ai
' âu	" âu	y o	y o	v o	v o	r o	a o	ā o	a o	āv o	o
' āu	" āu	y au	y au	v au	v au	r au	a au	ā au	a au	āv au	au